a greener life clarissa dickson wright and johnny scott

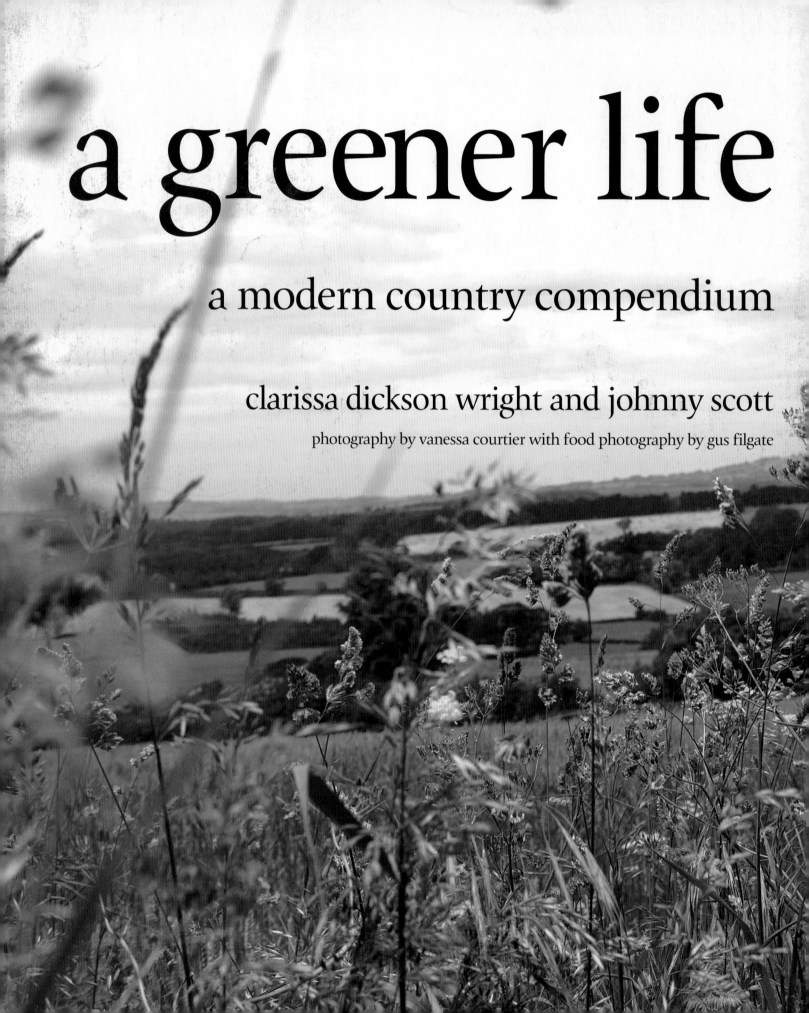

a greener life

a modern country compendium

clarissa dickson wright and johnny scott

photography by vanessa courtier with food photography by gus filgate

D&C
David and Charles

Dedication

Clarissa Dickson Wright:
To Tom Tibbitts, the energy spokesman for the Green Party,
for showing us all the way.

Johnny Scott:
To Rosie Scott and a dog named Jack.

First published in North America
by David & Charles
an imprint of F+W Publications, Inc.
4700 East Galbraith Road
Cincinnati, OH 45236
800-289-0963

First published in Great Britain in 2005 by
Kyle Cathie Limited
122 Arlington Road
London NW1 7HP

ISBN-13: 978-0-7153-2750-0
ISBN-10: 0-7153-2750-x

Library of Congress Cataloging-in-Publication Data

Dickson Wright, Clarissa.
   A greener life / Clarissa Dickson Wright and Johnny Scott.
      p. cm.
   Includes bibliographical references and index.
   ISBN-13: 978-0-7153-2750-0
   ISBN-10: 0-7153-2750-X   3754 6115   6/08
   1. Home economics. 2. Dwellings--Remodeling. 3. Household ecology. I.
Scott, Johnny, 1948- II. Title.
   TX303.D45 2007
   640--dc22   2007017540

Project editor and copy editor Hilary Mandleberg
Design Geoff Hayes
Picture research Sophie Allen
Home economy Jane Suthering
Styling Wei Tang
Index Alex Corrin
Americanization Delora Jones
Production Sha Huxtable and Alice Holloway

F+W PUBLICATIONS, INC.
Printed in Italy by Stige

Authors' acknowledgements

Clarissa Dickson Wright: Thanks to Douglas Wain-Heapy for his advice on vegetable growing and other gardening matters; to April O'Leary for help with spinning; to Marianne More-Gordon for advice on mending, weaving, knitting, and to Jane Burnett for advice on composting.

Johnny Scott: Thanks to all the country men and women who have shared their priceless knowldege with me.

contents

about the authors

Clarissa Dickson Wright came to most people's attention as one half of the BBC's Two Fat Ladies TV series but prior to being in the TV spotlight, Clarissa's focus was always on cooking and maintaining a connection with the kind of rural living she knew and loved as a child.

Johnny Scott's focus is also on rural living and his experiences as farmer, sportsman, and naturalist complement Clarissa's input in this North American edition of *A Greener Life*.

introduction to the US edition

Originally published in the UK, this edition of *A Greener Life* has been adapted for the North American market. The experience that the authors draw on in their writing is very rooted in a British "way of life" and although I have, wherever possible, provided American equivalents it is worth bearing in mind a few of the differences that distinguish our two cultures.

In the UK, where there are laws and legislation governing things like farming, these are generally set on a national level, whereas in the US these laws often vary from state to state so exact conversions do not always fit. For example, in the UK, the Soil Association sets the standards for organic produce and is accredited to the International Federation of Organic Agriculture Movements (IFOAM). In the US, however, there are various organizations that can confer an "organic" label on food products (some of whom are accredited to IFOAM), but the one defined by the Department of Agriculture ("USDA Organic") is the most common. Consequently, in these instances, I have tried to point you in the right direction for obtaining the relevant information.

Another contrast between the UK and North America is the impact of the Second World War, as while America surged ahead with industry, people in Britain took a long time to recover and survived on rationing for a good many years. I have lived in the UK now for 15 years and although my personal American upbringing was one of scrimping, my family did enjoy the luxuries of central heating, telephone, and a car in the 1950s —things most people in Britain did not have at that time. Consequently, those growing up in Britain were living a greener life without thinking about it and it remains as a strong point of reference within living memory. However, while this book is firmly rooted in this tradition, it also shows just how accessible and enjoyable a more self-sufficient way of living can be for everyone, no matter where you live.

Delora Jones, Americanizer for the North American edition

introduction

When I was a child in the 1950s, my family, like the majority of other rural families, was self-sufficient. They had to be. The working week was Monday to lunchtime Saturday, and stores were shut on Sunday. Few people had cars, and a visit to the nearest town was an occasional outing.

Most people kept chickens, ducks, geese, or bees. Many agricultural workers fattened a pig on their household waste. Bacon and the produce from the all-important cottage garden was the staple diet. The countryside was full of rabbits, and farmers were only too happy to allow ferreting over their land. Exchanging produce was commonplace. Those who had a surplus of one thing would exchange with someone who had a surplus of another. As farmers, we ate all our own produce and drank our own milk. When we killed for the house, there was always enough to share with the people who worked for us and, during the season, there was never any shortage of game.

the war years

To supplement their food, country people had been harvesting wild foods from hedgerows and from the woods for centuries. Nor was nature's bounty just for those who lived with it on their doorstep. A desperate shortage of food during the war years led the Ministry of Food to actively encourage the civilian population to make the most of the countryside through their publication *Hedgerow Harvest*. In Britain, rationing was with us until 1954 and urban dwellers had become as self-sufficient as their rural cousins, bottling, salting, and preserving produce through the growing seasons to bolster their diet through the winter.

In the 1960s and 1970s, advances in agricultural technology and intensified farming led to the destruction of much of the old rural landscape and an exodus of people from the countryside as machinery replaced manpower. Communications improved and with it came a dependence on out-of-season produce. This became available through the new and readily accessible supermarkets that started to crop up in every town—a result of Socialist policies to feed the nation on cheap foreign imports. All this led to a change in eating habits and standards. Myxomatosis destroyed the wild rabbit population and intensively-reared chickens replaced rabbits as the nation's cheap food. Lifestyles changed and, to meet people's economic needs, both adults in a family were now required to work. Even country people found there was less leisure time to spend picking wild produce and much country food lore became forgotten.

return to the countryside

Since the 1980s, an increasing number of people have moved into the countryside. Computers have removed the necessity of commuting, and distance from work is now no longer necessarily a consideration when choosing where to live. Many of the cottages once occupied by shepherds in this part of the world are now homes to people who earn their living connected by a computer to a London office.

With this new lifestyle, a growing interest has arisen in what country living has to offer. This has coincided with a complete turn-around in agricultural policy. Where the ministries of agriculture in Europe and America in the 1960s and 1970s spent millions destroying huge tracts of permanent pasture, moorland, marsh, and thousands of miles of hedgerow through reclamation schemes, the modern British equivalent, DEFRA (Dept. for Environment, Food and Rural Affairs), is spending similar sums putting it back as it was. The countryside has fewer farmers, but is beginning to look more as it did just after the Second World War.

Our book offers practical advice on how to be self-sufficient, giving this new generation of country dwellers the opportunity to live as their ancestors did, in harmony with the seasons and enjoying our rural heritage and the delicious wild food that nature has always provided.

the green
outdoors

growing your own food

If you want a garden you will find a way, so let us start on this exercise assuming that the desire is there and the spirit is willing. What I am dealing with here is a garden that will supply all or some of your needs. It is not about growing flowers but about feeding yourself, healing yourself, having a garden that smells nice, and squirreling away food for the hungry months. Just because you don't have a 5-acre garden it doesn't mean you can't grow some food. Community gardens can be rented in some areas (see page 22) and you can grow anything there from just potatoes, as some people do, to a year's supply of vegetables. Even in a small urban garden (see page 16) you can grow vegetables among the flowers in your borders and have a dwarf fruit tree or two.

basic principles

The word on everyone's lips at the moment is "organic." It is the new buzzword but as such should be viewed with caution. At one end of the scale there is pure organic gardening such as Prince Charles practices on his Highgrove Estate in Gloucestershire.

On announcing, at the age of 21, that his favorite ancestor was George III, everyone went on about lunacy, America, and Charles talking to trees. What I think Charles was referring to was the triumph of the Agrarian Revolution with its search for excellence in both plant and animal husbandry. George III himself had a keen interest in agriculture and was known as "Farmer George." At Highgrove, all the bits fit; it is organic production at its best. Even the air vibrates with health and life.

At the other end of the scale is the use of systemic pesticides, polyethylene and hydroponic cultivation, all of which dominate the production of what most people eat when they shop in supermarkets. In this world the vibrations are those of rape, ill-health, and misery.

Somewhere in the middle lies what is known in England as best practice, where you aim for the high altar of organic production but incorporate a layer of pragmatism. This tells you that you don't have the time or energy for true organic but you will do the best you can. If you adopt this path you will find the way easier and the progression to the pinnacle structured. You choose how you want to proceed. We are not offering you the lowest rung of the ladder—the totally non-organic approach—but you can pick any rung on the rest of the ladder.

what is meant by organic gardening?

This is the growing of plants and trees using only organic compost or manure, in other words, compost made using only organic matter and manure from animals that have been raised organically. These will both be in short supply until you provide your own.

You also mustn't use any artificial or chemical fertilizers and are limited as to what pesticides you can use, although there are plenty of alternatives available. Nicotine and pyrethrum are effective plant derivatives that are used in botanical insecticides.

The Soil Association sets the standards for organic produce in the UK, and is accredited to IFOAM (International Federation of Organic Agriculture Movements). In the US, there are various organizations that can confer the "organic" label on food products but the one defined by the Department of Agriculture ("USDA Organic") is the most common.

To tell you where I stand, my compost heap takes what it gets and my manure comes from people who use best practice. The meat and poultry I eat at home comes from beasts raised by best practice from known suppliers, but is not necessarily organic.

permaculture

The term permaculture was first used by the Australian ecologist Bill Mollison in 1978 and, like Topsy, the word grew. Now it is a great buzzword and woe betide the gardening course that doesn't include a section on permaculture.

We live in an age where we have developed a passion for renaming something and imagining we invented it. Permaculture has been around for a very long time; it is simply holistic gardening, which every good vegetable gardener has tried to achieve since time immemorial. Mollison describes permaculture as integrating human habitation with plant life, creating microclimates by the use of annual and perennial plants, and mimicking the patterns found in nature. I would have said that was simply a description of pre-20th-century gardening.

The growth in the use of chemicals and the shortage and increased cost of labor have led us away from these principles but ever since Lady Eve Balfour laid down the principles of organic gardening in *The Living Soil* published in 1943, it is what we have been striving for.

The use of plants, shrubs, and trees as windbreaks for more delicate plants isn't new and permaculture garden designers, with their layered growth, are echoing all the great vegetable gardeners of history. The Frenchman who plants a rose at the end of his row of vines, to attract pests and diseases and to make them easily identifiable before they attack the vines, is practicing permaculture.

Dr. Mollison is an Australian and the use of plants to cast shade and protect tender plants from wind dehydration, as well as the use of sheet mulching to preserve moisture, are all techniques my grandmother used in that self same climate. However, all credit to him. Anything that inspires people to more organic and better gardening practices is to the good. The one drawback I can see to layered permaculture however is in small gardens, where the yield will be reduced. But all things considered, I am glad that Bill Mollison has got us all buzzing about permaculture because it is the right way to garden.

lunar planting

Felicity, who ran the vegetable garden at Lennoxlove House in East Lothian, Scotland, where I used to work, was very keen on lunar planting, a.k.a. bio-dynamic planting. If you consider that the moon governs the tides, women's bodies, and many other things, why should it not also govern planting rhythms?

If you use lunar planting you will most certainly see your seeds germinating better and growing more strongly. To take advantage of the moon's power for promoting the growth of your crops, you must plant, and indeed transplant, your seeds and seedlings as the moon begins to wax, which is three days after you see a new, or crescent, moon.

There is no doubt that it works; I've even planted some seeds on a waxing and a waning moon and seen the difference with my own eyes.

tools

Don't stint on the quality of your tools or, as is always the case in life, it will prove more expensive in the end. Stainless-steel tools, though somewhat heavy, require the least maintenance and will last the longest, but they cost dear. If money is short, you can always start off with just a spade and a fork.

Secondhand tools are another option. I often go to flea markets and yard sales and there is always a stall selling old tools. I have found some of my dearest friends on such stands. They are especially good places to find inexpensive trowels, hand forks, rakes, and garden lines. They made things better in the past, so take a look. And remember, you can always replace handles if necessary. My marvel weedcutter, similar to a narrow cleaver, is perfect for splitting lobsters. My gardening friends gaze at it enviously.

the basic kit

1 a spade with a strong thin blade and a good step on top for digging

2 a round-pronged fork for digging and breaking up the soil

3 a flat-pronged fork for lifting root crops

4 a hoe or a scuffle hoe with a 4-inch blade

5 a trowel

6 a hand fork

7 a hand cultivator or a rake

8 a dibble with a steel point

9 pruning shears

10 a wheelbarrow—don't stint on this. You will use it a lot. Buy a wooden wheelbarrow or one of galvanized steel with a hard rubber tire

11 a watering can, preferably of galvanized steel with a screw-on brass rose (avoid push-on roses as they wear loose and can drown your row of precious seedlings). A dribble bar is a useful addition if you are watering on fertilizer or weedkiller. If you are buying a plastic watering can, choose the stiffest and best balanced you can find. Yard sales are often a good source of watering cans.

You may wish to add, at a later date, a 3-inch onion hoe, a spring tine rake, and a garden line.

If you can use a garden hose in your area, buy one with a reel to store it on and an adjustable spray head.

Look after your tools well. Always clean and oil them before putting them away and cover the handles with linseed oil from time to time to stop them from drying out.

small-space gardening

The excitement I just heard in our publicist's voice because at last she was to have a garden of her own said it all. Many of you will have or will be starting with a small urban garden. The main thing to remember is that you should not attempt to grow large crops or keep large animals in a small garden. Apart from that, the same principles apply as to a larger plot.

As if to prove the point, my nephew, who has a garden in south London, even keeps chickens in his. They come indoors and roost on the rack for drying clothes. His main problem is the urban foxes. He has rescued one of his chickens from the mouth of a fox. In England, urban foxes are a menace that the local government will not touch. Buy a country life magazine and find yourself a pest-controller with a silenced rifle is my advice. And before you scream at me, think of the danger fox mange poses to pets and children alike. Foxes are vermin; they are not, despite what anyone tells you, protected, except, impossibly, from fox-hounds!

organic or not?

You may be asking yourself if it is really possible to produce food organically in your small urban garden. Lynda Brown, in her brilliant and sadly out-of-print book *Gardeners' World Vegetables for Small Gardens* makes the point that while organic gardening is easier in a small garden, where everything interacts, it is in just such a garden that you want every lettuce and fava bean to count, so you should not feel guilty if now and again you use a few slug pellets or some inorganic pesticides.

raised beds

Your best way to grow vegetables is in raised beds, which are prettier than tire planters. I must say I don't really fancy tire planters myself; the smell of hot rubber on a sunny day doesn't appeal and I think the garden ends up looking rather like a junk yard. It's not that hard to build a small raised bed. The Chinese have used them for centuries where space is limited.

They need to be narrow, double-dug (see page 26)—hopefully your subsoil is not too full of rubble—and filled in with lots of compost and manure before the soil is replaced. This raises the soil above the level of the sub-soil so they look like tumulus mounds without the grass. In a garden I once had I took down the old air-raid shelter and filled the foundations with composted soil. It was fantastic. I grew Jerusalem artichokes, tomatoes, wild strawberries, and herbs. It kept me very happy.

You will need to edge the beds with bricks, log rolls, or old coping stones; use your imagination. Once the beds are finished you will never walk on them again so design them for easy access. You can make them any shape you like but you must be able to walk around them or at least reach across them. A bed about 4 feet long and 4 1/2–5 yards wide is probably the optimum.

Divide the beds with paths, not with grass as that would harbor slugs and snails and be impossible to cut. Wood shavings, gravel, bark, or bricks are all good. Make sure to leave room for yourself and of course for a wheelbarrow. Because the beds aren't walked on, drainage is better, yields are improved, the soil warms up quicker, rotation is simpler, there are less weeds, and the beds look wholesome and attractive.

Another attractive idea is to find an old cartwheel, treat it, paint it with non-toxic paint, build a raised bed to its measurements, lay the cartwheel on top, and grow herbs through the divisions.

If you don't want to restrict your garden to vegetables then grow the vegetables among other plants. Remember roses love alliums.

And remember that a garden with slugs does have some benefits. It is probably a sheltered garden with a microclimate of its own.

the disadvantages of an urban plot

The main disadvantages of an urban plot are too much shade, problems of access, and pollution. If trees overhang, you may cut them back but do remember to tell your neighbors first or war might ensue. If they are merely casting shade you have no right of light but talk to your neighbors or the appropriate person in local government and see if you can have them trimmed. If the tree is very tall, you could have some legal remedy as it may pose a threat to your house or to people. If all else fails, you can console yourself that you will have the ingredients for really wonderful leaf mold. If the shade really is too bad, you will simply have to grow what you can in tubs in the sunny bits, or perhaps in just one raised bed and a few containers.

Consider access carefully while you are planning your urban garden, especially if you have to bring everything through the house. You don't want to go off and buy a wheelbarrow which won't fit through the hall or an established fruit tree that could scrape your wallpaper.

As to pollution, lead is the main worry. If there is too much in the soil, plants may still grow but will have a toxic content that is harmful to children. Modern fuels are a lot less toxic but if you are worried, check with your local government to find out who could test your soil.

If your soil is polluted, always wash vegetables carefully, especially soft-leaved ones, and peel all root vegetables. If the soil is badly contaminated, the only solution is patience—grow green compost for several years and dig it in. Have the soil rechecked before growing any fruit or vegetables.

fruit and vegetable growing on a terrace

All the gardening shows on television, which I avoid like the plague, seem to advocate decking and slab terraces. Well, you can grow all sorts of things up the pillars of your decking—beans, squashes, and raspberries spring to mind—and you can easily grow fruit and vegetables in containers on your paved terrace. The advantage of a paved terrace is that it gets a lot of reflected light and heat, but remember to keep watering and feeding.

Good-looking terracotta pots are now readily and inexpensively available. You can get them in a variety of shapes and sizes, so choose what is best for your terrace and for the crop you plan to grow. Make sure you put a layer of small stones or broken-up bits at the bottom to help with drainage before you plant.

If you are growing in containers you will need soil that drains well but is not too fine. It would be nice to think that you have your own compost or leaf mold, or maybe you have a garden plot where you are composting or you have a kind and generous friend with lots to spare. If not, you will have to use potting compost. Alternatively, if you can, get your hands on some organic compost. A national composting association should be able to put you in touch with someone who can supply this.

I like to mix a little garden soil in with my compost for containers as I feel it helps drainage and root development. It's not the end of the world if you don't have any. Use a bit of fine gravel instead.

Don't feel confined to growing herbs in your containers, but read the fruit and vegetable sections carefully (pages 48–67) and select accordingly.

vegetables for your containers

Chiles of different varieties are good to grow in your containers as they look attractive and unusual and do well. I have a friend who grows Scots Bonnets, the hottest of all the chiles. He deep-fries them in batter and eats them like potato chips!

Pot marigolds are another good plant. They give off a scent which deters garden pests and are good for eating in salads and stews. **Nasturtiums** are another idea. They will hang down prettily over the sides of the container and are excellent in salads or eaten on bread and butter, as we did as children.

Dwarf beans thrive in containers and so do **tomatoes**. I have even seen some in growbags on the roof of Westminster Cathedral. For window boxes plant the dwarf variety. **Eggplants** and **peppers** make unusual plants for containers but look a bit stark in window boxes.

Horseradish is another option. As it needs to be grown in a bucket to keep it under control, it does well in a container on a terrace. Its lush leaves look very rustic and it will grow well in shade. **Tree onions** and **chives** also do well and give an unusual look.

fruit and vegetable growing on a balcony

You will have seen how much use people make of their balconies in foreign towns, albeit that they probably have more sun. Herbs, geraniums, squashes, beans, tomatoes, and even melons spring to mind as possible balcony crops. Your main drawback other than space is insect predation, especially the dreaded whitefly (see pages 44–47).

As well as pots, growbags do well on balconies but they aren't very glamorous and dry out quickly, so always remember to water. If you construct a wooden container for your growbag it will keep it structured and will look better.

fruit and vegetable growing in hanging baskets

I am not fond of hanging baskets but recently saw some at a friend's in Dorset. She had strawberries growing very well and happily there. There was no danger of slugs or damp rot and no back-breaking picking. I am told that you need to feed strawberries grown this way once a week with tomato food and add a meager teaspoon of sugar for bigger, juicier fruit. No doubt you may think of other fruit or vegetables which are suitable. As I have never owned a hanging basket, perhaps you would let me know!

window boxes and windowsills

It is amazing what you can grow in a window box—I have even grown dwarf leeks. Make sure your box is secure, that you can get to it easily, and remember to feed and water regularly.

Sometimes all you have is a windowsill, but do not despair. Herbs such as chives and garlic grow well while a pot of basil will keep away the flies.

large gardens

Large gardens really fall into three categories—open, walled, and partially walled gardens.

clearing an open garden

If you are starting to make a paradise from a common field then you will need to clear it. When I worked at Lennoxlove House in East Lothian, Scotland, the vegetable garden had not been touched in 15 years, so I borrowed two Tamworth sows that had been clearing bracken on a nearby hill and we penned them in with an electric fence. They cleared the whole lot in about 10 days, rootling out and eating all the couch-grass roots and nodes, and turning everything over better than any rotovator—and manuring as they went. So using pigs to clear and break up the ground is one option. Another is to use a crop such as potatoes which will help break up the soil, but in this case it will take you a year before you begin to see any results at all.

Possibly you will have inherited a garden rather than a field. Though it may be overgrown and weed-ridden, there may be a fruit tree or two in it. However gnarled they seem, don't grub out a fruit tree until you see what it can do. Pruning works wonders.

starting to plan the garden

The first thing to do with your open garden is identify the prevailing wind and see whether it poses any major problems. If it does, then you must create windbreaks. Whether these are walls, wattle fencing, quick-growing trees such a poplars (remember never plant a poplar close to a house—I can't tell you how many law cases there are about this), or a nice crop of densely sown Jerusalem artichokes, depends on you. Wind is not in itself a bad thing, as it disperses the spores of rust, mold, and blackspot, but it can be drying and in extreme cases destructive.

You will also need to note where the sun strikes your plot and plan your planting accordingly. On a large sheet of graph paper, mark out where you will put your greenhouse, cold frames, hot beds, and compost and manure heaps. Also mark out the paths—gravel, brick, or slab for preference—to give access to these and to the beds, and remember that box hedges will keep out rabbits and deer.

beds for fruit and vegetables

Decide where you are going to plant your fruit trees and canes and other permanent or semi-permanent plants such as rhubarb. Once all these are in place on the graph paper, divide the remaining areas into beds and decide what you want to grow. This is important as you don't want gluts and you may dislike some vegetables and fruit, in which case don't grow them. Work out how many people you are feeding and remember that freezers are all very well but green people search for seasonality. Now read the sections on crop rotation (see page 40), companion planting (see page 46), and What to Grow (see pages 48–75), and off you go.

partially walled gardens

These are gardens with one south-facing wall up which you can grow your tender fruit trees, and with box hedges to divide the garden from the rest of the surrounding land. They were common in poorer areas where there was less manpower available to build expensive, labor-intensive brick walls. The vegetable garden at Lennoxlove House was an example. Here, in good old Scottish tradition, rows of 8-foot-high beech hedges were grown perpendicular to the wall and at some distance from it. They protected the fruit trees growing against the wall from frost, allowed air to circulate, acted as a windbreak, and concentrated the sun.

If you have a partially walled garden, plan it as you would an open garden but bearing in mind the dictates of the wall and all that implies in terms of frost pockets and circular wind currents.

walled gardens

Walled gardens built for monasteries and the houses of the rich from the Middle Ages onwards vary in size from about 270 square yards to six or seven acres.

An old walled garden will probably have some form of greenhouse, cold frames, and possibly even double walls with flues running inside them heated by a coal-burning stove, though none of this will be working. The magnificent octagonal garden at Lafuness House in East Lothian, Scotland, built by French prisoners of war during the Napoleonic Wars, is unique in that as well as heated double walls, it has adjustable polished metal plates to direct the sun's rays onto particular parts of the garden.

If you are lucky enough to have a walled garden it may already be up and running, but if not, in the UK at least, there are grants available for restoration. There has recently been a revival of interest in getting them back to speed with a view to selling their vegetables into farmers' markets and to local community and restaurant outlets. A good way of getting help with the restoration of a walled garden is to enlist your local history group both for advice and volunteers, while your local authority will be able to advise you on grants.

planning

As with any garden, plan your garden on graph paper, starting with the permanent features and dividing up the rest of the garden to accommodate your other needs.

insect repellent

Early Egyptian gardeners daubed their garden walls with clay to keep insects out of the crevices. This is a ploy that is still practiced in France to this day. It is not as pretty as aging brick but is very practical and saves on the repointing.

community gardens

Community gardens are good news and and if you live in the US or Canada and would like one, contact the American Community Gardening Association (www.communitygarden.org).

Douglas Wayne-Heapy, my mentor in all vegetable matters, grows the most amazing vegetables on a dry windswept garden plot in Birmingham in the middle of England. On my birthday last year, his wife and I sat in the sun by the River Avon at Bridgnorth. Here we consumed a thermos of baby fava beans he had grown and which he insisted she bring me to celebrate the day. Everything he grows has wonderful flavor and with the aid of a freezer, he and his wife buy virtually no vegetables at all. So don't delay. If you live in a city and haven't done so already, track down your local community gardening organizations.

In a walled garden, the shade cast by the walls is used by gardeners for retarding plants to avoid gluts. The walls also provide somewhere to grow fruit trees against but be careful when hammering in nails. It is a good idea to use cast-iron nails heated in a roasting pan in the oven until they are red-hot, then thrown into cold linseed oil. This prevents the mortar sticking to them and pulling away. The French used to build sheep shanks into their walls and tied the trees to them. Today we use horizontal wires as supports but they still need to be attached to the wall. Remember, too, that walls have two faces so you can grow blackberries and hardier fruit on the outside of the wall as well as the more tender fruits inside.

Now we come to the center of the garden. This will need to be divided into beds. These can be any size but smaller beds are easier to work (see page 16) and make crop rotation easier, so they may suit best.

If your garden is very large, internal cross-walls and plant dividers may have been erected to prevent wind damage, however, high internal walls will create their own wind-current problems and mini-frost pockets, not too mention too much shade.

home to wildlife

Of course you may want your garden to be a home to some wildlife, too. If you wish to indulge in some beekeeping (see pages 130–131) you should place your beehives in a warm, sheltered south-facing spot.

Walled gardens are also useful for keeping poultry but seeing the damage the Bantams do to my beds when they are dust bathing and snacking, I would recommend keeping them cooped in a moveable run.

"Remember, too, that walls have two faces so you can grow blackberries and hardier fruit on the outside of the wall as well as the more tender fruits inside."

looking after the soil

It is important to identify your soil type and whether it is acid or alkaline as this will affect what you can grow in it. Soil types range from sandy to heavy clay. To find out what you've got, take a small handful and rub it between your fingers and thumb.

Sandy or light soil: This will not stick together at all as there are large spaces between the soil particles. It makes it easy to work but sandy soils dry quickly especially in windy conditions. They drain well but are difficult to keep together and will need manuring and having compost added. Sandy soil warms up quickly so is good for growing early crops but nutrients leach out of it very easily. As this soil tends

to be alkaline, add lime and check its pH (see opposite) every couple of years as lime washes away. Alliums and all root vegetables like light soils, as do salad crops, chard, and spinach. Apple and nut trees thrive in sandy soils too.

Clay or heavy soil: A clay soil has a shiny surface and when rubbed between your fingers and thumb, the very tiny particles cohere. This makes it heavy to work and the soil sticks together like glue. If allowed to dry, a clay soil sets and cracks like a piece of bad pottery, so mulch well in the summer to retain moisture. In cases of really heavy clay you may have to dig some sand into it. Only cultivate clay soil in dry weather and see

that your compost and manure are well rotted before you add them as decomposition will be slow due to lack of air in the soil. Turn the soil in the autumn where possible, so the frost will break it up. Peas and fava beans, strawberries, raspberries, pears, and plums all like clay soil.

Silt: This tests like clay but without the shine. A silt soil is easier to work than a clay one but it gets sticky when very wet and turns to dust when dry.

Loam: The most sought-after soil, loam is a mixture of small and large particles. It doesn't stick together or fall apart but is like perfectly made pastry crumbs. It is possible though to have a sandy loam or a clay loam. Loam holds moisture but also drains well. It is quick to warm and slow to freeze and all your fruits and vegetables will grow well in it.

Peat soil: This forms a brown springy ball between the fingers. It is formed from decomposed vegetable matter rather than rock, so it is very fertile but you need to watch the pH level (see opposite). Peat is slow to warm up and to freeze. It tends to be neutral or slightly acid.

Once you have identified your soil you can decide what to grow. Having said all this I have to confess that I have never used a soil-testing kit and although I count some legendary gardeners among my acquaintances, when I called them up, neither had any of them. The most crushing rejoinder I received was from my friend Isabel who told me that she simply looked at the weeds to tell her about the acidity of her soil. This is a very good point and one I shall deal with opposite.

Wild chervil grows where there is an excess of nitrogen and where there is too little, look for vetches and clovers. Compacted soils sport grasses while all types of buttercups, docks, sedges, and mosses are signs of poor drainage.

Many weeds contain minerals and if they are dug up before they seed and are left to dry on the ground, they are useful on the compost heap. The dreaded couch grass, for example, contains potassium as does yarrow which also brings iron, copper, phosphorus, nitrogen, and sulphur. Dandelions, nettles, mayweed, bracken, and horsetail are full of useful minerals and can be used for green compost (see page 40).

Deep-rooted weeds such as nettles and docks have the advantage that they bring up nutrients from deep in the soil for more shallow-rooted plants. Their root channels also help break up the soil and aerate it.

weeds

The main problem with weeds is that they are competition to your carefully planted vegetables. The greatest threat is during the first four weeks after planting. If you can keep them away from newly planted seeds and seedlings during this time, you don't need to worry too much.

Some "weeds" are actually quite useful, for instance stinging nettles, lambs quarters, and dock leaves are all great to use as pheasant and chicken feed.

Dandelions provide a delicious addition to your salad bowl as does common chickweed. The latter, made into a tisane, acts to clean the blood, as does pennyroyal, a type of wild mint that was once used as a substitute for tea. You shouldn't drink pennyroyal though if you are pregnant as it was once known as "the abortionist's friend." Dried moss is another useful weed as it can be made into an effective bandage or poultice.

Weeds are also a good indicator of the state of your soil. So what to look for? Acid soils grow sorrel, plantain, and knotgrass (knotweed). Alkaline soils grow poppies and field parsley, while nettles of all types, common chickweed, dandelion, and borage all indicate fertile soil.

Cow parsley

digging

If you possibly can, borrow a pig; if not, digging is weary work. If the ground is very hard and has been left idle, rent or borrow a rotovator. This will at least remove the hardship of double-digging in most cases. Remember, however, that digging is a much better and more long-term exercise for the muscles than going to the gym.

The trick with digging is not to rush into it willynilly and put your back out. Start gently and do no more than half an hour at a time until you have strengthened your muscles. And always buy the best and strongest tools you can afford. You needn't spend a fortune; at county shows and flea markets you will find stalls selling all sorts of secondhand garden implements. I have often found a cracking selection of spades, forks, and trowels, many of them much stronger than the latest gimmicky ones.

Spit-digging

The most effective way of digging a plot is spit-digging or single digging. It enables you to incorporate compost or manure into each spit or trench as you go along and before it is filled in. The spade has been developed to the depth and width it is as a means of achieving efficient spit-digging.

You will want to do your digging in the autumn after the equinoctial rains but before the first frosts so that they will break up the manure you have dug into your trenches.

Divide your plot in half either mentally or with a stretched piece of string. Starting nearest the string and working at right angles to it, dig out a spade's depth and width of soil and place it on the other side of the string. Put manure or well-rotted compost into the trench you have dug, then dig a second trench parallel to the first, putting the soil from the second trench on top of the manure in the first one.

Continue digging in this way the length of the first half of the plot. When you reach the end, dig in a reverse direction down the other half. The soil from your first trench will fill the one you dig last.

Double-digging

Double-digging is used to improve drainage and break up compacted sub-soil. It is particularly necessary when growing root crops. Mark out your plot in the same way as for spit-digging and dig your trenches in the same way, but make each trench two feet wide. When you have dug out the first trench, use a fork to break up the soil and dig out another spit's depth. Add manure as before and fill in the trench.

Non-dig method

As an alternative to all this back-breaking digging, there is a non-dig method. Simply cover your patch of earth with a thick layer of compost and plant your vegetables into this. You can continue like this for 2–3 years, but after that you will have no option but to dig.

Digging out a spade's depth and width   **Using a fork to break up the soil**   **Putting manure into the trench**

composting

This is the Holy Grail of the true organic believer. Indeed, Lady Eve Balfour (see page 12), the original organicist, had her spiritual awakening beside a compost heap in East Lothian, so it is very fitting— although they probably don't realize it—that East Lothian Council, where I live, runs a composting scheme to help and advise those who want to compost.

Once you have discovered the joys of composting you will never look back and will become quite obsessively boring (as I am) to those who haven't yet "crossed the line."

Composting is caused by the presence of bacteria which needs air, light moisture, and nitrogen. Your heap (or temple of fertility) must stand on the earth so it can draw nutrients out of the earth as well as worms. If you put it on plastic sheeting, it will rot and grow mold and fungi.

The optimum size for a compost heap is 3 feet square and 3–4 feet in height. You can construct one quite simply with stakes at each corner and chicken wire between them, or you can build a fine version with wooden slats for the sides, but remember to leave some space in between the slats to allow the air to circulate. I am not a great fan of purpose-built composters but . . . "chacun à son goût."

Choose the site of your compost heap carefully. Don't put one under drippy trees or they will keep it too wet, nor in full sun as the compost will dry out too quickly. It is advisable to have three compost heaps—one ready to take compost from, one maturing away nicely, and one that you are building up.

Build it up in layers of 6–10 inches and do not have a layer of all one type of material, grass cuttings or autumn leaves for instance, as this will slow the process.

Mix each layer well like a fruit cake, then cover with a thin layer of garden soil to supply the bacteria and, if your soil is acid, a sprinkling of lime to keep all sweet. When the heap has reached the right height, cover with a layer of old carpet to keep everything warm. Some people recommend plastic sheeting but I think that makes the heap too wet.

If the weather is exceptionally dry you may want to sprinkle the heap with water. A finished compost heap needs about six months before it is usable and after three months, if all your power sources fail, it's so hot you can cook in the middle of it, using the haybox principle. A compost heap in my village made only of grass cuttings spontaneously combusted once and burned, leaving the owner with nothing but ash!

Some people put autumn leaves on their compost heaps but I prefer to keep them separate and allow them to do their own thing and form leaf mold. It takes about 2–3 years to make proper leaf mold from the leaves of deciduous trees but is worth the wait. You can speed up the process by keeping your leaves in plastic bags for about a year. Personally, I prefer the slower-matured variety.

do not put on your compost heap

eggshells as they will attract rats.
any vegetable waste attacked by blight, e.g. club root in brassicas, alliums suffering from white rot, blighted potatoes, etc., as the disease may stay in the compost and be disseminated.
woody vegetation such as clippings from trees, shrubs, or fruit bushes, as this will slow down the decomposing process. If you have a proper shredder you can in theory add them, but I find the twiggy bits irritating when sifting the compost. Burn them instead, have a lovely bonfire, dance around it, roast potatoes in the embers, and you'll have nice ash to use as well, which will help keep out slugs as well as providing fertilizer.

Something else you can do is to grow lots of comfrey around the edges of your vegetable patch. This makes a wonderful addition to your compost heap as it helps the decomposition process. And add a few earthworms to your heap as well as they are great for breaking everything down and encouraging the bacteria.

manure

Don't balk at the thought of manure; if it is well rotted it doesn't smell nasty or indeed very much at all. One of the problems in organic vegetable growing is obtaining organic manure, in other words manure from cattle or pigs that have been raised organically. As the organic movement grows this naturally becomes easier, but it is still quite hard to find, and expensive.

Organic fertilizers used to be made of bone or fish meal which have now become pretty well illegal in the European Union. In any event, organic fertilizer used to attract foxes who dug it up and ate it, thus ruining your planting.

You cannot use fresh manure in your trenches as it needs to rot down. If it is not well rotted it will burn the plants. If you have your own animals, you will have a regular supply of organic manure after the first year but it is worth buying it to begin with. You can obtain horse manure from friendly riding stables. Although horses are not eaten as food in England and consequently are not raised organically, there is not much in their diet to offend, so unless you are going for commercial organic status, I'd use bought horse manure in year one. Personally I have always found the finest manure is well-rotted pig manure.

You can use spent mushroom compost instead of home-produced compost. I once had a car that grew mushrooms when it rained as a sack of mushroom compost I had in the back leaked and wasn't completely spent. Chicken droppings are

another alternative. It makes a very good manure for vegetables. Don't dig it in fresh but keep it for about three to four weeks. Grass cuttings are yet another possibility. You can put them into a bed intended for potatoes. Lay them at the bottom of the trench and fill in on top.

watering and mulching

Never water in full sun as this will burn the leaves of your plants. Early morning is best before the sun has any heat. The evening is also good but if the plants stay wet all night this may promote disease. Water closely around the roots so that the water doesn't dissipate, and on the leaves as well. Watering needs will vary with the different plants; brassicas for instance need $2^{1}/_{2}$–4 gallons a week in dry weather, whereas legumes don't need much watering at the seedling stage as this promotes leaf growth at the expense of flowers and pods. Once the pods are set however, they need watering to promote internal and external pod growth. Two and a half gallons of water per square yard per week, applied twice daily in dry weather, is about right.

A good way of feeding the plants while watering is to fill a rain barrel with water and throw in a good quantity of comfrey. Let it stand for a week or so and use it for watering. Use it in the ratio of about one part comfrey slurry to three or four parts water. You can also throw manure into your rain barrel which gives a rich feed, but use this sparingly and do not water the leaves with it.

Mulching, the practice of applying compost or leaf mold around the plants, is another good way of retaining moisture and keeping down weeds. Apply after the seedlings are well up. It is easy to remove any wind-blown weed seeds from the soft surface. Don't feel romantic about weeds; they leach both moisture and nutrition from the soil at the expense of your vegetables.

sowing seed

Unless you are sowing outside in the autumn, in which case the seeds lie dormant over winter, it is prudent to wait until the soil warms up a bit. The potato farmers of East Lothian used to pull down their trousers and rest their naked bottoms on the sod to see if it was warm enough to plant. It is all very well of me to say smugly that you should sow seed in March or April but if you have a year with late frosts and cold rains, it can hold back or arrest germination quite considerably. If the soil is too wet, the nascent seedlings may drown. It is all part of the frustrating adventure of gardening.

preparing the soil

In general though, once winter has worked its wrath on your soil, spring winds will begin to dry it out and break

down any large clods of earth to give you a friable soil surface. Then you need to advance this process. Using a hand cultivator if you have one or a rake if you don't, produce a tilth, working the top 6–8 inches of soil from both angles. Don't overwork the soil as you don't want the tilth too fine at this stage. If you are a cook you'll know what I mean by coarse bread crumbs.

Evenly apply a base layer of fertilizer, then use the head of a rake to break down any remaining clods. Only do a traditional foot shuffle on very fluffy soils.

Vegetable seeds can be sown directly into the ground or can be transplanted from seed trays (see page 32) in a greenhouse or cold frame. If you are planting directly outside, you need to cut out a drill to plant them in. To do this, put two pegs into the soil where you want the drill to be, string a line between them, then cut out the drill with a hoe following the line of the string.

sowing seed

Remember when sowing seed not to plant the seeds too deep. The bigger seeds like beans and peas will need to be dibbed in about a half-inch. Make sure that the soil is firmed down but not compacted over them. Smaller seeds really only need a thin drill made with the tip of a rake. Don't forget to put strings with tied-on pieces of aluminum foil across emerging seedlings to save them from pigeons and other birds.

Cutting a drill

Sowing seed

Always sow seed as thinly as you can. This cuts down on thinning, prevents competition between seedlings, and gives sturdier plants. Large seeds such as fava beans, pole beans, and corn can be sown individually in their final positions.

Sow the seeds and water them, then rake the soil back over the seeds.

Don't forget to label your rows. At the earliest possible moment, thin your seedlings (see page 32) and water the remaining seeds.

Watering

cloches

Cloches (see page 42) are a good way to bring seedlings on. They are like portable greenhouses, concentrating the warmth and focusing the sun's rays. Remember to remove them, however, if there is a scorching hot day as the sun may burn the seedlings, rather on the magnifying-glass principle.

planting seeds in seed trays and pots

If you are setting seeds in trays—and what is more exciting than watching the start of new life?—use fine potting compost. If your own compost is well rotted and friable, it will do nicely but pass it through a fine garden sifter to make the finest possible bed for your seedlings. Put the seed trays in a warm place and keep them just moist but not wet. Depending upon the species, your seedlings should start to show at ten days to two weeks.

Positioning of your seed trays is important. Some people buy a heated propagator, which I don't think is really necessary. A warm windowsill or a shelf in the kitchen with good light is usually enough. If you have a cold greenhouse, that is ideal.

I tend to plant the bigger seeds such as peas or beans straight into small shallow pots—allow 2–3 per pot—rather than seed trays.

When the seedlings are well above the surface you will want to harden them off before they finally venture outside. If you have a sheltered patio, this is perfect and unless the weather bodes very cold or wet, they can sit there until they are ready to transplant.

speeding up germination

When propagating seeds you may find a plastic bag comes in handy. My friend, Douglas Wayne-Heapy, who grows better vegetables than anyone I know, will put three or four larger seeds in a small pot of compost, water them well, and cover them completely with a plastic bag, which keeps the moisture in and helps them sprout. With all types of beans he lays a folded plastic bag on top of the compost to the same effect. Germination occurs much more quickly in this diminutive greenhouse.

thinning

One of the great questions is when to thin out your seedlings in their trays and really, like so many things, it's all a case of using your common sense. Remove any seedlings that show signs of deformity or weakness or don't straighten themselves out, and consign these to the compost heap. There is no place for sentimentality in gardening. Once your seedlings look strong enough and are showing signs of leaf growth, move them on to the next stage of their lives. If you are transferring them to individual pots, continue to use fine potting compost; if they are going to be planted outside, make sure that the soil is well worked.

watching the weather

My friend, Douglas Wayne-Heapy, says that when you have planted out seeds or are hardening them off under cold frames or cloches you must listen to the weather forecast continually. This season the frost was so bad in May in my area it actually got through the cloches and scorched the plants. Potatoes and most over-wintered plants will grow back if cut back by frost, but peas, beans and delicate or half-hardy plants won't, so it's a question of starting again. Douglas is a great believer in staggering germination to preserve against gluts. He sows his seeds at fortnightly or even monthly intervals so he can keep gathering his crops right through until October.

using seed you have saved yourself

One of the problems of saving your own seed is that it may have a low germination yield, either because you have taken the seeds too early or because they have not properly dried, so watch out for this when they are germinating. A good way of testing your seed in enough time to buy more if necessary is to put a few seeds in early and see how well they sprout.

transplanting

This is the moment when a cold frame will really come in useful. Transfer your seedlings to their pots and stand them in the shelter of the cold frame until they have 3–4 proper leaves before planting them out. This will give them the best possible chance of survival.

Obviously take the greatest care when transplanting seedlings to handle them gently. Hold the seedlings by the leaves rather than the stalk as leaves can regrow if damaged, but if you snap the stalk, you've had it. Make sure you allow yourself plenty of time when transplanting. Hurry or stress may not transfer to the plants but it will to your fingers!

trees

If you have the space you can grow a few useful trees, whether for wood, fruit, or nuts. I am always amazed at city-dwellers who think trees just grow in the countryside any old how. I usually point out acerbically that if Charles II hadn't planted his oak plantation in the midst of the New Forest we would have lost the Battle of Trafalgar because we wouldn't have had enough oak trees to lay the keels of Nelson's fleet.

Different trees are used for different things; wood has very individual uses according to the species. Trees are also good for drainage if your land tends toward wetness. One excellent tree that will grow straight and strong anywhere is the ash. I have two ash bookcases and an ash writing desk at which I am sitting at the moment, both made for me in Scotland. Ash is much used for furniture and has a lovely grain and a pleasing light color. Because of its strength and flexibility—it doesn't shatter or splinter under pressure—ash is mostly used for tool handles.

buying your trees

You will need to buy young trees; when choosing them try and ensure that the roots have been trained using the Airpot method. This Australian invention is a device for training tree roots that prevents root-spiraling problems and produces a better root system. In addition, the Airpot system reduces the shock factor that is caused by travel and planting, which means there is less chance of you losing your rather expensive investment.

alder

Alder trees are also good for drainage and produce a hard, waterproof wood. In the days when people wore clogs, the soles were made of alder, and boxes made from alder were often used for storing gunpowder. If you have alder containers in your kitchen, you can be sure that they will be moisture-free.

sycamore

Sycamore contains a built-in antiseptic and should be used for rolling pins and kitchen containers. Food put in sycamore bowls will not go bad on you.

locust wood

The English writer William Cobbett raved about the properties of locust wood. It has the great advantage that it doesn't rot so is excellent for fence stakes, barn footings, and indeed anywhere else where wood is set in earth.

beech

Beech is best for furniture. It is an easily worked strong wood, much used in country furniture. Of course its leaves make the best leaf mold and if you're lucky enough to have a beech forest, you should have mushrooms and even possibly truffles.

sweet chestnut

Sweet chestnut of course produces nuts but young limbs of chestnut trees are also cut for use as long straight poles. Its wood was much used for traditional rood screens, fireplaces, and minstrels' galleries as it carves very well.

oak

Oaks are always nice to have especially if you keep pigs, and I am told by the brilliant furniture-maker and designer Ben Dawson, whose work includes the inside of the Scottish Parliament and the Welsh Assembly, that oak is now back in vogue although most of it is currently from central Europe.

nut trees

While planning your tree planting, you might give a thought to growing some nuts if your garden is big enough. I like to see nut trees growing. There is something primitive about their presence which brings out the hunter-gatherer gene. Johnny talks about the virtues of growing hazel for coppicing (see page 80) but remember that fresh hazelnuts are quite delicious eaten whole, or dried and grated for cooking, both for breadmaking and in such delights as hazelnut meringues.

almond

Almond trees are elegant and have beautiful blossom in the spring. In colder climates the fruit won't ripen but if you have a walled garden or live in a warmer climate, you are in with a chance. Fresh almonds are delicious either plain or covered in sugar syrup or spices and dried in the oven, while ground almonds are a must in baking and a great help when cooking for a celiac.

walnut

There is a walnut tree in the garden where I live in Scotland and even though the fruit doesn't ripen most years, I am able to make lots of pickled walnuts and walnut ketchup from the unripe fruit. The wood of a good tree is valuable, too.

(see page 80)

large-scale planting

If you are planning to plant a large plantation you should seek professional advice. If you simply want trees to act as windbreaks or simply for beauty, you can easily choose varieties that will offer a useful end product, though you may have to wait anything from seven to 30 years for the result. Aosta in Italy is one of the major tree-producing areas of the world, the others being Oregon and North Florida.

If you live somewhere warmer, you will have lovely walnuts to eat and if you cut a growing shoot of walnut on St. John's Day, June 24th, in the Northern Hemisphere or Christmas Eve in the Southern Hemisphere, and put it in a bottle of eau de vie, you will make a delicious liqueur.

brazil nut

Brazil nuts are an important part of a vegetarian diet but will only grow south of the Equator.

cultivation of fruit trees

Although you can buy container-grown fruit trees, all the experts agree that it is best to buy dormant bareroot trees in the late autumn and early winter.

The care you invest in the planting of your tree will repay you many times over the years ahead.

planting

Make sure the hole is wide enough to spread the root system out. It needs to be at least 2 feet across but not too deep and no deeper than the hole from which the root was removed. You will be able to tell by looking at your tree; the graft point, the swollen bit on the bottom of the stem, should be just above the level of the soil. Put well-rotted compost or manure in the bottom of the hole before planting. Only unwrap the tree once the hole is dug and if the roots seem in any way dry, soak them for a couple of hours in a bucket of water. Trim off any damaged roots as they may let in disease.

protect from attack

Don't let pigs into your orchard until the trees are well established or they will dig them up. To guard against bird predation, hang old CDs in the tree or any glittery, tinkly items. Mothballs hung in the tree are good for keeping insects away.

Plant a treated stake alongside the tree and tie it to help support its early life unless of course it is against a wall or wires. Water well immediately after planting and in the early months, water often to help the tree establish itself. Fruit trees need pruning as soon as they are planted.

Keep a circle of soil around the base of the tree free of vegetation as a guard against disease for at least the first two or three years. After that, if you are letting the grass grow, let it grow longer around the trees as that conserves moisture better.

pruning

Pruning helps shape a tree and removes much of the risk of disease. It encourages fruit production and lets in light. Only prune in winter, except for apricots, nectarines, cherries, and plums, which must be pruned when they are growing vigorously to minimize the risk of attack by silverleaf.

Always cut out damaged, diseased, and cankered growth, and burn the latter at once. Keep your cuts as small as possible. As a general rule, prune vigorous shoots lightly and weak ones hard, which seems bizarre but heavy pruning encourages vigorous growth. If removing larger branches, cut at the collar—the swelling where one branch meets another. If the cut is particularly big, you may need to tar it to prevent disease.

For cones, fans, and espaliers, remember the principle of strong and weak shoots as you prune to shape the plants to fit along your wall.

spur or tip?

Before pruning an apple tree, check whether it is a spur-bearer (the most common), a tip-bearer (more usual in pippins), or a partial tip-bearer. Pruning tip-bearers usually requires the removal of old wood to encourage new shoots and tip-pruning branch leaders, which may otherwise break under the apple's weight, so that they form tip-bearing shoots.

For partial tip-bearers, cut back any strong lateral shoots that are longer than 10 inches to 5–6 buds.

pruning after planting

When pruning fruit trees and bushes after planting, cut the central leader so it just tops the tallest laterals, then reduce the laterals by two-thirds. In the tree's second winter, cut the laterals that you want as your main branches back by half. Remove any crossing and misplaced shoots and prune everything else back to 5 buds. In the third winter look at your framework and remove a quarter of the leader's new growth, prune weak laterals back to 2–3 buds, and strong laterals to 5 buds. Thereafter shorten weak leaders by half and strong ones by less than a quarter. Use your discretion.

thinning fruit

It is very important to thin your fruit once they are set. In midsummer the tree will shed some leaves anyway as nature's way of exposing the ripening fruit to the light. At this time go though the clusters of fruit removing any that are damaged or diseased and thinning out some smaller ones so that you will get bigger fruit. The remaining fruit should be 2–4 inches apart, depending on the species size.

pollination

Most of the time clever nature does the work for you. The color and scent of plants is all about attracting pollinators— just like short skirts and fancy hairdos or hipster jeans in clubs attract boys. However, there are a few things you can do to help nature along.

Having your own bees (see page 130) is one possibility of course. Nothing beats a hive in your own garden for ensuring that there is always a roaming bee, but beekeeping is not always possible. There are, however, hives all over the place, even in London. A beekeeping friend of mine used to sit in the garden of her

planting to attract bees

One way to ensure pollination is to grow plants that will attract neighboring bees. They will then wander among your plants carrying pollen on their feet or proboscis. But if you are trying to attract bees, remember all the precautions against drowning bees in you beer traps (see page 44) or otherwise damaging them.

Borage is a bee herb par excellence. It also happens to be a delicious salad herb and the leaves are good cooked as fritters in the same way as sage or comfrey leaves.

Also good is lavender, especially the cotton lavender varieties. You will notice there are always bees around lavender hedges. Borage and lavender are particularly beneficial because they flower during what we in England call the June gap—the barren period for flowering. Your barren flowering month may well be different; it depends where you live. In Scotland, for instance, the barren month is July.

Knightsbridge flat and watch the bees, as dusk drew in, streaming up to the roof of Harrods where someone kept several hives. The trick is to lure those bees to your plants.

problem pollinators

I have talked elsewhere of the difficulty of pollinating maize and corn (see page 73) due to the way the male and female tassels grow low down on the plant stalks. All wind-pollinated plants should be grown in blocks or at least close enough to cross-pollinate easily.

Fruit trees nowadays are usually self-pollinating but some of the older varieties may need a bit of help. Check from your plantsman to find out if any of your species need cross-pollinating, in which case you may need to plant two trees of the same variety. I have helped gardeners to cross-pollinate their trees using a soft sable paintbrush, but that is mostly a thing of the past.

Old varieties of fig trees needed a fig wasp for pollination. This is an insect which laid its eggs in the buds of the trees. The hatched grub would then eat its way out and cross onto another flower, thus pollinating the tree. This curious feature of the fig explains why trees of old fig varieties planted in areas where there are no fig wasps are frequently barren. This problem has largely been sorted out by hybridization but remember Christ's advice on the barren fig, and if you have inherited one, root it out and condemn it to the flames in a suitably biblical fashion.

planting to attract butterflies

Butterflies are another good pollinator. Plant stinging nettles to attract them and also a small buddleia tree. These are a great attraction to butterflies. Buddleia sprouted like weeds on all the London bomb sites of my childhood. They are extremely easy to grow just from a slip or leaf cutting. I have often stopped by building sites where old abandoned houses with neglected gardens are being renovated and have asked the workmen if I can take away a buddleia or two. They are always delighted. Be brutal with your buddleias or they will take over. No matter how ruthlessly you prune them, they will always bounce back.

"If the weather is very cold, there may be an absence of bees and if rough winds are shaking your darling buds of May, you may need to resort to using a paintbrush."

cloning

Some plants, mostly airborne varieties such as orchids, can be cloned. This is done using centrifugal force but while it is quite fun to witness the machinery at work, it is a very expensive process and is not really that much use for growing vegetables in your own garden.

You must keep a weather eye when the blossom is out to ensure that cross-pollination is taking place. If the weather is very cold, there may be an absence of bees and if rough winds are shaking your darling buds of May, you may need to resort to using a paintbrush. Accept that some years have better conditions than others for fruit-setting, resulting in variations in your fruit production, but if you continue to have low yields you may have to call in an expert.

cucurbit problems

The worst-case pollination scenario in your garden will be the cucurbits, especially melons and squashes. Usually these plants intertwine so that pollination does take place, but if you are having problems, you may have to pluck a male flower and thrust it into the female flower and shake it about. Make sure that the sexual bits actually connect. It's just like sexual penetration in humans, but less fun. Remember to cook the male flower afterwards—a bonus we don't enjoy, at least not since pagan prehistoric times.

rotation of crops

In order to prevent disease it is vital to rotate your crops. Vegetables grown in the same spot year after year will take the same vitamins and minerals from the patch of soil they are grown in, which will weaken subsequent growth. Moreover, if there is any trace of disease in the soil or of earth-bound pests such as eel and wire worms, these will stay in there and attack the same vegetables the next year.

> "Apply manure before potatoes but not before root crops such as carrots."

green nutrition crops

You may be wondering what I mean by overwintering nutrition crops in the table below. Let me explain. Any land that is left bare to rest is subject to erosion by wind and water as well as invasion by wind-borne weeds and rough grasses. These will leach nutrition from the soil and negate the reason for resting it. It is like the house in the Bible that is swept clean and waiting for more devils to move in. The best way to avoid such "devils" is to sow green manure crops—alfalfa, clovers, or winter tares. These can then be dug into the soil to provide feed for the next batch of crops.

the four-year plan

One common rotation plan that works best is a four-year plan. Divide the plot into four and plant as follows:

	Section A	Section B	Section C	Section D
Spring/summer	early and main-crop potatoes	carrots beets (chard and spinach are classed with beets) celery fennel parsnips	brassicas	legumes alliums
Autumn/winter	autumn-planted onions	phacelia or other overwintering nutrition crop	winter cabbage	winter tares (*Vicia villosa*) or other nutrition crop

Next year move everything around one space. Apply manure before potatoes but not before root crops such as carrots. Dig in the green overwintering nutrition crops before spring planting. Cucurbits, in other words zucchini, marrows, squash, pumpkins, and cucumbers, will go in the beds where the green manure has been dug in as they like a good layer of manure.

the greenhouse and its satellites

The greenhouse is a wonderful tool for a gardener. It enables you to provide a winter growing season, improve ripening conditions for some plants, extend the length of the growing season, isolate rare species from cross-pollination, and allow you to grow exotica.

Before we come to the greenhouse proper, let us consider growing under cover, with one word of warning which is to make sure you are not enclosing a plant that needs insect pollination.

cloches

These are portable greenhouses, transparent covers made of glass or plastic which can be moved around as needed. Cloches can be used to cover planted-out seedlings until they are hardened to the elements, and to place over tender plants if frost is a threat. They vary from ornate covers to cut-off clear plastic bottles. Even the plastic you see spread over fields of potatoes is really just a huge cloche. Use your imagination but make sure you give the plants plenty of room under the cloche.

polytunnels

These are sheets of polyethylene placed over hoops, open each end and facing east to west for maximum light. They are simply a variant of the greenhouse. I don't love them but they are very useful. I once had a

friend who ran a snail farm inside some polytunnels on the Mull of Kintyre. The snails flourished, which says it all really.

horticultural fleece

Nowadays horticultural fleece is a translucent fabric that acts as protection against wind and pest damage. It is supported on hoops or sticks to keep clear of the plants. Originally it was a poor fleece that was not usable for spinning. Dig the edges of your fleece into the earth and/or pin them down securely.

cold frames

Cold frames protect from wind and frost damage and are excellent for hardening off seedlings between the seed tray and the real world. At Lennoxlove House we had wonderful brick-built cold frames with hinged glass lids, but this is the ideal and not necessarily the reality. A few bales of straw to prop up some old glass or windows will do. Lay out the bales in a square and place a wooden board on top. Put another layer of bales on the board and top these with the glass. Cover the board with compost, and plant out seedlings in the compost.

hot beds and hot walls

Much used in more northerly gardens, hot beds—like cold frames but heated—and hot walls create extra warmth that enables you to force fruit or grow fruit, such as melons, that need a good amount of heat.

In the 18th century, growers put walls of deal planks in front of the brick garden walls against which fruit trees were growing, and piled dung into the gap between the wood and the brick. The heat generated by the rotting dung helped to force cherries, peaches, and other fruit.

In the 19th century, a company in the Suffolk, England town of Bury St. Edmunds patented a moveable glass wall to be used with fruit trees growing against a wall. A bracket with a cantilevered hook was screwed to the wall and this held the wall of glass in its wooden frame in front of the tree. The glass reflected the sunlight so the fruit tree benefited. Hot walls like these are still in use in heritage gardens around the world.

Although modern hot beds use electric cables, I prefer the green variety where the frame is placed on top of a bed of rotting manure. More manure is heaped around the sides. You can put these hot beds anywhere, even in a cold greenhouse or polytunnel.

Hot beds give you the opportunity to grow some unusual plants if you like. The first pineapple grown in England in the 17th century was grown in a hot bed.

cold greenhouses

The principle of a greenhouse is that the sun heats the greenhouse and it cools slowly when the sun has gone. The same principle applies to a lean-to, so if you are building one against a house, make sure it gets the sun.

You can of course buy a greenhouse or you can make your own, which is easier than it may sound. Old glass doors salvaged from dumpsters, old windows, sheets of glass or clear plastic and a little imagination are all you need.

You will need ventilation to admit insects and to prevent rot and molds, and you will also need to water your plants regularly. At times of frost you may want to leave a small kerosene heater or a halogen light or heater burning overnight inside. Another way of introducing some heat is to store your rainwater in large black plastic tubs in your greenhouse. These will act just like night-storage heaters. Alternatively, you can build a hot bed (see above), which will give off a lot of warmth.

Inside the greenhouse use compost not soil for your beds, top-dress them each spring and autumn, and practice crop rotation. Remove any diseased plants at once and observe the suggestions for tying back and stopping the various plants so that the foliage doesn't obscure too much of the light.

Tomatoes, cucumbers, peppers, eggplants, and chiles will all grow well in a greenhouse if you can keep it clear of whitefly (see page 45). Winter crops that do well sown in the autumn are carrots, chicory, Chinese greens, endive, and winter varieties of lettuce, including corn salad (mâche), peas, and perpetual spinach.

heated greenhouses

From the late 18th century onwards there was a passion for large heated greenhouses. The mid-Victorians in particular went wild for them, priding themselves on growing grapes and new potatoes in time for Christmas. They even grew tender peach trees such as the white Italian varieties.

Their greenhouses were ventilated via windows that opened with rotating handles and were heated with coal- or charcoal-burning stoves with hot pipes running under all the raised beds. They also had water pipes running through, either half-pipes from which the water would evaporate into the air, or pipes with holes in them running above the beds. These operated with plugs that could be raised or lowered to open or close the holes—a sort of early sprinkler system. Nowadays you can heat your greenhouse with electric cable running under the beds or with heaters, but why not a wood-burning stove in the middle?

pests and diseases

Nothing will bring home to you your organic status more than growing vegetables. The minute you embark on a vegetable garden you are at war—pigeons will want your brassicas and legumes, song birds will be after your soft fruits, and there will be insect predators galore. You will have to marshal your troops and enlist your allies carefully.

Gone are the days when you could simply blast everything with chemicals. In fact, you are probably reading this book in order to protect yourself and your children from the systemic spraying of food crops. We perhaps don't have to go as far as the great Lord Coke of Holkham in Norfolk who, in the 17th century, turned 200 ducks into a field of cabbages infested with caterpillars. The ducks ate all the creepy crawlies and the cabbages were saved. Bear it in mind.

slugs and snails

Just as Coke turned to ducks, you might care to encourage hedgehogs. You will be delighted when you realise quite how many slugs and snails these spiky predators will consume. I have always been kindly disposed to hedgehogs ever since I read about Mrs. Tiggywinkle and Fuzzy in the Little Grey Rabbit books. There was a tendency among country people to abjure hedgehogs as they believed they stole the milk from cows and brought bovine TB, allegations which have all now been proved to be untrue. Hedgehogs are fewer than they once were due to the growth of roads and car traffic, but they are still to be found. If, when the warm days begin and they are coming out

of hibernation, you leave out a saucer of milk mixed with a little chopped meat or dog food after dark, you may well lure them into your garden, especially if there is an early spring when there is not much around for them to eat.

You may also lure in the odd fox, in which case shoot it and make a nice hat like the one I'm wearing on the back cover. That one was shot by an urban Yorkshire butcher in his hen run.

follow the trail

Slugs and snails pose a major problem and they are your worst enemies early in the growing season. To locate them, follow the slime trails. Both these creatures need to feed to create slime, without which they die. They are hermaphrodite and therefore can impregnate their own eggs. If you

come across a batch of eggs, wait until daylight, then remove the stone they are under and give the birds a caviar feast.

If you put wood ash, ground seashells, or sawdust around your plants, this will help to deter slugs and snails. Copper wire and aluminum foil are also deterrents; use them to construct little fences around tender plants.

Slugs love beer, so sinking shallow containers of beer as slug traps is very efficacious, but hedgehogs are also partial to beer, so do make sure the traps aren't too deep for the hedgehogs to climb out of and leave a stick in for any beetles to climb out. (I'm not being "fluffy" about this— beetles feed on soft-skinned insects so you need them, too, to help you in your fight.) And if you keep bees, don't use beer traps in early summer as the young bees are attracted to them and may get drowned.

snail hunt

Another way of dealing with slugs and snails is to seek them out. My grandmother in Singapore used to keep me out of mischief during the afternoon siesta by getting me to swat flies at a penny a fly. Apply the same principle to your children or grandchildren and send them on a slug and snail search. Slugs and snails prefer to come out in the dampness of evening so this is the time to mount your torch-lit hunts. Children may not want to pick the creatures up by hand so provide them with chopsticks, rubber gloves, or tweezers as accessories. When you have located the enemies, drop them into a bucket of water to drown them, then compost them or feed them to your poultry.

eat your snails

While slugs make chicken food, snails can provide a tasty dish for you. In order to eat them, they need to be placed on oatmeal for 2–3 days to clean them out. Then boil them like whelks to remove them from their shells. After that you can cook them with garlic and butter or stew them with tomatoes in the Spanish fashion, or cook them in any other way you choose.

Most commercial snails come from Turkey but especially in chalk regions you find what country people call "wall-fish"—the land snails transported throughout their empire by the Romans to supplement their diets. If you have African land snails (sometimes the size of a dessert plate) in your area, they are also good eating but are tough so will need to be marinated for a day or two in pawpaw or pineapple juice.

frogs and toads versus slugs and snails

Other allies in your fight against the slugs and snails are frogs and toads, so build a small pond in your garden if you don't already have one. You may have to borrow some frog spawn from a friendly neighbor to get your frogs started. Don't forget to plant a few water lilies to shelter the frogs from marauding birds. You may also have to acquire a toad. Find a nice damp, cool spot for it to shelter during the day and you will be repaid one hundredfold.

Ponds do, however, attract mosquitoes which lay their eggs on the surface. This is another reason to encourage frogs as they will eat the mosquito larvae. Build a proper pond lined with clay in the old-fashioned manner, not one with a fiberglass or plastic lining. You will find your pond life does better in it.

birdlife joins the struggle

Thrushes and blackbirds are also your friends in the slug and snail war but in order to ensure their safety and encourage them to breed, you will need to kill or remove crows, rooks, jays, magpies, jackdaws, and squirrels, all of which prey on songbird eggs and chicks.

A Larsen trap or a small-bore rifle will do the job for crows and magpies. Jackdaws nest in chimneys, so sweep your chimneys as they are building their nests. This will destroy the nests before the eggs are laid and the jackdaws will quickly move elsewhere.

Squirrels are good eating in a stew with prunes and tomatoes. It's funny but once you actually start engaging with nature rather than watching it on televison or through your binoculars, you very quickly become un-fluffy. Take all these steps and your reward will be glorious birdsong, to say nothing of fewer snails.

"Squirrels are good eating in a stew with prunes and tomatoes."

keeping insects and other creatures at bay

There are many traditional ways of dealing with insect pests around the fruit and vegetable garden. To kill and prevent whitefly, I recommend a splendid remedy that was told me by my good friend Charlie. He cuts rhubarb leaves, puts them in a galvanized bucket, pours in boiling water, and lets them rot down. Then he sprays with the rather smelly liquid that results.

Another friend in the war against greenfly is the ladybug. In England, there are actually companies now that will send you ladybugs by mail. Put them on those plants that are affected by greenfly and the ladybirds will do the work for you. Don't order too many ladybugs, though, as they will reproduce.

insecticides

Then there are insecticides. Botanical insecticides are derived from plants and these are greatly to be preferred. Many work as well as synthetic insecticides and because they break down quickly, there will be less risk of residues on your crops.

There are, for instance, the nicotine-based insecticides deriving from *Nicotiniana tabacum* that work on the nervous systems of insects to kill them. Just be careful not to use them immediately before harvesting. Pyrethrum, made from the dried and powdered flowers of the daisy chrysanthemum, Cineranaefolium, is one of the safest of this type of the botanical insecticides, but make sure you get pure powdered pyrethrum as some formulas include piperonyl butoxide, which is not suitable for an organic garden. Derris dust is extracted from tropical and sub-tropical plants belonging to the legume family. It is a good general-purpose insecticide but is harmful to fish so don't use it near ponds or streams.

Soapy water is good against soft-bodied insects but must be sprayed directly on them. Spray when the adult insects are less active, either in the cool early morning or, if you have beehives, in the evening after the bees have gone to bed as the soap will hurt them. And only use soap, never dish detergent, which may damage your plants.

fighting plant disease

There is little you can do against fungal infections and leaf curls apart from spraying, but it is a general rule of thumb that the healthier your garden, the fewer the diseases. Composting, mulching, and weeding are the tunes to which a well-kept garden marches. These basic tasks will all help combat disease as will regular inspections and removal of infected material as soon as you see it.

companion planting

For most of my life modern notions have scorned companion planting as foolish country lore. Holistic gardeners, however, have long known that growing certain plants close together complements and sustains them while some species detest each other. Modern scientists who dislike what they cannot explain poo-pooh the idea and forget the maxim "there are more things in heaven and earth." Repeatedly nowadays I come across some "invention," "discovery," or "innovation" by some young Turk which was actually mooted centuries ago by Trusser, Markam, or Culpeper. If Alexander Fleming had read his mother's Mrs. Beeton's Cookbook he would have discovered penicillin a lot earlier: "the mold that grows on bread and oranges is excellent in the treatment of boils, carbuncles, and infested wounds." Companion planting works, so do try it.

● Grow marigolds among your vegetables as marigold roots secrete a substance that destroys nematodes and eel worms. If your soil is badly infested, grow a solid block of marigolds for a season then dig them in as green manure. If you make sure that you grow the edible pot marigolds, you'll have an extra food harvest, too.

● Nasturtiums are irresistible to aphids so use them to distract the aphids' attention from your vegetables, but make sure you plant them well away from the vegetable plot. As a bonus, nasturtium leaves, flowers, and seeds are all good additions to salads, too.

● Alliums of all sorts exude enzymes from their roots which are toxic to many pests, so plant garlic among your lines of vegetables.

● Rue, mint, tansy, lavender, sage, rosemary, and wormwood all deter a variety of pests so plant them among the rows, too.

● Nettles attract butterflies as well as the early aphids that provide food for ladybugs waking from hibernation. This means that nettles not only keep the aphids off other plants, but also encourage aphid predators to breed.

● If you plant nettles near your tomatoes they will help the fruit ripen, and remember that young nettles make good eating (see page 82) and are full of iron.

● If you are reclaiming field land for vegetables, there may be a real problem with click beetle so plant mustard for a season and dig it in as a green manure.

Another thing that will help is to keep some rainwater barrels. Use this purer water for watering and for mixing your sprays. If you look in the back of this book you will find the names of some providers of organic pesticides and plant sprays so you will be able to exercise control without breaching your organic principals. However, remember that, at the end of the day, you will never win completely. That is part of the adventure of gardening.

"If Alexander Fleming had read his mother's Mrs. Beeton's Cookbook he would have discovered penicillin a lot earlier..."

fruit

cane fruits

It is a great joy to grow fruit canes as they only need a little attention—just pruning and watering in dry weather as the fruit begin to color. You are also advised to protect the canes from birds with netting. It is very fulfilling—as well as filling—to pick your own berries and currants; pick one to eat yourself and two for the trug.

You can grow a variety of cane fruits, including raspberries, tayberries, loganberries, and gooseberries, and you can even grow thornless blackberries, although I prefer to pick my blackberries in the hedgerows. You might also like to grow red, white, and black currants. I always find that just as there are never enough raspberries, so there are never enough black currants. All of these fruits freeze well and you can make jams, jellies, and syrups with them, also.

raspberries

Raspberries prefer a neutral, very well drained soil. Plant the canes from late winter to early spring, once the soil has dried out. Set them in shallow holes, about 2 inches deep, and spread the roots out in the hole to encourage suckers that will form new canes. Plant the canes 1½ feet apart and the rows 6 feet apart. Once you have planted your canes, cut them back to about a foot above the ground, cutting to a good bud. Mulch well in the spring to conserve moisture.

Once the new canes appear, cut out the old ones. Allow about 6–7 canes per plant

buying the canes

When buying your canes make sure that they are guaranteed virus-free. All of these plants, with the exception of gooseberries, which grow as a shrub, will need support. Grow them either against a wire fence at the edge of your garden or hammer in stakes and string wires between them to support the canes. If space is limited you can twist the canes around just one post. The raspberry variety Autumn Blissa will grow without any support at all and can be grown as a container plant.

but do not select your canes until late spring as this is when you will be able to choose the best. Cut out any that show signs of disease.

As soon as they are tall enough, tie them to the wires (see box above). Weed well throughout the season. Harvest as and when the fruit is ripe.

When the plants have finished fruiting, cut back the brown woody canes as next year's fruit will grow on new wood. There are a number of varieties you may like to grow; talk to your plantsman about what suits your area best. Plants should last for around 10 years.

blackberries and their hybrids

Blackberries and their hybrids prefer well-drained but not dry soil. They like full sun best but will do all right in partial shade. Dig in plenty of manure or compost before planting. Otherwise treat as raspberries.

gooseberries

Gooseberries are little shrub-like plants that do well if neglected. I have gotten the best fruit off stunted little bushes that I have totally ignored, while I have had little or tasteless fruit off those that I've carefully nurtured.

currants

Tie up carefully to support the fruit bunches and to let the light get at them. Remember not to grow too many white currants as they fruit best and you will find that you end up adding them to your red currant jelly in despair.

soft fruits

strawberries

So called because a layer of straw spread around the plants helps them to ripen and keeps back slugs and snails. I prefer to grow my strawberries in raised beds because it prevents the crawlies and saves backache. Strawberries also do well in planters or containers.

They tolerate most soils except heavy, wet ones. They prefer a slightly acid soil and if yours is chalky or alkaline, you may have to feed for iron deficiencies (see page 25).

Plant in late autumn or winter and remove runners—this is how strawberries spread themselves—as they develop, to help the plant produce more fruit. The final distance between plants should be about 1½ feet. Harvest as soon as the fruit is ripe.

Plants crop best in their second year but should last four years. They benefit from a light dressing of ash, watered in. If you are careful in your selection of varieties you can have strawberries all summer and autumn. They do not store and do not really freeze well so unless you want masses of jam, aim for different varieties that will crop at different times.

wild strawberries

These make wonderful groundcover, are easy to grow, and do not need straw. Grow them on a very well-drained bank and you will reap a wonderful reward.

blueberries

These are excellent if your soil has a high pH reading—they will even grow in soils that are above pH6. They are high in anti-oxidants so are very good for you, and even babies love them as they aren't tart. Mixed with either strawberries, raspberries, or both, they make a visually attractive summer fruit salad. They love peaty soils, where they are found growing wild. Blueberries also do very well in tubs on your patio and are tolerant of either sun or partial shade. If you are planting them in a barrel, mix well-rotted coniferous bark or crumbled peat in with your soil.

tree fruits

apples

Considering mankind gave up earthly paradise for an apple or, as Lord Byron put it, "since Eve met Adam much depends on dinner," we should pay attention to this splendid fruit. It will be another joy to add to your new way of life. Supermarket apples are tasteless, horrible and have usually traveled around the world in heavily chilled conditions. An apple freshly plucked and ripe from the tree has a brilliant taste sensation.

choosing an apple variety

There are many great new apple varieties but I am fonder of the older types that I grew up with.

Worcester Permain – this is my favourite apple. I carry in my head the flavor of Worcester Permains picked from a tree in Sussex.

Costard – I wonder about this now-extinct apple from which the word "costermonger" (fruit seller) comes. It was the definitive apple of the Middle Ages in England.

Flower of Kent – also now lost to us but this was the apple that fell on Isaac Newton's head and changed the world.

Api – another favorite of mine and the most likely contender for the apple of the Garden of Eden. It was beloved of the Romans and features in their poetry and prose. It is a small, very pretty apple with a sweet but sharp taste and it keeps very well.

Blenheim Orange – I suppose this is the apple many of us carry in our mind's eye as it is the most frequently painted of apples. It is red and yellow with a crisp sweet flavor--the perfect Christmas apple.

Cox's Orange Pippin, Discovery and any of the **Laxton** family are good keepers for winter eating.

White Joanetting – named for Joan the Fair Maid of Kent, mother of the Black Prince, this was the Elizabethan favorite. It ripens in early July and has a beautiful aroma as well as a sweet flavor.

Gladstone – another reliable summer apple with a good scent.

Allington Pippin – this is a good example of the "pippins"—apples grown from a pip. Pippins usually keep well.

Bismark or **Granny Smith** – if you are reading this in North America, Australia, South Africa, or Chile, try either of these for tarts and fritters.

Egremont Russet – seldom seen nowadays but always worth growing as they are easy maintenance and good storers but are rustic rather than pretty. They are too misshapen for today's supermarkets. They vary from the largest, the Royal, a pre-17th-century type, through to the Golden.

Cider apples – virtually inedible and intended solely for the making of cider.

Apples are entirely a matter of personal taste. There are currently over 5,000 different species of apples to choose from so it is important to find a local plantsman to advise you. Ask about having a selection of early and late species. Or you can go to one of your local apple days—the Brogdale or Wisley apple days are some examples. Here you can taste a good cross section and make your choice. Remember, too, that apples need to be cross-pollinated so it is important that you choose trees that flower at the same time. Again, take advice on this.

Early apples do not store well but are excellent for eating. Later-ripening apples are picked as the first frosts come and are stored over winter. They become sweeter but less visually appealing as the months go by. You also want to include some cooking apples, though not necessarily Bramleys, which were developed by Victorian plantsmen to collapse when baked and are the best for purees and apple sauces. Instead you may want something that will make a splendid apple tart.

fitting your fruit trees in

Apples and other fruit trees can be grown in a variety of ways—as a full-size tree or a dwarf, as a fan, espaliered against a wall or along wires strung between posts, or as a cordon (a single shoot growing either straight up a wall or, preferably, at a diagonal angle so that you can fit in more trees).

Rootstocks

Apples grown from seed rarely succeed and take a long time to mature so it is best to buy young trees. Apples are grafted onto a variety of rootstocks which really dictate their future growth, eventual size, and what growth conditions the tree will need. Again, seek advice.

For dwarfing trees M9 and M27 rootstocks are probably a good choice. M27 will produce a squat shrubby tree and M9, which reaches 6 to 10 feet at most, is very good for cordons, although it is quite high-maintenance. M26 is slightly taller and good for three-tier espaliers and cordons. MM106 gives a nicely shaped tree up to about 18 feet in height.

pears

In the Middle Ages they preferred pears to apples and the great monasteries of France grew and developed many varieties. There have been waves of pear mania at different periods of history, the last of which swept New England in the 19th century. Although there is no native American pear, these "epidemics" have led to the development of over a thousand types of pears, both eaters and cookers.

Pears deteriorate very quickly and do not store that well, so they taste best when they are picked ripe, which is impossible for supermarkets to do.

Pears follow the same growing requirements as apples but unless you live in a very warm part of the world, grow them against a wall or, as I once saw in the late Lord Sefton's garden, as a chalice. This is a technique where the center of the tree is removed and the leaders are trained to grow upwards to form an open bowl, allowing the sun to strike the center of the tree. The lady gardener there was very proud of her achievement as it takes time, effort, and

meticulous husbandry to avoid disease and destruction by pests during the formation period.

Apart from the obvious ways of cooking and storing pears, they are very good cut in half and dried (see page 204).

pear in a bottle

I have always been fascinated by that strange French liqueur Poire William. In order to make it, a growing fruit is put in a bottle while it is still small enough to fit through the neck. The pear continues to grow in the bottle until it is ripe, at which point the pear is severed from the tree. The bottle is then filled up with eau de vie and left to stand until the alcohol is infused with the scent and taste of the pear. It is then ready to drink.

plums

It is a fine thing to have a plum tree in your garden. It is almost impossible to buy decent plums and there is nothing to compare with a ripe juicy one.

The main worry with plums is that they flower very early and the blossoms can be damaged by frost. If possible, cover the tree with a fleece or burn smoke braziers nearby to keep frost off the flowers.

There are many varieties of self-fertilizing plums so if you are just having one tree, make sure you choose one of these.

Plant plums as for apples, exercising the same degree of care. They like a sunny position and damp but not wet soil.

All pitted fruits are prone to silverleaf, a potentially fatal disease. Trees acquire a silvery sheen on the leaves which then spreads to the branches and then the tree dies. If this happens, cut out the affected areas. Any diseased branch over an inch wide will show a brown stain. Cut this wood out to well below the stained area and burn the prunings. Because of this tendency to disease, prune only where necessary and always in summer when the tree is growing strongly. Remember to thin your fruit at the midsummer shed (see page 37).

(see page 37)

plum predators

The worst predators for plums are wasps and pigeons. Other birds may strip the buds even before you have to worry about the fruit. Hanging discarded CDs and mothballs among the branches may suffice but sometimes the only answer is to net the whole tree or invest in a hawk. A wasp trap or a jar filled with beer are also useful as deterrents but not if you keep bees.

Plums for small spaces

If you live in a cold place or if space is limited, grow your plum as a cordon, fan, or espalier. For small gardens there is a rootstock called Pixy, which provides dwarf trees. These can be grown in pots. If space is limited, you can also grow the single-stemmed Minarette.

other pitted fruit

The rules for plums apply to all pitted fruit. Cherries, including geans (wild cherries for cooking) are a joy. One of the best things I ever ate was a wild cherry crumble made by my friend Alaphia Bidwell. I also love the Hungarian wild cherry soup.

If you have the climate or a wall to ripen them on, apricots are reckoned by some to be the taste of paradise. Damson plums are happily making a come back here. In the Lye Valley in Cumbria, England, they have a Damson Day for admiring the blossom, much as the Japanese do with their cherry blossom. Be careful when buying damson gin as many commercial producers use imported sloe and damson juice from Poland rather than steeping the fruit.

mulberries

I would put in a plea that you plant a mulberry tree, although you will have to wait nearly a decade for the first fruit. It is an attractive tree in its own right and quite delicious. The fruit makes wonderful ice cream and is very good dried as the Persians and Afghanis do. And of course, if you want a totally new way of life, you can always keep silkworms. I did this when I was young and although I never made much silk it was fascinating. I always love the story of how Napoleon, bored to tears during his brief stay on Elba, observed that black mulberry trees grow in profusion there and encouraged the establishment of a silk industry on the island.

melons

When I was at school at Brighton there was a splendid aged nun called Mother Peirquet who taught me Latin and Greek with a high Prussian accent and gardened magnificently. Her great pride was that in a good year she succeeded in growing melons outside. Hopefully many of you will be reading this where you can easily grow melons but for those of us in Britain it is possible, especially with a greenhouse or hot bed.

Sow your seeds ½ inch deep in individual pots in mid-winter. They want to be at about 68°F. Re-pot the seedlings when they have about four true leaves. If you are growing them inside, transfer them to their final position at this point. If growing them outside, harden them to the elements in a cold frame and plant them after the frosts are finished. Melons like a lot of farmyard manure, so dig in plenty of it.

Once the side-shoots have produced five leaves, pinch out the tips. Stop additional side-shoots at three leaves. You may have to pollinate as you would for zucchini, thrusting the male flower into the female. If you are training your melons up a frame, you will need hammocks to support the fruit. Netting is best but you can buy ferret hammocks at game fairs, which do very well. Old tights are all right too, but aren't very elegant. If you are growing them on the ground, grow them on a small mound. To prevent the fruit from rotting, put a slate or wooden slat under the fruit. You will know when they are ripe from the smell; the musky, erotic smell of a ripe melon is unmistakable.

grapes

If you are living in Britain, successful grape growing depends upon where you live. There is a fair-sized English wine industry and the Romans grew grapes in Lincolnshire, but for table grapes, you really need a hothouse. However my friend Henrietta Palmer, a descendant of the man who grew the first pineapple in Britain, grows a vine in her guest bathroom, a room with a lot of south-facing glass.

Grapes flourish on dried blood, either dug in around the roots of the vine or watered on. The great vine at Hampton Court, still thriving since the reign of Henry VIII, used to have the blood of an ox poured over the roots every few years. Today I believe they use the dried variety. When it comes to table grapes, Black Hamburg is my favorite.

citrus fruits

There is much theorizing that the fruit Adam plucked was actually an orange, just as people believe that Paris's prize to Venus was an orange rather than an apple. All of this seems pretty likely in the context of Mesopotamia or Greece.

If you are reading this in a hotter clime, picking the fruit in your own garden will always be a joy. I find nothing nicer when visiting friends in Spain than to go into the garden or even the street and pluck an orange or a lemon. On the Costa del Sol, the oranges grow in the streets as sycamores do in London. The silly ex-pat Brits step over the fallen fruit and go to the supermarkets to buy them instead. They look at me askance when I pick them up and take them home to squeeze for breakfast.

In the orange groves behind the hills on the Costa del Sol, you can get drunk on the scent of the trees but even a single one will give out the most lovely scent. If you live in the right place you can easily grow oranges, lemons, grapefruits, or any of the many other citrus species.

When I was a child and visited relatives in Australia, I loved the little kumquats that grow there. They make the most delicious marmalade, are very simple to grow, and are a compact size, which makes them ideal for terraces and patios.

A warm enclosed space is a good place for citrus trees and growing dwarf

varieties is a particularly good idea where space is limited. All the rules that apply to other fruit trees apply to citrus.

figs

Eating a ripe fig freshly plucked and warm from the sun is a truly sensuous experience. If you are reading this in a country where figs are easy to grow, I will not need to tell you much about their cultivation—they just get on with it themselves. All the usual information on bird predation, training, and pruning apply.

The most common fig grown in the UK is the Bardaic or Brown Turkey fig. It doesn't need caprification—a method of pollinating by a fig wasp—which many of the wilder varieties still require. Walled gardens sometimes have fig houses that are like vine houses, but figs can ripen perfectly well in a good year on a south-facing wall.

potatoes

Potatoes are in my genes. My father, a true gourmet, writing an introduction to a celebrity charity cookbook chose, of all things, to write about the potatoes of his childhood, while my mother's comfort food was new potatoes eaten with a bowl of double cream. It is such a joy to grow your own potatoes. You will taste the difference once you try.

In England, potatoes are classified as: "earlies," which are ready in June and July having been planted in March; "second earlies" for eating in August and early September; and "main crop," maturing in September and October. For information on grades of US potatoes for processing, go to www.ams.usda.gov/standards. There is a lot of information there so pull what you need from it, if what you're looking for is there.

"...any supermarket selling British 'new' potatoes other than Jersey Royals earlier than June is palming you off with last year's chilled, irradiated, small salad potatoes!"

vegetables

cultivation

To grow, manure your ground the previous autumn. Be careful not to plant potatoes in frost pockets and remember they need a deep tilth. Your seed potatoes should be about an ounce in weight and the size of a pullet's egg. Dig drills 2 feet deep and 2 1/2 feet apart and place your seed potatoes with the rose end upwards in the drills. Plant "earlies" 12 inches apart and all others 16 inches apart. Cover immediately and draw up the soil to make a ridge 4–6 inches high.

Water "earlies" at the rate of 5 quarts per square yard over a 14-day period and once they reach the size of a marble (check this by gently digging around in the soil), increase this to 5 quarts per square yard every 10 days. Main crop potatoes should be watered at this rate only at flowering time, as this will increase yield and will prevent scab; otherwise water them when the weather is very dry.

Potatoes are ready to harvest after three months, when the flowers are fully opened. Leave potatoes on dry soil or anywhere dry for 2–3 hours before storing. Lift all potatoes to prevent future disease. Store all the undamaged tubers in a frost-free building and keep them in the dark or under black plastic to prevent greening. For large quantities, store in an outside clamp. This involves removing the leaves after lifting, heaping the potatoes under straw and, after they have sweated for two or three days, mounding up the earth over them. Do not underestimate the danger of eating green potatoes; all solanums are quite poisonous in certain conditions and there is a direct link between green potatoes eaten by pregnant women and spina bifida, so keep your potatoes out of the light.

potatoes for small spaces

Don't worry if you live in a town or city; potatoes grow perfectly well in pots. To grow them this way, you must first chit them in early February by placing a single layer of seed potatoes, "rose" end up, in a box or tray in a light airy spot such as a cool greenhouse. By late March you will have strong, sturdy shoots. Take a large pot, at least 12 inches wide, and fill it with garden soil. Plant 2–3 chitted potatoes in the pot and keep in a slightly heated greenhouse until the frosts are past.

There is a fashion for urban gardeners to grow potatoes in planters made from old tires; personally I think this makes your garden look like a tinker's bothy but there is no doubt that it does work. In fact, many other vegetables can also be grown in this way. Put down your first tire and fill it with well-rotted manure or compost. Add another tire and fill with soil; add a third tire and put in a thin layer of manure or compost and more soil. Three tires will probably suffice. Don't completely fill the last tire as you will need to leave room for plant growth. Bury your chitted potatoes in the soil and cover with sacking or black plastic to promote growth.

When the time comes for harvesting, break down the tire structure, removing the potatoes as you go. This method works surprisingly well and offers the benefit of pest protection as slugs can't climb that high. It also avoids a lot of digging. Remember when planning crop rotation (see page 40) that potatoes, tomatoes, and eggplants are all from the same family.

(see page 40)

choosing a potato variety

Choose your variety of potatoes for joy and for keeping. Here are some of my favorites, but you will have great fun reading the catalogues and making your own choices.

Pink Fir Apples – a delicious choice if you have lots of space, but they are not great keepers.
Desirée – good flavor.
King Edwards – unbeatable for a main crop. They store well and cook even better, but are prone to blight, so watch them carefully.
Pentland Dells – I like these for "earlies."
Pentland Express – for "second earlies."

companion planting

Plant potatoes with beans and corn, but they dislike the company of cucubrits, squashes, Jerusalem artichokes, tomatoes, peas, and raspberries.

onions

You can never grow too many onions and in fact we could be facing future shortages. A few years ago there was a major onion shortage in India, which caused rioting in the streets. The soil for an onion bed should be finely tilled, reasonably fertile, but not freshly manured. Onions like a sunny sheltered spot and can be grown successfully from seed or from sets.

cultivation

Double-dig your onion plot in the late autumn or early winter and lay a 2–3-inch layer of manure in the bottom. A week before sowing, top-dress with twice as much potash as nitrogen. Onion bulbs sown the previous autumn do not require this; instead dress them sparingly with chalk in February. Sow the seeds thinly in drills about 3/4-inch deep and 10 inches apart and, if the soil is dry, water. Thin out the seedlings to 2–3 inches apart once they have straightened. Onions shouldn't need more watering unless the weather is dry in May and June, when you may need to water sparingly. It is, however, important to keep them free of weeds. In mid- to late August or early September, the stalks will flop over and turn yellow indicating that they are mature. In a wet summer you may have to bend the tops by hand to assist bulb maturity. Once the tops are yellow and withered, try to pick a dry spell for harvesting, then you can leave the onions on top of the dry soil to dry for a day or two. You will notice some onions are bull-necked and will not bend; never store these as they will rot, so eat them first.

growing from seed

Choosing the dates for sowing over-wintering onions is important as you want the seedlings to be strong enough to survive the winter and you need the

warmer soil for germination, but if they are sown too early, you will suffer attacks of bean fly. I find the first week in September best as there is usually a spell of good weather then. Sow the seeds thinly so that you can leave the thinning until early spring to produce bigger onions. If you sow seed in a greenhouse, sow in January, then harden the plants under a cold frame in March so that you can transplant to the bed in April.

growing from sets

"Sets" are partly developed onion bulbs stored over the winter and planted in the spring, when they grow rapidly. This method is most useful in areas with a short growing season. You can buy sets, but they aren't cheap, or instead you can keep back some of your own from the previous season, choosing firm onions about $2^1/_4$–$2^1/_2$ inches in diameter. Plant your sets in fine tilth in late March or early April in rows 10 inches apart. Your onions should be separated by 3 to 4 inches and only the tip should be visible. Firm the soil around the plants. If birds or frost should pull them out of the ground, replant at once.

onion pests

Onions' main pests are onion fly, which lays its eggs around the onions in early May, and eel worm. That is when you should treat your seedlings. If you are gardening organically, the best protection is a layer of ash both on and around the base of the plants. Be very careful to rotate your onions as pests will stay in the soil for a year or more.

onions for small spaces

If you live in an apartment or condo, or have a small town garden you can grow shallots, which take up less space for more gain. Scallions will grow quite happily in a pot on your windowsill or in a window box. These are sown from seed and don't need thinning except as you pick them for eating. The other type of onion for small-space gardening is the Welsh or tree onion which is a perennial and, as it grows up rather than out, does not take up much space. Tree onions are particularly good for companion planting, as, like all alliums, they emit a substance that is abhorred by aphids and many other pests.

storing onions

When you have lifted your onions from the ground, lay them on newspaper in a dry place until their stalks are completely dry and straw-like. Turn them every 3–4 days to ensure proper drying, then sort them and retain the perfect ones for storing over winter. Any with signs of fly, rot, mold, or bull necks should not be stored but used as soon as possible. In my drinking days, dear friends used to invite me over at the time of onion harvesting, as the fascinating (to me) task of sorting onions kept me off the gin somewhat, hence I was better company. I would then make large quantities of onion soup for eating or freezing with the "must use" ones.

When you have sorted out your storing onions, rub off any excess dry skin and braid the stalks together, reinforcing them with thin string, and then hang them by the string from hooks in a dry place. I think they look very gratifying hanging in a kitchen or pantry. Small onions and shallots can be stored in nets; old tights or stockings are good for this. A good onion crop should see you through the winter and when they start sprouting in the spring you can eat the green tops in salad as an anti-scorbutic. If you don't want to string them or hang them in nets, lay them in boxes in a cool, dry place and check them from time to time. When storing shallots, you may like to break apart the bigger bulbs as this will stop any tendency to rot.

garlic

Garlic is a true gardener's friend and is good for your health. In the 16th century, Culpeper, the herbalist, wrote that "garlic burns away the fat that is stored around the heart," so eat it as a cholesterol-controller.

Garlic likes sunny conditions and will grow happily in plots, pots, or windowboxes. Plant your garlic from bulblets separated from the main bulb in February or March. If planted in a plot among other vegetables, it will help with pest control but don't plant next to any legume. Harvest as for onions and store in nets in a cool, dry place. The bulbs are frost-hardy so can be left in the ground throughout the winter.

leeks

I live in Musselburgh, the land of the leek. Indeed the finest standard leek bears the name of my "honest town," a name registered by the great botanist, Mr. Scarlett, who lived at the end of my street. The Romans, who were great leek eaters, raved about our local leeks and one of the duties of the soldiers on the Antonine wall in Scotland was to guard leek shipments to Rome. By the church near me, there was a Roman cavalry fort and there is a temple to Mithras in our park, so I often muse over our Roman ghosts and their affection for our leeks. Leeks like a well-drained soil and not too much food as that makes them grow lush and floppy, which is fatal. They also do not like heavy or clay soils that hold the wet during winter months.

cultivation

Leek seeds mature very slowly, so it is best to sow them in trays in a warm greenhouse and harden them off under cloches. Sow in trays in late January to early February and prick out to other trays when the seedlings have straightened. Outside, sow seeds in drills 1/2-inch deep and 6 inches apart in late March.

Leeks should be planted out when they are as thick as a pencil and 6 to 8 inches high. Make a hole 2 inches wide and 6 inches deep with a dibber, insert your seedling, then do not put the earth back, but instead fill the hole with water. If you are sowing seed, you will need to mound up the earth around the rows to aid blanching. Leeks are virtually pest-free. Harvest them as needed from Christmas onwards. They can remain in the ground until May when they begin to sprout.

companion planting

Plant leeks with carrots, onion, and celery, but not with legumes.

carrots

Only for you, dear reader, would I write this section. We all have something we hate in this world and, long before Mr. Blair, my hatred has always been reserved for the carrot. So much so that Johnny's wife Mary teases with me carrot gifts. I have a magnificent handbag with a bas-relief of carrots on it, I have a carrot pepper grinder, and many such other joys. I love the gifts but continue to hate the vegetable. When I was a little girl my father would pull them from the soil, dust them off, and make me eat them, slugs and all. Today I would probably fry the slug in garlic and butter but the carrot remains a black spot in my soul. I know, however, this is irrational and I don't condemn you for liking them, so here we go.

cultivation

The carrot likes a light sandy soil which has not been manured for a year. Soil that is too rich will cause it to fork and heavy clay will make it rot. If carrots are deprived of water while they are growing, they become coarse and woody, but too much water encourages leaf growth which draws in the deadly carrotfly.

From early March, sow the seed thinly in drills about 1/2- to 3/4-inch deep and 6 inches apart, then cover with fine soil. Thin the seedlings regularly throughout the summer as they become ready to eat. Young and tender carrots I'm told are delicious! When weeding, take care not to damage the shoulders of the plants as this will encourage disease.

Harvest your main-crop carrots in October, cut off the foliage, and clean off the soil. Pack in boxes of dry sand, ensure the carrots are separate, not touching, and keep in a cool, dry, frost-free place. They should last until March. Don't attempt to store damaged or diseased roots; burn the latter and compost or eat the former.

carrot pests

The carrotfly is attracted by the smell of crushed foliage, so thin in the evening and do not leave the removed leaves lying around. The carrotfly has two main seasons, May and August, so bear this in mind. Apart from planting onions as companions, the only organic remedy is to liberally sprinkle the leaves and shoulders with wood ash, replacing the ash during fly seasons if it is washed away by rain. The ash deters the fly from laying its eggs. Don't even bother growing carrots south of the River Tamar (bordering Devon and Cornwall) as the damned carrotfly flies all the time. That's why traditionally Cornish pasties should not contain carrots.

carrots for small spaces

If you live in a town or city, you can easily grow carrots in a growbag on your balcony or in shallow pots.

companion planting

Plant carrots with onions, peas, herbs, tomatoes, and radishes. Strangely, they dislike dill but this herb eats well with carrots! I do hope you have a good crop but don't invite me to share it!

parsnips

Soil for parsnips must not have been manured before sowing; if it is too rich they will fork. They require little nitrogen and like a sunny spot, although they will tolerate light shade. Unless you are growing a short-root variety of parsnip, you will need to dig deep to prepare the soil for planting as parsnip roots can go down as much as 2 feet. Dig a spade's depth and loosen the soil below this with a fork.

Two weeks before sowing in late February to early March, apply a dressing of general fertilizer. Try to avoid sowing in cold, wet weather but if the soil is dry, water before sowing. Use new seed each year as parsnip seeds lose fertility quickly, and plant 3–4 seeds together. Then, when the first true leaves appear, leave the strongest plant in each grouping.

The seeds take anything from 10 days to 4 weeks to germinate, depending upon soil temperature. Don't let your parsnips get dry throughout the year as this will cause splitting, and when hoeing the rows, take care not to damage the shoulders of the plants as this can let in disease.

You can harvest when the leaves die back in late autumn or early winter, but they are much improved by frost. Leave the plants in the ground throughout the winter and harvest at will. If you have to lift them, you can store as carrots but they tend to go soft and are only really useful for soup once that happens. Lift any remaining parsnips in March to make way for other vegetables.

parsnip pests

Parsnips are also prone to carrotfly so treat as for carrots.

parsnips for small spaces

In a town garden, parsnips can be grown in tire planters or in deep frost-proof pots.

the secret of borscht

In Russia and other parts of central Europe the beets are stored in barrels on the roof where the cold causes them to ferment. I firmly believe this is what gives true borscht its special flavor.

beets

A wonderfully versatile cropping vegetable, sow beets any time between February and June. The small, round-crop varieties will be ready in 12 weeks to adorn your summer cold table and salads. Plant on well-drained ground that isn't freshly manured or intersperse between rows of other vegetables or even, in a town garden, between other plants. Plant and thin as for parsnips.

Protect the seedlings from sparrows with black thread and take care when hoeing or weeding as damaged roots will bleed badly. Your main crop can be left in the ground through the winter, covered with straw against frost, or it can be harvested in October and stored in sand boxes. Inspect regularly for deteriorating roots.

companion planting

Beets love onions and cabbage or other brassicas but dislike beans.

"...long before Mr. Blair, my hatred has always been reserved for the carrot."

brassicas

This large family covers a huge range of vegetables—cabbages, brussels sprouts, cauliflower, kale, rutabagas, and turnips, broccoli, and, my favorite of all, purple sprouting broccoli. I am torn between this and asparagus for my funeral; debating the merits of each as the seasons come and go will probably keep me alive forever.

cultivation

There are certain key principles involved in growing brassicas. Plant them in a seedbed and transplant them at 5–7 weeks, or buy established plants. They like a fertile soil and should not be planted in the same plot more than one year in three. For preference, grow them to follow legumes as they benefit from the nitrogen in the soil.

All brassicas like a firm ground so cultivate and manure early in the winter or, if for some reason you must cultivate later, feed the soil and firm it down well. How? you ask. Use your feet.

The seedbed should preferably be open, sunny, and sheltered. Manure it well in the autumn and rake it over before using. Water if dry. Firm the soil and rake again to produce a fine tilth. Sow in drills 6 inches apart and 1½ inches deep. Germination takes 7–12 days. Thin to 2 inches apart as soon as possible, keep weed-free, and water if dry. Firm the soil down after weeding or thinning and remember to label the rows if you are sowing different varieties at the same time.

Double-dig your permanent main bed to between 1½ and 2 feet. Brassicas get very

thirsty and this will allow deep, well-formed root structures, which aid water intake and are more resistant to disease. Transplant your seedlings when they have 3–4 leaves and are about 6 inches tall. Take care not to damage the roots when transplanting, water with a rose, and, if it is very dry, make puddle holes and plant into them. Remember to firm down the soil; a gardener we had when I was a child said brassicas are just like small children, they like to be tucked well into their beds.

brassica diseases

The main reason for moving your brassicas to a fresh plot most years is the danger of club root infection; should this occur, carefully root up and burn infected plants and do not grow brassicas again on that spot for at least seven years.

> "I am torn between purple sprouting broccoli and asparagus for my funeral..."

cabbages

Never underestimate a gardener's passion for cabbage. I remember when once we were staying in Barbados, the West Indian gardener who had all the lovely Caribbean plants at his command would present us proudly with his cabbages, which I am ashamed to say we rather spurned. Having said that, I am very fond of cabbage when cooked properly, and cooked with partridge, it is a delight.

spring cabbage

Sow in late July or early August, to transplant between mid-September and mid-October. Plant 12 inches apart for hearted plants or 4 inches apart for spring greens. You can get the best of both worlds by removing two out of three greens in February and sprinkling with sodium bicarbonate, then with sulphate of ammonia or wood ash in early March. Plants will keep in the ground until June.

summer cabbage

You may not bother to grow summer cabbage as there are lots of alternatives to eat at this time of year and summer cabbage is the most prone to club root. If you do want it, sow between February and May for transplanting between April and May, and for harvesting between July and autumn. Be particularly careful at all stages of sowing and transplanting, as damaged roots are more prone to disease. To my mind, the main reason for bothering to grow summer cabbage is to eat sauerkraut.

cauliflower

This is the most difficult of the brassicas to grow successfully as it is very demanding in its soil, moisture, and food requirements. It is less hardy than other brassicas and in a bad winter even the over-wintering varieties will be damaged or killed by adverse weather. I suspect this is a gardener's vegetable, grown for pride—a head of mature "curds" looks impressive—but it is not a cook's dream as it is difficult to cook interestingly and tricky to store. However, if you are a vegetarian and aren't too worried about appearances, it is a godsend as it holds flavors well and has a different texture to other vegetables.

winter cabbage

Savoys and other winter varieties are the hardiest and thrive better on poorer soils than other brassicas. Sow in May and transplant in July. Water frequently and harvest from October onwards. In August, as they begin to heart, tie up the outer leaves with raffia.

red cabbage

Grow as spring or summer cabbage, cutting mature heads long before any frost. Take care not to grow too many red cabbages as a little goes a long way, even if you are pickling.

storing cabbages

Red and white cabbages will store well in a frost-free area. Dig up the whole plant, cut off the roots and the coarse outer leaves, and store so the cabbages are not touching. Inspect them from time to time to make sure they are not rotting.

brussels sprouts

In your new green world, you will want to grow the older varieties of brussels sprouts which mature irregularly on the same plant so that you can keep picking throughout the season. The new hybrids are designed for the freezer or for the farmers' market where you will see whole stalks being sold. Brussels sprouts freeze well on the stalk. I remember picking them with frozen fingers and they went tinkle plonk into the pan as we threw them in.

Sow in March or early April to transplant in May or June. A week before transplanting, dig over the site and rake in fertilizer at 4½ tablespoons per square yard. Hoe and weed regularly, but only water them if very dry. Pick the sprouts as they mature from the bottom up, and when all are picked, cut off the tops to use as greens. Dig it up as soon as you have finished with it as the plants draw heavily on nutrients in the soil. Dig up the woody stalk and burn it (don't compost it as it won't rot down well and may cause disease).

cultivation

A deeply dug, fertile soil, rich in humus is essential, and a heavy dressing of manure helps to provide food and retain moisture during growing. Cauliflowers should never be allowed to dry out as this will produce poor heads. During dry periods they need 5 quarts of water per square yard per day. If other brassicas don't heart, you still have top greens you can use, but with cauliflowers you are left with diddlysquat!

Dressings of sulphate of ammonia or wood ash should be watered into young plants before the curds form, to promote vigorous healthy growth. Sow summer cauliflowers in March or early April to transplant in June and harvest in August and early September. Unless you live in a mild, dry area, don't even think about winter cauliflowers as they hate heavy soils and bad weather.

sprouting broccoli

Unlike cauliflower, purple and white sprouting broccoli are very hardy and happy with the poor soils and cold areas that other brassicas disdain. Moreover they are totally delicious and are among those gratifying vegetables that you really have to grow yourself as the short season means the supermarkets avoid them. Sprouting broccoli matures from January to May and in very mild areas you may even get them for Christmas. Their main predator is the pigeon, who can decimate a crop, but with a gun and a little luck, you can have a perfect dinner. They are also useful plants to intersperse in an ordinary garden as they are out of the way quite early.

cultivation

The seeds are planted in April or May for transplanting in June and July. Harvest the plants as they mature, picking the central spear first at about 4 inches long but before the flowers begin to open, then picking the side shoots as they mature. Pick every two days and you will harvest for several months. The white variety crops later and is less prolific.

broccoli

I rather sided with the first President Bush when he said that he would never serve broccoli at the White House. I'm sure it is clever American marketing that, in order to tackle the damage he did, has persuaded the health-obsessed that broccoli is better for you than any other brassica. Why this is, no one has explained or as far as I know, proved. The large green head is in season from August until October and takes 12–14 weeks to mature, although with a mild autumn it will crop until the first frost.

cultivation

Sow in April and May and transplant in June. The seedlings should be planted in rows 18 inches apart with 18 inches between the plants. Harvest as the head's seven side-shoots mature. An ideal plant for freezing.

kale

This is an extremely hardy and useful winter plant, tolerant of club root, root fly, and poor soils. It is also beloved of pheasants so the old poachers' trick of using brandy-soaked raisins to lure pheasants into the kale will supply your whole meal. The old Scots expression, "Have you had your kale yet?" meant "Have you eaten?" and the Highland vegetable plot was known as the "kale yard." Kale soup is delicious; it was a staple of the Scots' diet before the Industrial Revolution, and is far healthier than the Scots' current obsession with deep-fat frying! Remember, the fashionable cavalo nero is only black kale! The larger leaves of kale can be bitter but are good for soup or for slow-cooking with other vegetables. Kale is happy with an open site but in areas of high, cold winds some windbreak is advisable, though having shot pheasants in East Anglian kale fields with the wind arriving straight off the Siberian steppe, I suspect it is not vital.

cultivation

Sow kale in April and May to transplant from late June to early August. Plant 16 inches apart in rows the same distance apart. Harvest after the first frost, selecting young shoots and discarding woody or yellowed stems. Inspect from time to time.

legumes

This group of plants is vital to a green garden as they are the best providers of nitrogen for your soil. They should not be grown on the same site two years running and after cropping has finished, cut back the plants to 4 inches above the ground and compost the vegetation, then dig or rotate the rest back into the ground. All legumes have little tubers attached to the roots which will restore nitrogen to the soil.

green beans

When I was a child, these were regarded as a delicacy and my mother, who loved them, was viewed as rather eccentric for growing them and serving them at dinner parties. Now they are fairly

commonplace and easy to grow. We used to call the round ones bobby beans, but now they all tend to be classed together.

Green beans do not thrive in cold soils and will rot if too wet. They grow best in a well-drained, fertile soil but I find that farmyard manure or compost dug in the winter before is usually enough, with no top-dressing needed. Don't grow them in the shade, and choose dwarf or climbing varieties to suit your garden.

cultivation

Don't sow before early May, and protect under cloches until they are established. Continue sowing until July and you will have beans all summer. Sow dwarf beans 18 inches apart, space the seeds 2 inches apart in drills 2 inches deep, and water the bottom of the drills. Sow climbing beans with a 2-foot gap between the rows and plant 3¹/₂–4 inches apart.

In June, give the plants a good mulching. Once established, unless it is very dry, do not water until the flowers appear, then water well allowing 5 quarts per square yard per week during flowering and pod-setting. This will give a good crop. Regular picking ensures a continuing crop, so pick while they are young and tender, and snap cleanly off the plant. Protect against aphids and burn plants infected by mold—never save seeds from diseased plants.

beans for small spaces

They grow very well on terraces, balconies, or decking, twining happily around the trellising and providing the sweet smell of bean flowers. In 18th-century England, Londoners used to walk among the bean fields of Chelsea to smell the lovely scent.

support for climbing beans

Climbing beans will grow up virtually anything—bamboo poles, teepee frames made of poles, or just some string strung between poles.

"In 18th-century England, Londoners used to walk among the bean fields of Chelsea to smell the lovely scent."

flat pole beans

Cultivation is as for green beans but pole beans will need stronger supports. Twist the plants counter-clockwise around the supports and they won't need much tying. They are insect-pollinated, so remember this when spraying. Sow in a sheltered, sunny spot, after the frosts are over. During cropping they will need picking every day.

fava beans (broad beans)

These were sacred in ancient Greece. I think I love young fava beans more than anything. You cannot buy really good fava beans; they are so much better when you pick them young and eat them at once.

The birthday beans from my friend Douglas (see page 22) were from overwintered plants sown the previous November. More usually they are sown under cloches in February for picking from late June onwards. Remove the cloches when the seedlings reach the glass. While they tolerate relatively poor soils, a better yield is obtained from rich, well-drained soil. Avoid cold, wet soils especially over winter, as the seeds will rot.

cultivation

Fava-bean seeds are very large and don't need a finely prepared bed. Plant them in 3-inch-deep holes in double rows, about 5 inches apart with 18 inches between the rows. The plants are quite frost-resistant and will germinate at soil temperatures of 41°F. Successive sowings will ensure beans throughout the summer.

When the plants are in full flower, pinch out 4–6 inches of shoot to reduce the danger of blackfly and aphids and to produce a more uniform pod. These pinched pickings are delicious cooked up in a little butter with salt and pepper.

From mid-June, pick the pods while they're young and supple. After harvesting, cut to 4 inches above the soil, compost the cut material, then dig the stem bases and roots into the soil to add nitrogen.

When you have shelled the pods, cook them and put them through the mouli or stew them whole in their pods. They also freeze very successfully.

peas

This group includes green peas (garden peas), marrow-fat peas, petit pois, snow peas, sugar snap peas, and asparagus peas. For me, green peas fall into the same category as fava beans: they are only really wonderful when freshly picked because the sugar in them turns to starch really quickly so even when bought in farmers' markets or the best produce markets, they are less than perfect.

cultivation

Peas must be grown on fertile, well-drained soil. Any waterlogging and the seeds will rot. Peas can be grown as "earlies," "second earlies," and main crop. From sowing to picking, 'first earlies' take 12 weeks, 'second earlies' 13–14 weeks, and main crop 14–16 weeks. You can also plant "late earlies" in early July for picking in early October if you live in a warmer climate.

Sow early peas in November for overwintering, then sow successively from early March until the end of April. Peas will germinate at 41°F but an intrusion of cold weather will knock them back and may lead to fungal disease.

Manure the ground the winter before planting. Pick when the pods are an inch long; if they are left until they are too big, they become fibrous and inedible.

pea support and protection

The taller varieties of peas give a better crop. Traditionally they are grown up pea sticks which are thin hedgerow twigs, but if you don't have access to these, grow them up netting instead.

Seeds and seedlings are prone to attack from birds and mice so use a guard of netting against the birds and sprinkle liberally with white pepper to keep the mice at bay. This tip was discovered accidentally by my mother, who didn't want to put down poison because of the dogs we had. It works very well against cats and foxes, too.

a choice of peas

Petit pois—best for canning so are worth growing for stocking up.

Marrowfat peas—these dry well and were used to provide a useful staple for soups and stews as well as for mushy peas throughout the winter.

Snow peas, sugar snap peas, and **asparagus peas**—fine if you have the room. I would go for the asparagus peas as they are more unusual.

soybeans

These are an excellent source of non-animal protein. Take particular care to plant when the frosts are past, and harvest in the autumn when the leaves turn yellow. The beans can then be threshed and eaten fresh, or frozen or dried.

tomatoes

You can grow tomatoes anywhere that has access to the sun—in greenhouses, on balconies, on windowsills.

cultivation

Sow the seeds thinly into seed trays and cover with finely sifted compost. Keep moist but not waterlogged. Ten to twelve days after sowing, when they have true leaves, transplant the seedlings to individual pots. Water to firm them up, then water little and often. Liquid-feed the plants before planting out when the plants are 6–10 inches tall and the first flowers are just opening. Water well before and after planting. Do not plant out any diseased plants. Alternatively you can buy ready-grown plants at this stage.

Snap off any side-shoots that develop or cut off with a sharp knife. When the plants are 4–5 feet tall, cut away the lower leaves with a sharp knife to allow light into the bottom of the plants and to guard against the risk of fungal diseases. In hot weather, water little and often, 3–4 times a day for pot and growbag plants, mixing feed in with the water.

If you have difficulty pollinating, spray with a fine spray of water or shake the cane or string gently to disseminate pollen. Stop your plants at the fourth truss by pinching off the plant two leaves above this point. In greenhouses, the plants should be stopped when they reach the roof, usually the sixth truss. For whitefly, use the rotted rhubarb cure (see page 45) and if the leaves turn yellow, water in a pinch or two of Epsom salts.

Pick the fruit as it ripens, but if you have unripened tomatoes in September, you can either de-stake the plant and lay it on straw covered with a cloche, or pick the tomatoes and lay them in a dark drawer to ripen, or put them in a brown paper bag with a banana. If you have small green tomatoes, you can crystallize them or even make chutney.

tomatoes for small spaces

In small spaces, tomatoes are best grown in 8½-inch pots or in stone circles with a plastic base. Lay out your plastic to protect your terrace or balcony, lay a circle of stones around the edge, and pile soil in the middle of the circle. They can even be grown on bales of straw with the aid of a little compost. They always need feeding with liquid manure (think back to your comfrey slurry—see page 28) and also need to be staked securely and protected from the wind.

marrows, squashes, zucchinis, and pumpkins

All of this family of plants, though different in appearance, have roughly the same habit and produce from June (early zucchini) until September. They all need well-drained soils and preferably a sunny sheltered position.

Unless you live in a warm climate, do not plant outdoors before mid-May—you must wait until the frosts are over. Dig your holes 5 feet apart for trailing varieties and 3 feet apart for bush varieties. Fill the holes with well-rotted manure or compost and replace the soil to form a mound over each hole. Sow 2–3 seeds in each mound and when each seedling has 3–4 leaves, remove the weakest seedlings leaving just one. They can also be chitted (see page 55) and transplanted later.

If growing early in pots, transplant one plant to each mound. Keep well watered and feed as the plants start to swell. Pinch out the growing points of laterals at 2 feet and train them at will.

You may need to pollinate them early in the season. The male flower is smaller and only produces pollen, so pluck these and brush the female flowers with them before frying the males in batter or stuffing them.

squashes for small spaces

In town or city gardens, squashes can be grown up trellises while one zucchini plant on a balcony will keep you supplied all summer. A single pumpkin plant on a terrace is dramatic and productive, especially if you plant a miniature variety. Pattypan squash look like tiny flying saucers, so they are fun to grow as well as delicious.

a cough mixture and children's tonic, but it was during the war that a commercial initiative was started by the Government, which remains with us today. In America, they boil rosehips and eat them as a vegetable with butter.

rose hip syrup

MAKES 2.5 QUARTS

2¹/₂ quarts water
2¹/₄ cups rose hips
2²/₃ cups sugar or honey

Boil 2 quarts water. Grind the rose hips in a coarse meat grinder or food processor, and put immediately into the boiling water. Pour into a crash (coarse cotton or linen) jelly bag and let it drip until the bulk of the liquid has come through. Return the residue to the pot, add 1 quart boiling water, stir, and let stand for 10 minutes.

Pour back into the jelly bag and let it drip. To make sure all the sharp hairs are removed, return the first half-cupful of liquid and let it drip through again. Put the mixed juice into a clean pot and boil it down until the juice measures about 1 quart, then add the sugar or honey and boil for another 5 minutes. Pour into hot, sterile bottles and seal immediately.

If you are using corks, boil them for an hour previously and, after insertion, coat with melted paraffin wax. Use small bottles as the syrup will not keep for more than a week or two once opened.

ramsons or wild garlic
(Allium ursinum)

In England, after the snowdrops have died back, a thick carpet of wild garlic appears beneath the alder and willow trees growing along the banks of the stream that runs through the farm. From late spring to early summer, beautiful white flowers appear on stems protruding from the clusters of broad green leaves. These give a very powerful acrid scent that can be smelled from a considerable distance. The bulbs are too tiny to be of any use but the leaves, which one can pick as soon as they appear in early spring, have a delicate garlicky flavor, which we sometimes eat with steak, fried in the pan juices, or added to a salad.

wild garlic to serve with steak

SERVES 4

¹/₃ cup (³/₄ stick) butter
steak juices from the pan
24 wild garlic leaves
²/₃ cup heavy cream

Warm the butter in a pan with the steak juices, stirring well. Tear up the leaves to release the flavor. As the butter begins to bubble, add the leaves. Stir well and when they have gone soft, remove from the pan. Let cool slightly, stir in the cream and serve.

mushrooms

Nothing evokes the period of mists and mellow fruitfulness and the musty smell of fallen leaves more than fungi. There are several thousand different species of fungi worldwide, of which only about 50 are deadly. Around 150 or so are good to eat and it is symptomatic of the lack of knowledge about the countryside that most of these are wasted.

Much of this is to do with fear. Fungi, by and large, look sinister: some resemble decaying human body parts—ears, sexual organs, and bits that one knows exist, but would rather not think about. Others have the reputation for being spectacularly toxic, like death cap (*Amanita phalloides*) and destroying angel or death angel (*Amanita virosa*), or for having hallucinogenic properties—fly agaric (*Amanita muscaria*) and liberty cap (*Psilocybe semilanceata*) or magic mushrooms are examples. Furthermore, fungi require other plants—usually dead ones—to supply them with carbohydrates, so they tend to grow in dank places among the rotting vegetation of mature woodland or in old pasture. They do, however, more than reward the time spent learning to identify them and the effort in searching for them.

My advice is to learn to identify positively twenty or so of the most common edible species and stick to them. Always remember to take a knife when you go foraging for fungi and cut them off at the bottom of the stem. As always in nature, don't take everything. Next autumn's crop is in the spores of those you leave behind.

some common edible mushrooms

● **Meadow mushrooms** (*Agaricus campestris* syn. *Psalliota campestris* – top left) and the larger horse mushrooms (*Agaricus arvensis* – top center)—these are the most recognizable mushrooms and the earliest to appear, often on pasture that has been grazed by horses.

● **Cèpes** (*Boletus edulis* – top right)—these bulbous, brown, thick-stemmed mushrooms grow in conifer woods, especially spruce. They used to be sold in fruit and vegetable markets in Britain and still are in many other parts of the world. Cèpes are one of the most popular fungi in Europe, with large quantities dried for winter additions to soup and stews.

● **Yellow chanterelles** (*Cantharellus lutescens* – bottom right) —exquisite and found in leafy woodland, particularly among beech trees.

● **Horns of plenty** (*Craterellus cornucopiodes*) —these are graveyard-gray and, like the chanterelles, are found in leafy woodland.

● **Giant puffballs** (*Lycoperdon giganteum* syn. *Calvatia gigantea* – middle left)—these pop up where you least expect them, on the edge of woodland or in the corner of a field. They must be picked while they are still vibrant white.

● **Hedgehog mushroom** (*Hydnum repandum* syn. *Dentinum repandum*)—these are delicious and creamy colored. They come from coniferous and deciduous woodland, and are commonly sold at farmers' markets in Europe.

● **Shaggy mane**, also known as shaggy ink caps and lawyer's wigs (*Coprinus comatus* – middle center)—these are found all over the place, by the roadside, among garden rubbish, or on lawns after a spell of rain. They are best while the gills are still white, and they make a delicious base for oeufs en cocotte.

● **Chicken of the woods** (*Laetiporus sulphureus* syn. *Polyporus sulphureus* – middle right)—these are a great delicacy in North America, Germany, and Poland. They are thick, fleshy and yellow and grow at the base of deciduous trees, particularly oak, sweet chestnut, and cherry.

● **Wood blewits** (*Lepista nuda* syn. *Tricholoma nudum* syn.)—these are lilac-coloured and are found in deciduous woodland, at the bottom of hedgerows and in rings in old pasture land. They are strongly scented and are excellent fried in butter.

● **Field blewits** (*Lepista saeva* syn. *L. personata* syn.)—these are lighter colored than wood blewits and are found in the same habitat.

● **Parasol mushrooms** (*Lepiota procera* syn. *Macrolepiota procera* – bottom left)—these are sweet tasting and buff-colored with a flaky skin.

● **Oyster mushrooms** (*Pleurotus ostreatus* – bottom center)—these are fragile, blue-gray mushrooms that grow in clumps on the stumps of beech trees.

"...don't take everything. Next autumn's crop is in the spores of those you leave behind."

wild mushroom crêpes

(MAKES APPROXIMATELY 10)

This is a good dish for mushroom hunters. If you find lots of mushrooms, you can have lavish crêpes, and if you don't find any, then you can just have crêpes.

For the batter
1¹/₃ cups self-rising flour
2 medium eggs
³/₄ cup milk
salt and pepper, to taste

3¹/₂ tablespoons unsalted butter
12 ounces wild mushrooms
a little oil for frying

Mix all the batter ingredients together and let stand for 1 hour. Meanwhile, melt the butter in a frying pan and fry the mushrooms until they have softened and all the liquid has evaporated. Keep back a little batter as the first crêpe is always for the dog. Let the mushrooms cool slightly and mix in with the rest of the batter.

Heat a small frying pan, smear with a little oil, and cook the first, plain crêpe. Discard. Add more oil to the pan if necessary, then pour in enough mushroom batter to coat the bottom of the pan. Cook for a minute or so, turn, then cook the other side. Serve immediately or stack the crêpes between waxed paper and put in a very low oven to keep warm while you make the rest.

mushroom pies

(MAKES 6)

1 pound pastry dough
1 pound wild mushrooms
1 shallot, peeled and very finely chopped
½ cup grated grated cheddar cheese
pinch dry mustard
2 tbsp. olive oil
1 egg, beaten, for glazing
salt and pepper

Line 6 deep tartlette molds using ²/₃ of the dough. Chill. Preheat the oven to 400°F. Heat a pan of boiling water and dip your mushrooms into the water for 2–3 seconds. Drain and pat dry on paper towels. Put the mushrooms in a bowl and mix with all the remaining ingredients, except the egg. Fill the tartlette molds

with the mixture, cover with circles of dough made from the remaining pastry dough and seal. Glaze with the egg. Make a small incision in the middle of each pie. Bake until the crust is golden, about 15 minutes.

Eat warm.

trapping, shooting, and fishing

Current agricultural policies in Europe and America are geared towards landscape enhancement and away from food production, so there have been substantial grants for tree planting and much land has been allowed to revert to nature. This has created a habitat that encourages all bio-diversity, but game in particular. Game has always been a harvestable natural food source. It is intrinsically organic, low in fat, high in protein, and has never been more accessible to both urban and country dwellers than it is today.

Most game that you can buy has been shot. If you are a novice who wishes to shoot, no matter what your age, you should join your local association for shooting and conservation. In North America, the National Shooting Sports Foundation (NSSF) has developed the website www.huntandshoot.org to help new or experienced hunters and shooters find the information they need. It offers advice on how to get started, how to find an outfitter, where you can enrol in a safety course and locate a range where you can practice target shooting, the cost of a license in any state and good places where you can find public land open to hunting.

In America anyone can shoot what they want on national parkland subject to acquiring the necessary licenses relative to the different game species. However, the landowner's written permission is required for hunting and trapping on private land, regardless of whether the land is posted. Permission slips are available at Division of Wildlife district offices and some license outlets.

gutting a rabbit

A rabbit must be gutted—have its intestines removed—as soon as possible after killing.

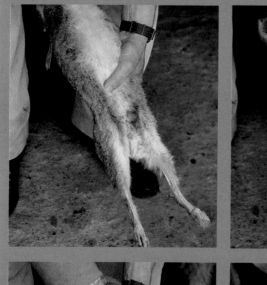
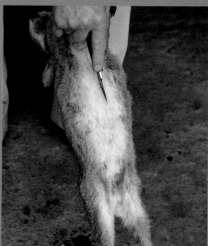
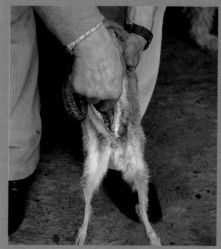
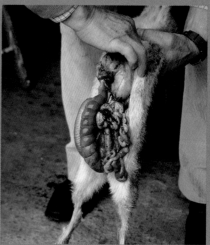

Hold the rabbit, head upwards, between your legs and squeeze the belly down towards the hind legs so that the bladder empties. Make an incision in the middle of the stomach where it joins the brisket or sternum. A skinning knife is scalloped towards the point to facilitate this. Run the knife straight down and over the pelvis, trying not to puncture the intestines. Insert a couple of fingers and remove the intestines.

rabbits

As well as shooting them, rabbits may also be snared, provided the snaring regulations are complied with. For example in Britain snares may not be left unattended for more than 12 hours. You should check your local regulations.

The first task is to find your rabbits. They like to establish their burrows in rough ground, and they venture out at dusk and dawn to find better grazing. They invariably follow the same route, leaving a distinct track through the grass and under fence wires. You can trap them using snares made of strands of copper wire formed into a noose. These are set beside one of these tracks. One end of the wire is tied to a small stake pushed firmly into the ground while the other is looped over the track and supported by a twig. The loop, or noose, must be at rabbit head height and it must be the diameter of its neck.

The other way to catch rabbits is by making them bolt out of their burrows into nets with a ferret. Ferreting is a wonderful way for children to learn about the countryside and to become a provider for the household before they are old enough to have a shotgun licence. Unless you intend to breed from your ferrets, I would recommend having a hob (male) and a jill (female), both of whom have been neutered. Ferrets should be kept in as big an area as you can spare but they must not be able to get out of it. They love to run about and play. I used to keep mine in an old stable with a sleeping hutch filled with hay and all sorts of tubes, balls, and some branches for them to amuse themselves with. If you live in an urban area, a hutch measuring 5 feet x 20 inches x 20 inches will suffice if the ferrets are taken out and handled often enough. The hutch should have a wooden sleeping box at one end, weld mesh sides, a hinged waterproofed wooden lid, and a wooden floor with a 1-foot-square area of weld

skinning a rabbit

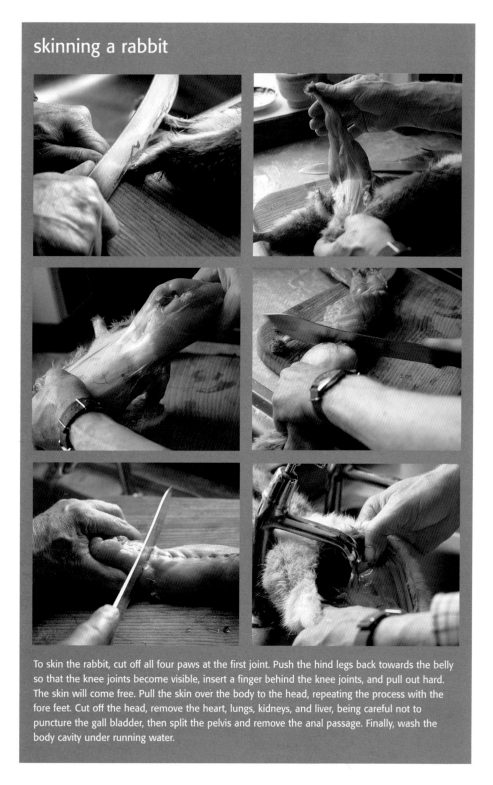

To skin the rabbit, cut off all four paws at the first joint. Push the hind legs back towards the belly so that the knee joints become visible, insert a finger behind the knee joints, and pull out hard. The skin will come free. Pull the skin over the body to the head, repeating the process with the fore feet. Cut off the head, remove the heart, lungs, kidneys, and liver, being careful not to puncture the gall bladder, then split the pelvis and remove the anal passage. Finally, wash the body cavity under running water.

edge that enables them to be stretched open and spread over the rabbit holes. The end of the string is attached to a wooden peg, firmly pressed into the ground to the side or above the holes. Once you have the net in place, slip the ferret into a burrow. His subterranean hunting will make the rabbits bolt out above ground and, as they come rocketing out, they become entangled in the net. Then take hold of the rabbit by its hind legs, remove the net, and hit it hard across the back of the neck with the side of the hand. This "rabbit punch" dislocates the neck, killing the rabbit instantly.

Another very effective way of catching rabbits is with a long net. Rabbits often graze a considerable distance from their burrows and the long net is set up, rather like a tennis net, near their burrows while the rabbits are out feeding. Once the net is in position, the rabbits are driven back towards their burrows and become entangled in the net.

deer

The change in agricultural policies worldwide has benefited all bio-diversity, but deer in particular. In Britain we have the majestic red deer, once a forest animal, which live in herds on the open moors of Exmoor, parts of Cumberland, and across the highlands of Scotland. We have other species too, fallow and roe deer—which were almost extinct in the late 19th century—sika, muntjac, and even Chinese water deer, all living in increasing numbers throughout the rest of the country. Continental Europe has these same species, as well as great herds of elk, in the northern forests. North America has white deer, tail deer, mule deer, wapiti, little prong horns, and moose, while New Zealand now has so many deer that the government is considering another national cull.

Deer are no respecters of agriculture or forestry and have to be controlled, not just to protect crops and young trees, but also

mesh for them to dung through as they are very clean animals. Properly handled, ferrets can become enchanting pets.

Again, your local association for shooting and conservation will be only to happy to

give advice on ferreting, but the basics are as follows. Once you have located an area—usually an earth bank—where there are a number of burrows, approach quietly and peg out the purse nets. These have a drawstring running around the

to ensure that a reasonable balance is maintained between deer numbers and available grazing. As with any other form of stock, old and ill animals have to be removed as part of normal animal welfare procedures and the correct ratio of males to females must be preserved.

In Britain, stalking the red stag in the Highlands is considered the sport of kings and is priced as such, but there is any amount of hind, roe, fallow, and sika stalking to be had at very affordable prices. Muntjac are such a pest that farmers would probably pay you to come and shoot them.

The situation is the same across Continental Europe, North America, and New Zealand. In America, the population of each species is assessed by the wildlife departments in each state and licences are issued to reflect the number that need to be killed. In Britain, the BASC are the best people to contact for information on deer stalking and there are similar organizations in America, Continental Europe, and New Zealand.

Once a deer has been shot, it should be gralloched, or disemboweled, bled, and the guts buried on the spot. Gralloching is done in the same way as when dealing with a rabbit, in other words, by cutting the deer open from the brisket to the pelvis. This is done to lighten the carcass for carrying and to avoid the risk of internal damage tainting the flesh. Your local association for shooting and conservation will almost certainly run deer management courses which include instruction on skinning.

pheasants, grouse, pigeons

The same expansion of wildlife habitat has led to an increase in the number of pheasants, partridges, quail, woodcock, and the different species of grouse. The pigeon and dove populations, on the other hand, increase most where there is agricultural expansion, particularly with

the planting of winter-sown crops. The famous red grouse population of Scotland and northern England relies on the management of heather through rotational burning every year to provide them with the habitat and food to sustain their numbers. All these species are available for the pot depending upon the regulations and laws governing wildlife in each different country.

fishing

Angling is globally the most popular participant pastime and, like all other field sports, is a vital contributor to the economy of countries worldwide as well as a key part of the socio-economic fabric of many rural areas. For example, rod-caught salmon from the River Tweed is worth £10,000 to the economy of Roxburghshire, Scotland (equal to about $19,000 in 2007). The fish itself is only worth a few dollars per pound, but its total value lies in the money spent by the anglers and their families who come to fish on one of Scotland's great salmon rivers.

Three and a half million people, encompassing all ages and social backgrounds, fish in Britain alone. Some £3.5 billion (equal to about $6.65 billion in

2007) are spent by anglers in an industry that employs over 6,000 people. Similarly, in excess of €10 billion (equal to about $13.1 billion in 2007) is generated by expenditure on field sports across the EU countries with fishing as a principal contributor. The 36 million anglers in North America spend $34 billion each year on their sport and provide employment for over a million people. But then, North America has some of the best and most varied fishing in the world.

There are three forms of rod fishing available in Britain and these are basically the same worldwide. The only difference is in places such as America and the Falkland Isles where the fish are bigger and there are more of them. The first is coarse fishing, which uses a bait, for the 15 species and numerous sub-species of freshwater fish, from carp to pike, other than the members of the Salmonidae family. These fish are found in canals, ponds, lakes, and sluggish rivers. The second is sea fishing, from boat, beach, or pier, for the 24 saltwater species, which range from bass to conger eels and their sub-species. And finally there's game fishing, which is fishing with a fly for grayling, salmon, brown trout, rainbow trout, sea-trout, whitefish, and char. These species of fish live in fast-flowing rivers and rely for their food on insects that settle on the surface of the water.

The opportunities for becoming involved in any of these sports and filling the freezer, is limitless. Possibly no other sport induces such passion among devotees from Iceland to New Zealand and a novice will find no shortage of helpful advice in getting started.

livestock

Of all the elements of a home producer's life, none is more satisfying than rearing one's own livestock and eating one's own produce. There is something cathartic about being governed by the reproductive cycle of the animals—spring for birth, summer for growth, autumn for harvesting, and winter for mating—and about experiencing the highs and lows, exhilarations and dramas that are part of every livestock farmer's daily existence. Your choice of livestock will be limited to the size of your holding: bees, a few chickens, or some pigeons can be kept in an average-sized garden while only five or ten acres are needed for a more adventurous enterprise. I hope my simple advice on keeping a cow, sheep, goats, pigs, rabbits, ducks, geese, chickens, and bees, and how and when to kill them and the best way to get rid of unwanted pests, will entice the new home producer to embark on this rewarding and enjoyable experience.

animal health

Anyone wishing to keep animals, whether it is a chicken, horse, or pig, must appreciate that they have complete responsibility for their welfare. Livestock are a total commitment. They wake with the dawn and, in the wild, start to feed soon after. Domestic animals are the same, but if you keep animals it is you who must be prepared to be up and about early to see that they are well and to feed them when necessary. You will have to know what, when, and how much to give them and will need enough basic veterinary knowledge to carry out an annual health plan. Making a soil analysis to determine what minerals may be deficient is an important first step.

I would not advise anyone to try and keep stock without first going on one of the many courses that are available to the home producer at agricultural colleges. It is not fair to the animals, it will be counter-productive to you, the producer, and, if things go wrong, which they almost certainly will, lack of knowledge could land you in court. What is more, lack of knowledge is no excuse for the ill treatment of animals.

some signs of animal ill-health

You will need to be able to spot signs of animal ill-health and react to them immediately. Most of these are a matter of commonsense.

● Loss of appetite is the most obvious. A healthy animal is a hungry one. Why is it off its food? Are there signs of discolored scour (diarrhea)? Is it hunched up indicating internal pain?

● Is it lame and is this lameness an injury or due to joint pain?

● Mucus around the nose and wheezing indicate pneumonia.

● Frothing at the mouth means it has eaten poison.

● A dull, staring coat – one that is lacking in bloom—could be caused by internal worms or a lack of essential minerals. Stockmen refer to a healthy animal as being "bloomy."

● An animal standing alone with its head down in the corner of a field is a sick creature. .Animals are, by and large, gregarious, so this is a sign there is something wrong.

● Pale, anemic gums indicate a worm burden or ticks.

● Long, overgrown feet or hooves will lead to lameness and foot rot.

● Scratching or rubbing against a fence or tree suggests lice or worse, the debilitating scab mite.

● A dry hot nose in a dog is a sign of ill-health.

"Livestock are a total commitment. They wake with the dawn and, in the wild, start to feed soon after."

choosing a breed

If you want a house cow, your choice of cow will be influenced by the quantity of milk you require as a family and how adventurous you wish to be. There is little point in going for a high-lactation dairy cow like a Holstein as that would give far too much milk for the average family and the carcass quality of the calf makes for poor beef. A Jersey is a lovely choice, with her superb butter-rich milk, but again, the calves have poor carcasses.

In Britain, there are several alternatives to choose from among the old dual-purpose breeds. Devons, Welsh Blacks (bottom right), Shorthorns (top right), Red Polls, Herefords (center), and even Highlanders (top left) all are good milkers and produce a nice calf, but my personal choice would be a long-legged Dexter. Dexters, which originate from the wild Celtic cattle of Ireland, are the smallest breed in the British Isles: even the long-legged Dexters only stand around 3¹/₂ feet at the shoulder. I wouild recommend that you go for the long-legged variety as the short-legged ones are quite difficult to milk. Dexters are hardy, low-maintenance, and docile, and will easily become a family pet. These dual-purpose cattle will provide about 3¹/₂ quarts of milk a day and will rear a calf. A steer will fatten off grass at 24 months and the small-jointed, well marbled Dexter beef is some of the best I have ever tasted.

COWS

"Dexters, which originate from the wild Celtic cattle of Ireland, are the smallest breed in the British Isles: even the long-legged Dexters only stand around 3½ feet at the shoulder."

For most of my life, I have been fortunate to have had access to fresh milk straight from the cow. As a small child, we kept a house cow, as most farms did in those days, and I remember being taken to watch her being milked. Matthew, our retired ploughman, sat on his three-legged milking stool with his cap twisted around so he could press his head into the flank of the venerable Ayrshire cross, chatting to her as if she were a human. The rhythmical munching as she chewed hay from the rack and the "splooshing" sounds as warm milk shot into the stainless-steel pail are still fresh in my memory. Once, bored with my chatter, Matthew squirted a jet of milk right across the milking parlor to catch me full in the face. After Matthew and the cow both went, we got milk in cylindrical aluminum containers with a lid from a neighbor who, in the 1960s, was making a decent living from twenty cows. Later on, when I farmed in lowland Scotland, my neighboring shepherd kept a house cow and we collected fresh milk from him.

keeping cows

To keep a small cow and calf, you will need half a good hectare of land and a suitable dry building, with water and electricity, to milk her in and house her overnight during the winter. Unless there is some form of natural shelter, a three-sided open shed is also important.

Ideally, you are looking to buy a four year-old, in-calf cow with a calf at foot, early in the spring. To find one, first decide on the breed that is suitable for your requirements and then look up the contact information in the directory on the website www.breederworld.com/beef for the cattle association relevant to that particular breed. They will have a register of cattle for sale and addresses of all their members, one of whom is bound to live within reach. Once you have located an animal that sounds about right, ask the owners to show you how to hand-milk her if you don't already know how to do so. This is an opportunity to discover if the cow can be handled and whether there are any bumps or lumps in the udder indicating mastitis. If you buy her, ensure that you have her pedigree certificate, and a certificate of guarantee that she is in calf, that she has been tested for tuberculosis and is brucellosis-free. She must also posses the necessary passport documents.

When you get your cow and calf home, they will be stressed after the journey, so tie the cow up in the cowshed and give her lots to drink and a good feed. Spend some time with her, letting her get used to you. The following morning, after she has been milked, let her out into the paddock. She will rear her own calf and supply ample milk but it would be worthwhile teaching the calf to drink from a self-feed bucket with a rubber teat, containing a mixture of three parts mother's milk and one part warm water. This will keep the calf occupied and contented while you are milking the mother. After a few weeks, offer the calf some decent meadow hay and then a little palatable concentrates in pellet form. By the time the calf is six months old it will be fully weaned.

milking

Your cow must be milked twice a day every 12 hours without fail. It should be a pleasant experience for both of you. Tie her up so that she has access to some good hay or cattle cake and where she can see her calf. Thoroughly wash any dung off her tail and hindquarters and gently wash her udder and teats with warm, soapy water, then dry carefully. Make sure your own hands are clean and dry.

Sit down beside her on a stool facing towards her hindquarters, with a sterilized stainless-steel bucket beneath her udder, and gently take the two forward teats in either hand. Encircle the top of the teat where it joins the udder with thumb and forefinger and squeeze. This is to stop the milk inside the teat from going back into the udder. Bring the other three fingers around the teat and in towards your palm. Milk will squirt out of the end of the teat and when it does, release your fingers, allowing milk from the udder to seep down into the teat. Alternate all four teats until the flow stops. It takes a few days to get the hang of hand-milking and it pays to practice on a rubber teat before starting on the real thing, but from then on, you will do it without thinking.

feeding your cow

An acre or so of permanent pasture is more than enough summer grazing for a small breed. It is advisable to divide it with a couple of strands of electric fencing and alternate her between the two patches. Apart from giving her a little hay and cattle cake while she is being milked, the pasture is all she will need from spring to autumn. If she goes down in condition—losing the shine to her coat is always a sign—or the milk yield drops away, you may need to increase her diet. If poor condition persists, call the vet.

For winter feed, your cow will need 9 pounds of good meadow hay a day and the calf will need 4$\frac{1}{2}$, making a total of about 2,400 pounds over six months. They will also both need a concentrate supplement of 2$\frac{1}{4}$ pounds for the cow and about a pound for the calf—a total of 560 pounds through the winter. Keep them in overnight after the evening milking during winter as there is no feeding value in grass at that time and keeping them off the ground for 12 hours saves it from getting poached, or broken up into wet, muddy patches. It is also less work to have the cow already dry and undercover for the morning milking.

calving

A cow has a gestation period of nine months and the trick is to calve her in late spring so that she and the calf benefit from summer grass growth, or in autumn, when it will be up to you to feed her but the calf will wean onto grass. She needs to "dry off," or cease being milked, at least eight weeks before calving to allow her to put on condition. Remember to freeze enough milk to cover you for this period.

A four-year-old cow should calve without any assistance from you but be vigilant around her calving date and be sure to

see that the calf is suckling well for the first three days, while the cow is producing the all-important yolk-like colostrum—the mixture of antibodies and organisms essential for the calf's survival. There will be an excess of this colostrum, also known as beistyn or beestings, which can be used to make the most delicious custard tarts. Once the colostrum is clear, normal milking may continue.

A cow comes into heat every 21 days and should not be inseminated until her second cycle, to give her time to recover from calving. In the absence of a local bull, insemination is done artificially. The breed's cattle society can provide details and will advise on specific bull semen.

A cow has one pregnancy a year which may be either a bull calf or a heifer. Either will require to be ear-tagged and registered as soon as possible after birth. In the case of a bull calf, castrate him by fitting a rubber elastrator ring over his testicles. A heifer can be sold at 15 months or may be kept to breed from. It pays to halter-train her from an early age.

A bull calf has got to be for the deep freeze. He will be ready at two years but could be kept for another six months. It rather depends upon whether he is a spring-born calf, in which case he would have another six months to fatten off grass. If he is autumn-born, the extra six months would be on expensive winter feed. When you decide to slaughter him, make sure you are properly prepared for the sudden influx of meat and that you have enough freezer space.

It is simply not feasible to risk slaughtering a valuable stirk (yearling) oneself. Ask other owners of the same breed for a convenient local slaughterhouse where they would be prepared to hang your beast for at least four weeks and butcher it according to your specifications. And don't forget to ask for the hide back. Slaughtermen regard this as part-payment for killing and butchering a beast. Some leather is always a valuable commodity to have around the place to use for mending a strap or making a belt.

castration using an elastrator

The elastrator is one of the many innovations in animal husbandry to come from New Zealand. It resembles a four-pronged pair of pliers with a very tight rubber ring attached to the prongs. When the handles of the pliers are squeezed, the prongs open and the ring is stretched wide. The stretched ring is placed over the scrotum of the animal, after ensuring that the testes are contained in the scrotum.

The handles are then released and the prongs removed with a downward flick of the wrist, leaving the rubber ring in place. The rubber ring contracts to its original size, constricting the flow of blood to the testes. Eventually, the testes wither and drop off.

By law, the elastrator must be used within one week of birth.

"...be sure to see that the calf is suckling well for the first three days, while the cow is producing the all-important yolk-like colostrum..."

guyanan beef stew

(SERVES 6)

In hot countries it isn't possible to hang meat (neither, of course, do supermarkets) so one must do something to compensate for the meat's toughness and lack of flavor. This is a really good dish I learned in the Caribbean.

6 x 8-ounce steaks cut from the rump or sirloin
1 cup orange juice
1/4 cup oil
4 small onions, finely chopped
4 garlic cloves, finely chopped
sprig of thyme
3 tbsp beef stock
salt and pepper

Let the steaks marinate overnight in the orange juice in a shallow dish.

Remove the steaks from the dish, reserving the orange juice, then dry them. Heat a heavy lidded pan, add the steaks, and seal the steaks quickly on both sides. Season then remove them. Heat the oil in the pan and sauté the onions, garlic, and thyme until the onions are soft and just colored.

Place the steaks on top of the onions, and add the stock and the orange juice. Cover and cook gently over a medium-low heat for 90 minutes or until the steaks are tender.

Serve with mashed sweet potatoes.

brisket pot roast with almonds and anchoid chiles

(SERVES 6–8)

This is a Mexican dish given to me by a school friend Lydia García who lives in Chihuahua. My friend Jan McCourt at Northfield Farm in Leicestershire produces beautiful beef and often cooks brisket. Last time I dined there he added chickpeas so I have stolen the idea and added them to this dish. Anchoid chiles are large dried chiles with a smoky flavor. They are not that hot and are much used in Mexico.

3¹/₂ pounds brisket of beef
1¹/₂ tsp blanched slivered almonds
4 ounces unsmoked ham or bacon, cut into slivers
3 large anchoid chiles
sprig marjoram or oregano
6 crushed peppercorns
4 peeled garlic cloves
2 tbsp red wine vinegar
1¹/₄ cups water
¹/₃ cup lard or bacon fat
2²/₃ cups chickpeas, soaked overnight

Preheat the oven to 325°F.

With a sharp knife, make slits in the beef and insert the slivered almonds and slivers of ham or bacon. Set aside.

Dry-toast the chiles on a hot pan then cut them open and soak them in water for half an hour. Drain the chiles and transfer them to a food processor or blender, or to a mortar.

Add all the remaining ingredients except the lard or bacon fat and the chickpeas. Blend or mash to a smooth paste. In a large pan, melt the fat and brown the meat all over. Then transfer to a casserole dish and set aside.

Cook the chile paste in the fat for 5 minutes, stirring as you go. Scrape the chile mixture over the meat. Place in the oven and cook for 2 hours. Add the chickpeas after 1 hour and baste the meat. At 2 hours turn the meat and baste again, adding more water if necessary. Return to the oven for an hour.

Serve with rice, potatoes, or corn dabs (see page 189).

deviled lamb cutlets

SERVES 4–6)

I suppose the 18th-century passion for deviling meats was a forerunner of the 20th-century passion for curry. I love deviled cutlets, especially for breakfast.

12 thin lamb cutlets
2 tbsp mustard powder
2 tbsp walnut ketchup (see page 202)
3¹/₂ tbsp butter
2 medium shallots, very finely chopped
1 tbsp soft brown sugar
1 tbsp Worcestershire sauce
²/₃ cup dark beer or stout
1 tsp cayenne pepper
salt and pepper

Mix the mustard to a smooth thin paste with the walnut ketchup. Smear all over the meat and let it stand for at least 1 hour. Season.

Put the butter and all the other ingredients in a small pan and cook gently to a thick syrup. Spread half of this over the chops and cook them in the broiler pan (not on the rack) under a hot broiler for a few minutes. Turn them over, spread on the rest of the mixture, and cook for a few minutes more. Eat with a good cup of coffee for breakfast.

horses

In the first decade after the Second World War, it began to look as if many of the hundreds of different breeds of horse and pony were going to become at best, endangered species and at worst, die out altogether. Apart from ceremonial duties, the cavalry—the arme blanche—of the world's armies had all become mechanized. For farm, dray, and forestry work, tractors and trucks had largely replaced heavy horses, and though we still had a pair of Suffolk Punches on our farm, we were an exception. There was little place for any of the magnificent driving breeds—the Cleveland Bays, Norfolk trotters, Hackneys and the hundreds of different types of vanner that used to pull tradesmen's carts. Apart from the few animals kept for hunting, show jumping, eventing, racing, and polo, horse and pony numbers worldwide seemed to be in a terminal decline. As someone who grew up with horses, I am delighted to say that nothing could now be further from the truth.

why have a horse?

Owning a horse opens up a huge range of possibilities and such is the love between man and horse that every discipline in the history of equitation has its devoted following. There is the complicated and ancient art form of Haute Ecole as well as polo, polo crosse, eventing, show jumping, dressage, and endurance riding. Heavy

"Owning a horse opens up a huge range of possibilities..."

horses are now used for timber extraction once again and, occasionally for plowing and pulling harrows and other farm implements, and there is a worldwide resurgence of interest in carriage driving. Hunting, the bedrock of all racing, is as popular now as it ever was.

children and horses

Any child wishing to own a horse or pony and to learn to ride should contact their local branch of the the United States Pony Club (USPC). Founded in America in 1954 and now with over 600 clubs and over 12,000 members, it is responsible for encouraging the ever-growing interest in riding among the young.

Pony clubs teach children to be well rounded horse people with complete knowledge of riding on the flat, jumping, riding in the open and horse care. Many programs are offered including eventing, dressage, mounted games, horse management, quiz, polocrosse, show-jumping, tetrathlon, and vaulting. Children have to have access to a horse or pony but they do not have to own one in order to be a member.

The clubs also include unmounted meetings where children are taught about the health and care of their horses, such as feeding, shoeing, and veterinary care. One of the beauties of the club is that it encompasses children from urban as well as rural backgrounds and apart from gaining riding skills and a knowledge of horses from experts in the field, the Pony Club has provided generations of young people with a unique social experience, based on fun, friendship, training, and the priceless responsibility of looking after an animal.

global horsiculture

Horsiculture is a global growth industry, with riding holidays, ranging from basic trekking holidays in beautiful parts of the British Isles, Europe, and North America to mounted adventures in Africa, South America, Mongolia, and unexplored parts of Eastern Europe, becoming increasingly popular. In Britain, a recent survey showed that the equine population exceeded one million, of which 65,000 were owned professionally in the racing industry and by riding centers, with the rest privately owned. These figures may be replicated across Europe, North America, Australia, and New Zealand.

adults and horses

There are also many opportunities for adults to learn to ride and become involved in a variety of equine sports. There are any number of riding clubs and equestrian associations that can provide help and advice on choosing a riding school but it is worth checking first with "Horsemasters," the adult arm of the United States Pony Club. This is dedicated to developing adult volunteers for Pony Club activities but its purpose is also to point anyone interested in horses in the right direction, offering a list of recommended riding schools and livery yards and providing an "adult connect" social atmosphere.

In the United States, there are hundreds of spectator events throughout the year—point to points and hunter trials, one-, two-, and three-day events and polo tournaments. See the United States Eventing Association (USEA) website for details.

choosing a breed

Britain

● The British thoroughbred is the world's most famous and valuable horse. Its ease of action, speed, stamina, and courage have underpinned a racing and breeding industry which is now multinational.
● The thoroughbred evolved from stallions imported from Syria, Turkey, and Egypt during the late 17th and early 18th centuries.
● Three exceptional stallions—the Byerley, Turk with the Darley, and Godolphin Arabians—are considered the foundation of all racehorses.
● The thoroughbred's superb qualities are used worldwide to improve many other breeds. A classic example were the hunters and eventers bred by my father. He took Welsh Cob mares to the Queen's Cleveland bay stallion, Mulgrave Supreme, and crossed the progeny with a thoroughbred. The Welsh Cob provided hardiness and common sense, the Cleveland, size and jumping ability, and the thoroughbred, quality and ease of action.

France

● The Selle Française is another famous competition horse using thoroughbred blood. The rather common all-purpose light draft Norman was crossed with an Arab and then with a thoroughbred to produce this excellent show jumper.
● The white horse of the Camargue, a very ancient breed improved with Moroccan Barb blood in the Middle Ages, is one of France's most famous breeds.
● The Landais and the Pottock are two indigenous French pony breeds that have been improved with Welsh and Arab blood.

Germany

● The Holstein, originally a carriage horse, has been improved with blood from the famous Yorkshire Coach Horse and the thoroughbred, to produce a first-rate show jumper and cross-country horse.
● The Oldenburg, particularly suited for driving and dressage, evolved from a cross between the French Norman, the Friesland, and the thoroughbred.

Spain

● The Andalucian or Spanish horse was the most influential improver across the whole of Europe until it was superceded by the Arab.
● These are the horses used in the famous Spanish Riding School and were the foundation stock for the white Lippizaners.
● Andalucians were bred from the native Sorraias crossed with Barb stallions during the Moroccan conquest of Spain.

Australia

● Australia has the splendid Waler or Australian stock horse. There are a number of different categories—pony, light, medium, and heavy.
● Walers originated when thoroughbreds were exported to Australia in the 1830s and were crossed with the hardy light draft horses that were already in the colony of New South Wales. This resulted in a tough, stylish stock horse with a bit of quality and a good temperament.
● Walers provided most of the cavalry horses for the British army in India and today. They are still used for stock work but are also popular as polo ponies, for endurance riding, show jumping, and dressage.

The Americas

● The foundation of many South and North American horses were the Spanish horses brought over by Cortés in the 16th century and from which hardy breeds like the Rocky Mountain Pony, Criolla, Appaloosa, Mustang, Palomino, Quarter Horse, Colorado Ranger, Paso, and Pinto descend.
● Crossing with thoroughbreds produced very stylish riding horses like the Saddlebred, Narragansett Pacer, Missouri Fox Trotter, Tennessee Walking Horse, and the supreme stock horse, the Quarter Horse.
● One of North America's most famous breeds, the Morgan, evolved from a Welsh cob crossed with an Arab and a thoroughbred.

Top left: thoroughbred cross child's riding pony
Centre: Suffolk Punch mare and foal
Bottom left: A pair of Shire horses

looking after a horse

Looking after a horse or pony is an enormous responsibility and no one should keep one without first acquiring a thorough knowledge of equine welfare. Centuries of breeding have resulted in horses suitable for carrying riders or pulling wagons and carts. A horse may be compared to a superb athlete and, just as any athlete must take care with his or her diet, exercise, and health, so the same applies to caring for a horse. The British Horse Society or a similar national organization will be able to advise you and there are, of course, societies for specific breeds who can also offer help.

In general you will need to ensure that you can offer proper stabling and grazing and you will also need a tack room and feed store. In terms of time and money, it is a big commitment, but the rewards and broadened horizons are incalculable, and who knows, you might start breeding to help cover some of your costs.

chickens

I would thoroughly recommend a few fowl to any would-be home producer. It takes a lot to beat a free-ranging brood of hens, or even a paddling of ducks (see page 124), a gaggle of geese (see page 126), or a rafter of turkeys. They are fun to keep and create an atmosphere of frenetic energy with their industrious search for food, their squabbling, egg-laying, and dust bathing, and the way they vocalize all their activities with raucous exuberance. Many have beautiful plumage, and the Phoenicians and Greeks kept chickens as religious ornaments, living symbols of the gods Athena, Persephone, Eros, and Hermes. What is more, chickens are productive and the flavor of the eggs and meat from a home-reared bird bears no relation to any mass-produced specimen.

keeping chickens

Chickens are a woodland bird and, assuming your vegetable and flower garden is rabbit-fenced, your chickens will thrive best running free, hunting for food in rough grass, eating weed and grass seeds, and scratching for insects. During the summer this is all they need, plus a little mixed grain and some scraps to keep them manageable.

Their housing is obviously of paramount importance. The main requirement for poultry is that they are protected from predators and the weather, and that they have adequate ventilation. They need to feel safe and comfortable. Like all stock, chickens are prone to stress and their performance will drop off if they are

unhappy. Lastly, though it is a secondary consideration to the welfare of the birds, the hen house should be easy for you to use.

Some people may have old, unused farm buildings which could be converted into poultry housing but generally speaking these tend to be too close to the house and away from the area where the hens should be grazing. In any case, I like to see chickens with their own house.

There are plenty of companies making poultry housing that is ideally suited to the small farmer. I would recommend a solid, decent-sized, purpose-built freestanding shed with skids on the bottom so it can be dragged to a clean new site when necessary. It must be easy for you to get in and clean and so will need a door for your own access. I

choosing a breed

There are so many breeds of chicken available today, thanks to the 19th-century craze for exotic breeds and the endless experimentation by geneticists, that a novice has plenty to choose from. My advice is to go for a traditional tried-and-tested, old-fashioned dual-purpose breed. This will provide more than enough eggs for the average family and delicious table birds at two years. Light Sussex are my favorites; they are hardy, independent, great table birds and capable of producing around 200 eggs a year. Rhode Island Reds are another traditional dual-purpose breed, while French Marans are wonderful, slow-maturing table birds and good brown-egg layers. The blue or buff Orpingtons are reliably meaty birds but produce fewer eggs while the white, black, and brown Leghorns, Barred Plymouth Rocks, Scots Greys and Wyandottes are all excellent, long-established dual-purpose chickens.

suggest having a hen house that is 5 feet square and 5½ feet high at the front, sloping to 4¾ feet at the back. It should have a wooden roof covered with tarred felt. In addition you will need a ramp and hatch for the hens, and lighting. This is particularly important if you live in the north where the days are shorter and if you want an extended laying period. You will also need a 3-gallon plastic drinker and an ad-lib galvanized feeder that can be attached to the inside of the door, plus a broody coop and integral run, and 16-inch-deep external nesting boxes complete with a hinged lid. Be sure to position the hen house on a dry, free-draining site.

breeding

You have various options for starting a flock. These include hatching eggs under an incubator, rearing chicks, or buying half-grown pullets or point of lays—birds that are ready to lay—in September. I would suggest buying point of lays. A cockerel and eight hens is a good starting point for a dual-purpose family-sized enterprise.

Make your purchase either privately, at an auction, or through one of the many businesses specializing in poultry and poultry equipment. When you get your hens and cockerel home, shut them in

the hen-house for four days so they can become acclimatized, making sure that they have plenty of food, fresh water, a little hay in each nesting box, and small, clean wood shavings on the floor. On the morning of the fifth day, open their hatch, scatter a little feed down the ramp, and let them find their way out. Feed scraps and a little wheat in the afternoon near the shed, so they get used to the idea of being in its vicinity when it comes to shutting them in before dark.

Realistically, pure-bred dual-purpose pullets are unlikely to give many eggs before the spring, particularly if the home producer lives in the north. Sunlight influences a hen's productivity and as the hours of daylight diminish, fewer eggs are laid. I have childhood memories of the bottling activities of the autumn. We preserved the eggs in isinglass—a form of collagen made from the swim bladders of certain tropical fish and still used today as finings in the brewing industry—and stored them in big glazed earthenware crocks for the lean winter months (see page 183). My hens in southern Scotland tail off into November and start laying again in early February, with just one or two laying sporadically through that period. To ensure a flow of eggs during winter, create daylight artificially by using a timer to set an electric light to come on for a few hours before dawn and then again at dusk.

I feed my hens standard layers pellets from the ad-lib feeder in the hen-house during the summer, plus wheat and household scraps in the afternoon. I increase the wheat by feeding them twice a day during the winter period. In spring and summer, in addition to the layers pellets, my hens get a large percentage of their protein from insects and weed seeds. You also need to give the hens access to grit to help eggshell production. They like a dustbath to clean their feathers and help get rid of mites and will find their own if they are running around freely. As long as the hen-house is cleaned out scrupulously, your hens will be disease-free.

With egg production starting in the spring, the second phase of the dual-purpose poultry enterprise begins when one of the hens turns broody, squatting on the nest with tail feathers erect, refusing to move and clucking in outrage at being disturbed. Now it is time to prepare the broody coop by cutting a turf, turning it over, making a depression in it, covering it with broken straw and putting it inside. Move the broody and her eggs into the coop. Fresh water, grit, and a dustbath made of dry soil, ash, and sand should be made available in the run together with a daily feed of wheat.

Eggs take 21 days to hatch and for the first ten, keep the hen off the nest for twenty minutes while she feeds. For the next eleven days, keep her off for 30 minutes. While she is feeding, turn each egg to stop the fetus adhering to the side of the shell and check that the turf remains damp. Always feed her at the same time each day.

after hatching

When the chicks hatch, they should not be fed for at least 48 hours while they live off the membrane that is left in the egg. After that they need plenty of fresh water and chick-crumbs feed pellets for a month.

Divide the run with a slatted partition to keep the hen separate and move the divider every day to give the chicks some fresh ground.

How you look after the chicks from now on depends on the amount of time you are able to devote to them. My view is that the sooner they get out and learn to forage with the hen the better. They will scuttle about the place with her and she will hide them away at night in some long grass. As they become older, they will begin to feed with the rest of the hens and will be roosting with them in the hen-house by the autumn. There is obviously the risk of predators when you have young chicks running about like this; the alternative is to keep them in an enclosure, feeding them growers pellets for up to 14 weeks.

How many hens you allow to turn broody and rear a clutch depends on the number of table chickens you require. Of an average clutch of ten, roughly half will be young cockerels. To take a hypothetical example, three hens will supply fifteen pullets and fifteen cockerels in the spring and early summer. The cockerels will all be killed in the following autumn and winter. In January the flock will stand at 33 hens of which eight will be entering their most productive second year, to be culled as boiling fowls at the end of it. Seven pullets or a combination of pullets and second-year hens that have proved to be poor layers will not be needed and could be culled. When more hens than are required for breeding turn broody, a trick to stop them is to feed them in a small wire or slat-bottomed coop raised off the ground. This is so uncomfortable that within a few days they lose the desire to squat and within two weeks will return to laying.

Young cockerels from the brood will be ready to eat at 18 weeks. It is well worth putting a couple in the broody coop and fattening them for two weeks on a three-times-a-day feed of a fattening ration. The same applies to the boilers that have passed through their second laying season.

When handling a chicken, pick it up by the body with the wings closed. If they can't flap their wings, they remain quite calm. Place the bird under your right arm and press her gently against your body so the wings are kept closed, and hold her feet together with your hand.

To kill a chicken, hold it as described, take the head in your left hand and in one fluid motion, jerk the right hand back and the left hand down, twisting the head to the left. The neck will snap instantaneously as the body is pulled rigid. Hang it up by the legs until cool and pluck (see page 128).

turkeys and guinea fowl

Another breed of fowl for the home-producer to consider is the guinea fowl. These are kept much like free-range chickens, to which they make a delicious alternative. Turkeys, however, are extremely delicate creatures, difficult to rear among other poultry and fatally susceptible to diseases which your other fowl may carry but be immune to. Unless turkeys are going to be the sole enterprise of your fowl yard, they seem hardly worth the trouble.

chicken for the table

Of all the differences that will bring home to you your altered lifestyle I suspect it will be chickens that provide the biggest shock. You will have been used to the bland but tender meat of a supermarket roasting bird or the more tasty but still tender free-range bird sold to you by your butcher. This is all about to change. You will now be keeping hens for eggs and killing them for the table when they have stopped laying. The problem with this is that such a bird will have a wonderful flavor but if you simply roast it, it will be as tough as old boots. Instead, you will have to slow-cook it, braise it, pot-roast it, or poach it. An old cockerel can also be delicious if it is properly cooked.

What, you cry, am I never to eat roast chicken again? And of course you are. In the spring when your chicks hatch you will find among them a proportion of cockerels; there is no point keeping these long term as they will simply kill each other. You have various options: either to kill them young and eat them roast or caponize (castrate) them and kill them at about 8–9 pounds. To my mind a caponized cockerel is one of the most delicious things you can eat. It produces a layer of fat under the skin which melts during cooking, sef-lubricating the bird while it is roasting.

The practice of caponizing fell out of favor 40 or so years ago because farmers started using hormone pellets for this purpose, which raised (quite rightly) all types of anxieties. However, no hormones are used in US chicken production as The Food and Drug Administration strictly prohibits the use of hormones in broiler-fryers. Capons have been around since Ancient Greece. In fact, the Athenian City Council passed a sumptuary law that forbad the eating of fattened hens as it was regarded as a waste of grain.

hindle wakes

(SERVES 8)

I love this medieval recipe which can only be made successfully with an old fowl. The name of the dish comes, I believe, from the lost Derbyshire town of Hindle which, due to absence of water, failed to survive the Industrial Revolution, and not, as some would have it, from Hen de la Wakes. Whatever the naming, it is scrumptious. The dish was designed for Wakes Week—a traditional summer holiday celebrated in Lancashire—as a cold dish to cut and come again. I have cooked it overnight in the bottom of an Aga using light ale instead of water and it was even better. I have used chicken blood like the original recipe and as we're being true to self-sufficiency I suggest sorrel instead of lemons unless you have retired to the sun or have gotten the orangery up and running.

1 stewing chicken 4–5 pounds
2 1/2 cups wine vinegar
2 tbsp brown sugar (for purity use honey)
salt and a handful of peppercorns

For the stuffing
1 pound large prunes, pitted and soaked but not cooked
8 ounces fine white bread crumbs
2/3 cup chicken's blood mixed with a little vinegar to prevent curdling
1/3 cup blanched almonds, roughly chopped
3 1/2 tbsp fresh mixed herbs, chopped
50g suet, chopped
2 1/2 cups beer
salt and pepper

For the sauce
1 tbsp cornstarch
1 cup chicken stock
2/3 cup verjuice (see page 151) or rind and juice of 2 lemons
2 eggs, well beaten
salt and pepper

Mix all the stuffing ingredients in a bowl and stuff the fowl both under the breast and in the cavity and sew up. Place in a large pot of cold water and add the vinegar, brown sugar, salt, and peppercorns. Bring to a boil and simmer for 4 hours. Let it cool in the liquid. While the chicken is cooling make the sauce.

Mix the cornstarch with the stock, bring to a boil, and stir in the verjuice as you do this. Season and cook for 2–3 minutes. Remove the pan from the heat, let it cool slightly, then beat in the eggs. Cook a little longer but do not let it boil. Let the sauce cool. Place the chicken on a dish and pour the sauce over it.

braised hen

(SERVES 6–8)

This is a dish our cook Louise Leeds used to make when I was young. She was a remarkable woman and most of what I know is based on the foundations she laid for me. I suspect that, as my mother was an elegant woman who bought her clothes in Paris and Louise was the one to show me all the benefits of cooking, Louise was more my role model than my mama! She had a great deal of energy and a fine, enquiring mind.

1 stewing chicken
3–4 strips bacon
scant cup dry white wine
3 pounds potatoes, peeled and chopped
1/2 cup (1 stick) butter
20 small shallots
1 1/4 cups chicken stock
125ml double cream
salt and pepper

For the marinade
1/2 cup olive oil
2 tbsp finely chopped chives or scallions
4 shallots, finely chopped
3 garlic cloves, crushed
salt and pepper

Mix all the marinade ingredients and leave the chicken in the mixture for 1 day, turning from time to time. Place the bacon strips in the bottom of a large, heavy pan, place the chicken on them and pour in the marinade. Season, add the white wine, cover, and cook over a low heat for 3 hours.

Meanwhile, fry the potatoes in 2/3 of the butter. Fry the shallots in the remaining butter until colored and set them aside. After 2 1/2 hours add the potatoes and shallots to the chicken pot, then heat the stock and pour it in. Finish cooking. Remove the chicken, carve it and place on a dish with the shallots and potatoes. Boil the remaining juices vigorously until reduced. Remove from the heat, stir in the cream, heat through, and serve the sauce separately.

rabbit hotpot

(SERVES 4–6)

This is a good warming dish made with belly pork. Now that you have turned off your central heating you will need dishes like this to keep you warm. The dish is of French origin and calls for Dijon mustard but I prefer the strength of English mustard. The choice is yours.

1 pound skinned belly of pork, sliced, skin reserved
2 carrots, chopped
2 onions, finely chopped
1 clove garlic, crushed
1 tbsp each fresh parsley and thyme, chopped
1 bay leaf
2 cut up rabbits
²/₃ cup dry white wine or dry cider
²/₃ cup stock
1 tbsp white wine vinegar
4 egg yolks
1¼ cups heavy cream
2 teaspoons prepared mustard
salt and pepper

Arrange half the pork on the bottom of a large ovenproof dish. Add half the vegetables and the garlic and sprinkle with herbs. Season and add the bay leaf. Lay the rabbit pieces on top of this and add the remaining pork and vegetables. Lay the pork skin on top. Pour in the wine or cider, stock, and vinegar. Cover and cook at 350°F for 2¹/₂–3 hours.

Remove and discard the pork skin. Remove the rabbit pieces to a dish and strain the cooking liquid into a pan. Remove any excess fat and reduce the cooking liquid by one-third.

In a bowl, beat the egg yolks with the cream and mustard and add to the reduced sauce. Heat to thicken but do not boil. Pour the sauce over the rabbit pieces and serve.

fish

If you have running water on your holding—and it is surprising how little you need—you could create a mini fish farm. Fish farming goes back centuries; the Chinese had been at it for several thousand years before the Normans brought it to Britain as part of their culture of the living larder. The "stew pond" was essential to every medieval castle, manor house, and monastery, with the monastic houses specializing in carp husbandry. Carp are hardy, prolific, and fertile and there was fierce competition among the monasteries in the breeding of bigger and better strains. Stew ponds remained in use until well into the 19th century, when railways made sea fish readily available.

making a fish pond

A pond is a lovely thing to have and creates a whole new bio-diversity. Apart from your fish, there will be dragonflies and clear wings, newts and frogs and, in the winter, mallard and teal may come there to feed.

You need to give some careful thought to the size of your pond and how you manage it. Cost is largely determined by the soil type in your area: sandy soil will require waterproofing by plastic sheeting whereas with clay, you can probably avoid that expense. I made a pond a couple of years ago that was about 16^1/2 yards, with a 6^1/2-foot earth dam. It was rectangular in shape as this helps improve water circulation which, in turn, aids the growth of nutrient life. I then had a happy time planting willows (*Salix*), rabbitear iris (*Iris laevigata*), flowering rushes (*Butomus umbellatus*) broadleaf and cattail (*Typha latifolia*), as well as buckbean (*Menyanthes trifoliata*), sweetgale (*Myrica gale*)—to keep the midges away—and Canadian pondweed (*Epodea canadensis*), which fish love. The pond lily (*Nuphar lutea*), whose flowers have a brandy-like scent and fringe lilies (*Thysanotus tuberosus*) were other favorites. This is a manageable size of pond for carp, rainbow, brown trout, or sturgeon. If you intend to use the pond for a regular supply of fish, it would be as well to have a sluice built into the dam wall so the pond can be emptied periodically, enabling you to check your fish stocks and clear excess weed.

A pond this size could be stocked with about 60 juvenile 18-ounce fish, which would put on about a pound a year. If you feed them every day at the same place, they can easily be caught in a net at feeding time or you can have a bit of fun with a rod and line. Nicholas Cox, writing in 1679, recommended a bait made from bean flower, cat's flesh, and honey for carp. Colin Willock, in his *New ABC of Fishing*, suggests worms or bread.

eels

There is every chance that you might get an unexpected bonus in the form of eels. They are delicious, highly underrated, and plentiful. There are several ways of catching them. The first is to use a rod, stout line, and a fine hook, baited with fish, meat, or organ meats. Or you can trap them in a baited pot like a lobster pot, but with a very fine nylon mesh covering to stop them wriggling through. Another method is "dabbing"—gathering together 20 or so earthworms and weaving them into a ball with strong woolen yarn attached to a piece of string. You should end up with a tangle of worms, string, and woolen yarn. Tie this onto another piece of string fastened to a stick and "dab." Eels have inward-pointing teeth like a snake, which become tangled with the string and wool. This method of catching eels is very popular in the West Country of England. Another couple of techniques, which also take advantage of the angle of an eel's teeth, is to make a small bag out of a jute sack, fill it with fresh chicken guts, tie the neck firmly with strong string, and throw it out into a pond on the end of a piece of rope. The eels get caught when they bite into the sack. Or, make a big ball of absorbant cotton pads. Tie it to a stick and soak it in fish essence, obtainable from a fish tackle shop, then dab using this.

Like all fish, eels should be killed as soon as they are landed with a sharp blow to the head using a short weighted stick, known as a "priest."

stuffed trout

(SERVES 8)

I thought I would never do anything to brown trout but eat it plain until I worked for my dear boss Rebeka Hardy. Her husband Lawrence and their son Allen caught so many brown trout that one needed to vary things. Rainbow trout, which isn't so tasty, should usually be stuffed.

8 trout, each 6 ounces
8 ounces veal forcemeat (about 1 cup), or the same weight of bread crumbs mixed with herbs and 1/3 cup (3/4 stick) butter
1/2 cup (1 stick) butter
1 tbsp flour
2/3 cup white wine
1 tbsp capers
1 tsp lemon juice
salt and pepper

Stuff the trout with the forcemeat or herbs and bread crumbs and sew up or close with skewers. Place the fish in a buttered ovenproof dish, season, and dab on 1/3 cup butter. Cover and cook at 350°F for 30 minutes, basting from time to time. Remove trout to a serving dish, reserving the cooking liquid. Melt the remaining butter in a saucepan and make a roux with the flour. Gradually stir in the strained cooking liquid and the white wine. Stir until it just comes to a boil and add the capers and lemon juice, then season with salt and better. Simmer to cook the flour for 2–3 minutes and serve with the trout.

dogs and cats

dogs

I was brought up to believe that one should never have a dog unless it was going to be used, as a result of which I have owned many sheep dogs and terriers over the years and the occasional gun dog. Whatever breed you decide to have, remember that dog ownership is a big responsibility, particularly in Britain where, since November 2004, a series of nonsensical laws were passed through Parliament, making it illegal for a dog to chase mice, hares, deer, foxes, and squirrels, but not rats or rabbits. Anyone now wishing to own a dog should familiarize themselves with any dog laws of their country and check what a dog might unwittingly do to criminalize its owner.

Before buying any dog you need to be aware of the downsides of each sex. Bitches can be a bore when they are in heat as they have to be shut up and they are messy around the house. They lose some of their working instinct if they are spayed. Dogs on the other hand are a nightmare if they take off whenever they scent a bitch in heat, though it is rather the luck of the draw. I have had some dogs that never left and others that could scent a bitch from ten miles away.

Once you have made a decision, the options are to buy a dog that has already been broken or an eight-week old puppy, and learn how to train it. Your local agricultural college should be able to advise on this. If you have chosen a Beardie (see opposite), he should learn obedience in his first year but will not

choosing a breed

Assuming that you are a home producer looking for a dual-purpose dog to help with your various livestock enterprises, to control vermin—within the letter of the law—and to be something of a family pet, I would unhesitatingly suggest the smaller type of working Bearded Collie, favored by shepherds in Peebleshire, Scotland. Beardies are an incredibly ancient breed and were the dog used by all shepherds in Britain until the 19th century, when flock masters began establishing enormous flocks of sheep on the heaths and moors of northern England and Scotland. Beardies move sheep by using energetic body movements and so creating a perceived threat, but this was found to be too hard on sheep being driven through heather. I suspect a setter was then crossed with a Beardie to create the Border Collie, which moves sheep through "eye" and with its sinuous cat-like movements.

Beardies are enchanting little dogs whose joie de vivre makes having one around a positive joy. They are less obsessive and more adaptable than Border Collies. They are highly intelligent and although, like all sheep dogs, their instinct is to round up sheep and bring them to you, they readily learn other skills. I have a friend who uses one to retrieve shot game. One of my best hill dogs used to drive the hens into their shed at night, was a great ratter, and I regularly took him ferreting. Beardies will help you with all your livestock except pigs—goats, sheep, cattle, even ducks, geese, and chickens. But never take a dog near pigs: it will simply attack them.

"The old adage 'familiarity breeds contempt' is no truer than when applied to dogs."

begin to work until he is a year old—although he will probably start rounding up the ducks and chickens at three months, which should be encouraged.

Remember that this is a working dog and a dog will only work for you if he believes you are a superior sort of dog and the leader of the pack. Beware of making him into too much of a pet. A dog should earn your affection and the old adage "familiarity breeds contempt" is no truer than when applied to dogs.

caring for your dog

Beardies have a thick coat which needs to be trimmed several times a year, but even so, they will get pretty dirty. They should have a good straw-filled bed clear of the ground, in a dry, draft-free place or a custom-made kennel with a run. My sheepdogs are fed 12 ounces or so of a working sheepdog compound mix containing vitamins, minerals, flaked maize, dried meat extract, and dried vegetables.

Dogs must be inoculated when they are puppies against the major canine diseases—distemper, provirus, leptospirosis, canine hepatitis, and kennel cough. Without documentation to prove that they have had all the essential inoculations, no responsible boarding kennel will accept your dog should you wish to go away. A dog should be wormed every three months in addition to which all the usual signs of animal ill-health should be looked out for and veterinary advice sought if necessary. Look after your dog well and it will give you many years of loyal service.

cats

The traditional farmyard cat was an extremely useful creature who lived in the farm buildings, well away from the farmhouse. This semi-wild cat was never fed once it was out of the kitten stage and was expected to live off the mice and rats it killed around the farm buildings. There are still cats doing sterling work in farm buildings across Britain, Europe, North America, Australia, and New Zealand.

If you must have a cat, make sure it is spayed if it is a female or neutered if it is a tom (toms stink and get smellier as they become older), otherwise you will have kittens everywhere. If you provide a kitten with a warm box in an outbuilding and three meals with plenty of milk, it soon accepts its surroundings as home and won't come into the house unless encouraged to do so.

A non-pedigree kitten is easier to acquire than a common cold. Your local paper will be full of ads for kittens being offered to good homes. Be sure to have the little creature inoculated against feline enteritis and cat flu.

the story of Heartless

When my children were small, I was persuaded to buy a kitten from a neighbor. It was the progeny of a highly expensive pedigree Burmese and a traveling farmyard Tom, a one-eyed veteran of hundreds of testosterone-fueled fights. The kitten grew into a beautiful creature and a serial killer. The children christened her "Heartless" because of the quantity of little birds she brought into the house. Periodically my terriers felt they ought to chase her, just to show they weren't getting soft on cats and Heartless happily entered into the spirit of the thing, licking them clean when they came in wet and muddy. However, while she lived we had none of the little song birds—blackbirds, thrushes, robins, or wrens—nesting in the garden and I have never had a cat since.

unwanted visitors

ants

● The bruised leaves of sage, mint, pennyroyal, or thyme will drive ants away if they have invaded a pantry or dry foods cupboard, these plants grown by doorways will stop them entering a house.

● I hate destroying ant nests, but if you have to, boil up any of the above, make an opening, and flood the nest with the liquid. Alternatively, mix a strong solution of alum or even of ordinary salt and pour into the nest.

● Paint a ring of eucalyptus oil or pure turpentine around the bottom of fruit trees to keep ants away.

badgers

In Britain badgers have gone from being one of our best-loved woodland animals to being a serious pest species. Increasing badger numbers have led to a shortage of their natural food sources—slugs, amphibians, baby rabbits, and other small surface-dwellers, like hedgehogs, which have completely disappeared in some parts of Britain. Badgers here are now a liability to small livestock, particularly fowl and lambs, to say nothing of the thousands of flowerbeds that they dig up nightly in their search for bulbs.

● A determined badger will get through any fence, electrified or not, and virtually nothing will deter them. Not long ago, when one broke into my chicken house, I tried putting heaps of dried powdered wormwood mixed with rue and cayenne pepper where a run passed under the bottom wire of a fence. The theory was that the poor old badger would get a face-full and would totter off sneezing. It worked for a night or two, but then they came in from another direction.

birds

● The only effective way of keeping birds from damaging seed beds, emerging plants, and small fruit trees is to cover them with fine netting. I have not found any bird scare that works for any length of time.

cockroaches

I once had a job loading sheep carcasses into the cold-storage holds of ships in the Auckland, New Zealand docks and there were enormous cockroaches scuttling about in the freezers. I have never understood how they survived the sub-zero temperatures but it gives an indication of how difficult they are to get rid of. Even our ancestors, who had so much knowledge at their fingertips, relied on biological control. Until the beginning of the 20th century, there was a weekly trade in caged live hedgehogs at London's Leadenhall Market. The hedgehogs were put down in cellars and dry-food stores and lived off the cockroaches there.

● There are a number of sugar-based herbal recipes for killing cockroaches—recipes using powdered dried black (*Tamus communis*) and white bryony (*Bryonia dioica*) and white henbane (*Hyoscyamus niger*) are examples, but these are poisonous and likely to be eaten by the family pet.

● Fresh leaves of black hellebore (*Helleborus niger*) or black horehound (*Ballota nigra*), scattered on the floor of a pantry are very effective; their drastic purgative and narcotic properties usually have the desired effect.

● Mullein (*Verbascum*) leaves are another possibility. The powdery down covering the leaves is said to ball in their throats and choke them.

deer

These are becoming an urban pest, particularly in Britain and parts of North America. There are more deer in the USA now than there were when the Pilgrim Fathers arrived. Roe deer and muntjac regularly predate on gardens in the suburbs of London and other major UK cities.

● To keep deer out, one option is deer fencing.

● Deer repellents are another option. A mixture of olives, cloves, oil, and lemongrass, can be effective.

● Planting shrubs and flowers that are distasteful to deer is another possibility. Rosemary, sage, tulips, lupins, buddleia, daffodils, and Siberian squill (*Scilla siberica*) are a few examples.

● Medieval flowerbeds and vegetable gardens had low box hedging planted around them which deer found visually confusing.

If you live in a rural area and have the appropriate firearm certificate, you can sit up and wait for the deer with a rifle at dawn and dusk, when they come out to feed. If you do not have a firearm certificate, I am sure a neighbor will put you in touch with someone responsible who does.

fleas

The general standard of hygiene nowadays has reduced the risk of human fleas, but you can never be too careful.

● In medieval households, European alder (*Alnus glutinosa*) leaves, which have a clammy texture, were spread among rushes on the floor in spring to catch fleas.

● Bunches of fleabane (*Pulicaria dysenterica*), hung up in the corner of a room or the smoke from burning dried leaves were also used to repel fleas, as were bunches of common wormwood (*Artemisia vulgaris*), rue, pennyroyal (*Mentha pulegium*), and fennel—dry or fresh—as well as borax and oil of turpentine.

● To prevent dogs from getting fleas, wash them in infusions of rue, wormwood, or walnut leaves.

● Several hill shepherds I have known worm their sheepdogs by giving them a whole unpeeled clove of garlic. They claim that this, done often enough, also keeps their sheepdogs free of fleas and, more importantly, ticks.

flies

● European black elderberry (*Sambucus nigra*) leaves, strategically placed around the house in bowls will deter flies.

● A border of common rue (*Ruta graveolens*) or basil planted under a kitchen window helps keep flies away from food.

foxes

Foxes are as destructive as badgers, are considered vermin, and are becoming, like coyotes in some parts of America, an urban pest. Until recently, the fox population was controlled by foxhound packs, as they are in America, Australia, Ireland, and large parts of Europe. Of the available options for control, this is recognized as the most humane. In Britain foxes may be shot at, snared and poisoned or driven from cover with no more than two dogs in England and more than two dogs in Scotland. This enables hunts to continue providing a historic service to farmers and the rural population, so if you are having trouble with foxes, contact your local hunt kennels.

In America, coyotes and foxes are the principal pest to small livestock. Australia has its dingos, foxes, and feral pigs, while in New Zealand, feral pigs are the worst offenders. All these are disposed of by whatever means is most suitable to the species and location.

mice

● There is nothing better than a good cat for mousing, but they tend to be selective. Some days they might feel in the mood for a mouse while on others, mice are completely ignored in favor of a small bird.

● A terrier is a useful deterrent, but uniquely to Britain, it is currently illegal for a dog to chase a mouse.

- Another alternative mouse deterrent is to use fresh leaves of dwarf elderberry (*Sambucus ebulus*) or dried wormwood (*Artemisia absinthium*) or rue (*Ruta graveolens*). Crumble the leaves until you have a powder, push as much into the mouse hole as possible, and blow it in with a set of bellows or a tube made from a rolled-up newspaper. Be generous.

- I have achieved astonishing results using the same technique with cayenne pepper.

moles

Having been a hill farmer all my life, I have never regarded a mole as an agricultural pest in the way that an arable farmer would. In fact "nature's drainage expert" was a welcome sight on damp moorland and a friend of mine used to buy live moles that he put down on damp areas in the hope that water would drain away into the mole runs. If a mole appears, I suggest trying to drive him away rather than killing him. There are a number of ways this can be achieved.

- Moles have an acute sense of smell so anything with a powerful smell, like oil of eucalyptus, poured into a run will see them off.

- They rely on their whiskers to pick up vibrations of worm movement so the vibration transmitted from a child's windmill stuck in the ground above a run can be enough to drive them away. When I was a child, an old man used to arrive on a motorcycle, lower the tire pressure, ride onto the lawns, stick a pipe connected to his exhaust into a mole run and sit there revving the engine. It was highly effective.

moths

Nothing is more irritating and destructive than the common clothes moth, which gets into closets and feasts on anything woolen.

- We always put little cheesecloth bags filled with rosemary, sage, lavender, and a pinch of orris root, in all the clothes drawers and hang bunches of thyme or rosemary closets.

- Leaves of wormwood (*Artemisia absinthium*) and southernwood (*Artemisia abrotanum*) are other good moth-repellants.

- Clothes that moths have just begun feeding on can be saved by putting them in the deep freeze for a few hours. This kills both the moths and their eggs.

rats

If you have livestock, rats are an inevitability. As I have always had dogs around the place, I have never risked using poison but have always relied on good ratting terriers to keep rats down.

- Rats live in dread of ferrets and a jill (female), small enough to enter a rat hole, will either kill the rats underground or bolt them into the open to a terrier. A ratting ferret will need careful looking after and any scratches or nips must immediately be disinfected as a rat bite will nearly always turn infectious. Remember that a ratting ferret is no use for rabbiting as they kill underground, rather than bolting the rabbits out.

- An alternative to a ratting ferret, but not nearly as effective, is the live trap. This is an oblong cage with a hinged trapdoor, connected to a balance plate to which bait is fixed. When a rat mounts the plate to eat the bait—strong cheese or fish such as kippered herring—the trapdoor closes. The rat can then be humanely dispatched.

wasps

- The simplest way to get rid of wasps is to stop them coming into the house in the first place. Make a solution of wasp sugar, by boiling 5 cups of dark brown sugar in $2^{1}/_{2}$ cups of dark beer. As soon as the mixture comes to a boil, add $1^{2}/_{3}$ cups of molasses. Simmer for five minutes and decant while still warm into a tin. Put spoonfuls of it in dishes slightly away from open windows.

- Pure turpentine or oil of eucalyptus mixed with glycerol and poured into the nest will destroy it.

weasels and stoats

Both these beautiful little creatures are terrible egg thieves and gamekeepers wage permanent war on them. I find them utterly enchanting and a constant source of fascination. They are totally devoid of fear and think nothing of attacking animals many times their size. A family of stoats or weasels will clear a farmyard of rats quicker and more effectively than anything else, but they will extract a high payment in eggs, chicks, and sometimes hens. A stoat will kill just for fun and can play havoc in a hen house.

- Keeping a dog around the place will deter weasels and stoats from breeding nearby.

- A cage trap as used for rats and baited with fish or fresh rabbit liver is the only real recourse against weasels and stoats.

the green you

making and creating

I don't know why it is that I always feel that other people can create things but that I can't. I imagine it's simpler living in remote tribes or communities where one is obliged to have a go or else you have to do without. I suppose it is fear of failure in an age where political correctness is trying to erase the word "failure" from the language. It's OK to fail isn't it, but only if you've tried? What is so bizarre is that when one does try, one rarely falls short. Obviously some people do things better than others but if it gives you pleasure, then so what? As my grandmother used to say, "patience and perseverance made a bishop of his reverence!" So don't say you can't make candles or soap or that you can't spin or weave until you've tried it. As for mending, well, if you're following greener principles and not throwing everything away, then you have no option but to make do and mend. After all, the only way to get rid of shopping malls and supermarkets with their food miles is for people not to shop in those places and the way to cure this mercenary mercantile world is to make your own things.

candle making

Lest you should think that candle making is just a hippie thing to do, you should know that the world's fifth largest yacht is owned by a candle maker and is called *Paraffin*. As a teenager this yacht-owner made his first candle for his mother. It was spotted by a neighbor. The boy sold the candle to the neighbor and bought enough material to make two more candles. He gave one to his mother, sold the second one and never looked back.

Older candles have an interesting history. Primitive people rose with the sun and went to bed with it or used the light of the fire for simple activities (sex and dancing spring to mind!). Once the need for extra light arose—for example for cave painting—simple artificial light evolved. The most primitive form of light was a hollow stone filled with animal fat into which a wick was inserted. Examples of these early lights, some made out of quartz or lapiz and some from carved soapstone, have been found in many prehistoric digs.

The first form of advanced lighting was the rush light, which people probably developed when they learned skills such as sewing and weaving and needed light to work by for longer periods.

candles—the next step

From the rush light it was a short step to making candles with cotton or linen wicks. These however needed constant trimming as the tallow burned away faster than the wick. Then someone discovered that if you braided your cotton wick, it bent over as the candle melted down and was consumed in the flame. All modern candles have braided wicks.

The finest candles are made from beeswax. These were the preserve of the church and the very rich. They smell beautiful, unlike tallow, and give a good clear light. The principle for making them is the same.

dipping candles

This is the traditional way of making candles and I find that dipped candles burn better than molded ones. Melt your beeswax in a saucepan over a very low heat. Loop a length of wick around a piece of doweling and support the doweling across the back of two kitchen chairs. The wick will hang down, giving you two lengths to dip. Make sure each length is the same. Dip the wick in the wax for a minute, then remove it and let it dry for a few minutes, until the wax hardens. Repeat until the candles are the desired thickness. Leave them until completely hardened before using.

molding candles

If you prefer, you can use candle molds. Almost any shape container will do, but you may want to go down the store-bought-mold route. Such a mold has a depression in the bottom, which gives you the point of the finished candle.

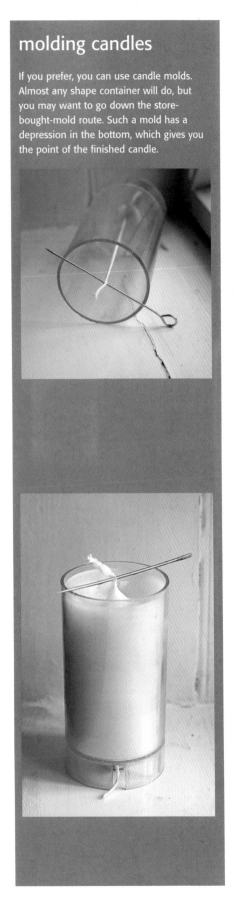

making a wick

Hammer a nail into a small board, measure off the length of candle you want, marking the board to ensure the right length. Attach three strands of cotton to the nail and braid them.

making a rush light

Take a rush and peel off most of the outside skin, but leave a strip of peel down one side to strengthen it. The pith provides a good wick which you then dip into melted tallow, that is to say, animal fat. When the tallow cools you have a rush light. A 16-inch light will burn for half an hour and two or three of them give enough light to read or sew by. They are smoky and smelly but faute de mieux. Mutton tallow makes the best rush lights, which suited the English, a nation whose economy was based on sheep.

"The finest candles are made from beeswax. These were the preserve of the church and the very rich."

lye and soap making

As a child I used to visit the west of Ireland and I remember the strong smell of the cottagers making lye, an alkaline solution used for the washing of clothes and particularly for removing grease and heavy dirt from linen. Lye is made by straining water through wood ash or bracken (fern) ash and was one of the main uses for cut bracken.

lye

Drill holes in the bottom of a wooden barrel and place it on top of a galvanized bucket. Put a layer of gravel in the bottom of the barrel to strain the lye and cover with a cotton or linen cloth. Half-fill the barrel with wood ash from hardwood or the ash from burnt bracken. Pour in water and leave it to drain through to the bucket—it takes a surprisingly long time.

Now boil down the lye until the liquid is strong enough to float an egg (see box below). In Ireland you could buy blocks of bracken potash which I was told would keep for 20 years.

checking the strength of a saturated solution

If you are ever making a saturated solution of brine, in other words, one that is strong enough to float an egg, take a short stick and add a weight to one end. Drop this into the brine and the stick will stand up straight. At the point where the stick emerges from the water, make a notch. You can then use the same stick to check the strength of your lye solution. When the lye is the correct strength, the notch will be level with the top of the liquid. This stick will save you from having to float an egg on your brine or in your lye.

special precautions

Take care with lye; it can give you a really nasty burn. You must handle it especially carefully if you are using it for washing fabric. Once the fat is added to make soap, it stops being caustic.

soap

Until the second half of the 19th century soap was a luxury because it was made with fat and fat was needed for the making of candles. Indeed, soap was quite heavily taxed to deter people from using too much of it. Instead, sharp sand and fuller's earth were used for washing such clothes as were washed.

When you consider that Elizabeth I was thought eccentric by her contemporaries of the 16th century because she bathed once a month, you can see that there wasn't much demand for soap. It wasn't until the 1860s that commercial soap became readily available.

making soap

For this it is necessary to ensure that your lye is the correct concentration. Pour the lye into an old pan. For every 2 cups of lye add gyros of melted clean beef or mutton drippings, or lard or vegetable oil. Believe me, the animal fat makes better soap. When you have asked yourself why cosmetic companies buy the fat that drips off $3\frac{3}{4}$ cups will know that I am correct. Boil this solution together for about three hours. As the mixture starts to cool, stir in a pound of salt. This will fall to the bottom of the pan but acts to harden the soap. Once the salt has settled, add scent and/or colouring if you plan to, and pour the liquid soap into wooden molds lined with a damp cloth, leaving the salt behind in the pan.

scenting and coloring

At this stage, but before you pour the soap into the molds, you can mix in herbs for scenting—lavender flowers, rosemary, and lemon balm are all good. If you have fresh herbs, shred them, otherwise use a distillation of the oil or an aromatherapy oil. If you like you can also add vegetable coloring. The juice of beets, carrots, and spinach were traditionally used. Don't add anything in alcohol as this will ruin the soap. Let the soap set. It will keep well in a cool airy place.

Soap can also be made with caustic soda and there are some herbs that are alkaline enough to replace the lye. In South Africa soap was made with ostrich fat and a member of the buckthorn family called seepbos (soap bush).

bath oils and fragrances

to make a herb bag

One of the easiest ways of transforming a bath into an aromatherapy experience is with a herb bag. Different dried herbs have a different effect. Peppermint, sage, chamomile flowers, and rosemary soothe a fevered brow. Others, such as nettle leaves, elder bark, valerian root, and comfrey relieve muscle tension. Oatmeal or bran can be added to the bag to soften the water.

Make a 5" x 3½" bag out of cheesecloth and fill it with dried herbs of your choice. You can close the bag with either a drawstring around the top or simply by tying it around the opening with a piece of string. Ensure that the string is long enough so that when it is attached to the hot faucet, it dangles in the water flow. In that way, the scent of the herbs is released as the water fills the bath.

The use of flower petals, aromatic herbs, and bark as scents and fragrances to sweeten bath water is as old as civilization. The knowledge of how to prepare them moved westward from China about 5,000 years ago and the first documentation of their use is from Babylon, in 2000 BC. These skills were acquired and improved upon by the Egyptians and Greeks and reached perfection with the Romans, who loved strong, sweet-smelling scents.

flower-scented bath oil

Take two handfuls of flower petals and bruise gently between your hands to release the scent. Place in a wide-necked container such as a 1-pint canning jar, and cover with 1½ cups sunflower oil. Seal and place in sunlight for at least three weeks, shaking the jar daily. In the absence of sunlight, a warm area will do. Strain through cheesecloth, making sure to squeeze out all the oil. Repeat, adding another two handfuls of petals. The more often you add petals and the longer you leave it, the more intense the scent will become. When you are ready to use it, mix three parts of glycerol to one part of scented oil to your bath water.

herb and fruit-scented bath oil

The leaves of rosemary, lavender, camomile, sage, fennel, yarrow, peppermint, eau-de-cologne mint, elder, nettle, lovage, marigold, raspberry, and black currant are other wonderful additions to your bath oil. The variety and possible permutations are endless. Follow the instructions as for the flower-scented bath oil, but crush the leaves with a rolling pin or put them through a meat grinder. For lemon or orange bath oil, remove the zest of the fruit using a sharp knife, making sure you do not include any of the pith. Twist the peel to release the oils as you put it in the canning jar with the oil, then follow the instructions as before.

sweet waters

Sweet waters are a very ancient method of capturing the scent of flowers and herbs. In their simplest form, sweet waters are basically the petals or leaves of flowers, herbs, and spices infused and allowed to cool in boiling water. The scent only lasts a week or two, but while it does, sweet waters make a refreshing hand or face wash and can be added to the bath. Fill a quart jar with rose petals or any other strong-scented fresh or dried flower, herb, or spice. You could try lavender, rosemary, lovage, a handful of crushed cloves—the options to experiment are limitless. Cover with boiling water, strain when cool, and add a couple tablespoons of rubbing alcohol, which helps to hold the scent.

scented verjuice

Verjuice is similar to wine vinegar and in the Middle Ages, scented verjuice became popular. This precursor to eau-de-cologne is wonderfully refreshing on a hot day. I remember elderly ladies dabbing themselves with it through the summer when I was a child. Add 2 cups of the best white wine vinegar to the same amount of water and heat until nearly boiling. Remove from the heat and add a couple of handfuls of dried crushed herbs or flowers—lavender, violets, rosemary, lemon balm flowers—or the zest of lemons or oranges. Leave overnight and strain through cheesecloth. Add more herbs or flowers and repeat the process if you want a stronger scent. Witch hazel or chemical alcohol, which in some countries requires a prescription to purchase, may be used instead of vinegar.

organic cleaning materials

Sir Humphrey Davy invented sodium hydroxide in 1807 and borax was discovered in Death Valley, California, following the 1849 gold rush. Both of these discoveries revolutionized kitchen cleaning. Until then dishwashing was more about hot water, elbow grease, and abrasive materials like sand, ash, chalk, and salt. Soap and the use of leaves and roots of the soapwort plant were reserved for cleaning the body and textiles.

Pewter plates and cast iron pots and pans were scrubbed with the plant, horsetail, (*Equisetum*) or scoured with fine sand, in England using either "Calais" sand or "Silver" sand from Galloway in Ireland. With the arrival of stoneware, china, porcelain, and copper, the acidic properties of vinegar—nature's marvel—verjuice (see page 151), and rhubarb were much appreciated for breaking down grease and giving a shine. China and porcelain dishes, for example, were cleaned by rubbing off detritus with a wet cloth and rinsing them in water to which a little white wine vinegar had been added. Nowadays lemon juice makes a pleasant alternative.

traditional cleaning techniques

● For copper pots and pans, wash, dry, then rub with lemon, vinegar, or rhubarb leaves. Let stand for an hour, then polish with a clean cloth.

● For stainless steel or aluminum, rub with rhubarb leaves, with the cut ends of rhubarb stalks, or with half a lemon to remove stains. For persistent marks, keep dipping the lemon in salt.

● For wooden cutting boards, rub vigorously with a cut lemon to remove the smell left by chopping garlic, onions, fish, or meat.

● Silverware should be washed after use in very hot water, dried with a soft cloth, and wrapped in any non-woolen cloth (wool absorbs damp in the atmosphere).

● To clean tarnished silver, rub with wet salt or a paste of distilled water and powdered chalk.

● With bone-handled cutlery, only their blades should ever be washed otherwise the shank will rust through. Stand them upright in a pitcher full of boiling water, dry, then wipe the blades over with olive oil.

● If your cutlery has old-fashioned stainless-steel blades and they become dull, rub them over with half a lemon dipped in salt.

● Before commercial oven cleaners appeared on the market, people cleaned their ovens much more frequently using a paste of salt and water or salt and vinegar if the oven was very greasy.

● Lemon juice or white vinegar will remove most stain and water marks from bathtubs, sinks, toilet. Rub vinegar on with a cloth or use a cut lemon directly on the surface. Leave it for an hour for the acidic action to work, then wash off.

● For persistent stains on bathroom fixtures, rub with a cut lemon dipped in salt or mix some pure turpentine with linseed oil and rub on. Leave it for a couple of hours and wash off with soapy water.

● For those awkward places around taps that build up with dirt, use a short, stiff 5mm paintbrush to apply lemon juice or vinegar, then scrub with a toothbrush—bristle is more absorbent than nylon.

● What with your homemade bath oils (see pages 150–151), sweet waters (see page 151), and the vinegar, lemon juice, and turpentine, your bathroom should smell

beautiful and a hundred times better than if it had been cleaned with commercial detergents. In extremis, don't forget lighting a match in the toilet bowl to get rid of any unsavoury odours.

● To clean wooden floors, sweep away loose dirt and dust, then scatter fine sand and brush it off in the direction of the grain.

● When I was at school, the kitchen staff kept all the tea leaves, which the cleaners spread across the floors before sweeping them up.

● For washing floors, white wood ash mixed with warm water was used and then rinsed off.

● Take rugs and carpets out frequently and beat them on the reverse side, then turn them and brush.

● Scatter tea leaves on rugs and carpets, then brush off to lift dust and grit. Hard snow would do the same job.

● Clean wallpaper with a loaf of stale bread, moistened on the cut surface or with a lump of flour and water mixed into a thick mass.

● Glass surfaces can be cleaned with an

onion cut in half, then washed down with a solution of white wine vinegar or cider vinegar, then dried.

● Fresh fruit stains and red-wine stains may be lifted by the quick application of salt. If some of the stain remains after the salt has been brushed off, dampen with boiling water and repeat. Milk is also a good vehicle for drawing out stains.

● Grease and oil on fabric should be scraped off with a knife, then covered with a paste of Fuller's earth or fine wood ash and allowed to dry. If the marks are still visible, dampen with a mixture of water and vinegar and add ash or dry Fuller's earth.

● Oil and grease on fabric can be shifted by placing brown paper above and below the stain and ironing with a hot iron.

the best silver polisher

My grandparents had a butler called Mr. Wild who was the best silver polisher I have ever come across. He polished everything with his forefinger, with his middle finger crossed over the top of it to keep it rigid. He believed that there was an interaction between the heat generated by rubbing and natural human oils in the skin that created the brilliant shine that he achieved. He also kept a tin full of cigar ash that he collected from the ashtrays. This he used with water to make a paste for removing discolorations and for working into ornate silver pieces with a brush made from badger hair. If a number of spoons became discolored after boiled eggs had been eaten, he soaked them in sour milk.

plain and purl

You are now ready to knit your first row, which you do by repeating the casting-on process but putting the new stitches onto the left-hand needle. This gives you plain stitch.

For a purl stitch, you put the needle through the back of the stitch instead.

yarn and needles

You can knit wool, silk, or cotton and can knit using two needles, four needles, or circular needles. Knitting yarn basically comes in five weights—2-ply, which is very fine, 4-ply, which is still fine, double knit, which is the middle range, Aran, which is traditionally used for pull-overs, and chunky, which knits up quickly. There is now also an extra-thick wool, which knits up really fast.

Wool can either be untreated, in which case it retains its lanolin and is very waterproof, or washed.

Needles start at the finest, No. 1 (2.25mm) and go up to 50 (25mm). They are made of aluminum, wood, or plastic.

Check your pattern to make sure that you buy the correct size of needle; larger needles mean larger, more open stitches and a looser knit.

Boleros, capes, and other similar seamless garments are made on circular needles of varying sizes and circumferences. Socks, mittens, and so forth are knitted on needles with points at both ends so that you can more easily turn a heel. These needles are sold in packs of four.

crochet

I am afraid that for most of my life I was not much interested in crochet. At primary school we were taught that strange craft in which you hammered four nails into a cotton reel and, with the aid of a crochet hook and different colored wools, made yards of colored woolen worms. The woolen worms served no useful purpose but were great fun to make and, as I can now see, encouraged dexterity. This was my first brush with crochet.

At boarding school I greatly coveted my friend Carrots' multi-colored crocheted bed covering known as Aunt Letts' Blanket. It taught me the meaning of the Tenth Commandment. I had no desire to replicate the blanket, only somehow to obtain it. I never succeeded and ALB now keeps Carrots' children snug.

I have never much liked babies and couldn't see the point of crocheting beautiful shawls for them to puke all over when a bit of old blanket you could throw in the wash would do just as well. Nor was I drawn to crochet when I moved to Scotland and was exposed to the beautiful crocheted Shetland shawls. This is surprising because I am deft with my hands and enjoy that type of work.

However, dear reader, don't despair. Somewhere in my fifties I learned that something similar to crochet is used to make nets for rabbiting and ferreting and also for Haaf-netting—that wonderful type of fishing where you stand in a river up to your neck and wait for the fish to swim into your net, which is suspended on a sort of cedar-wood cross of Lorraine. As a result, I have become quite keen on crocheting.

"I have never much liked babies and couldn't see the point of crocheting beautiful shawls for them to puke all over..."

yarn and needle

You will need a ball of wool or thread and a crochet hook. Hook sizes range from B-1 (2.25mm) to S (19mm). Practice with fairly thin wool or even string. Crocheting is all about maintaining tension and for this you must find a comfortable way to achieve an easy flow between needle and hand. As you get more skilled, you can use different-sized needles and heavier or lighter yarns.

to make a double stitch

Pick up the first chain stitch on your hook, then loop the yarn over the hook and pull it through.

Loop the yarn over the hook again, and pull it through both stitches.

getting started

Before you start, promise me that you will persevere until you have successfully crocheted ten rows. The point of this request is that, to begin with, crocheting is maddeningly frustrating and you will be tempted to throw the whole lot away and give up just as you are on the verge of succeeding. Ten rows are all it takes and you are off.

turning a row

When you have enough stitches for the width you want according to your pattern, you need to turn the row. To do this, make an extra chain stitch at the end of the row before turning to prevent bunching.

To increase the length of your rows, for example to make a piece widen out, work two stitches through one stitch of the previous row. To decrease, miss a stitch and work into the next one.

Make a loose slip knot and insert the hook through the loop. Assuming you are right-handed, hold the needle in your right hand about halfway along the shaft, as you would a spoon or a pencil, whichever you find most comfortable. Take the unused thread in your left hand, loop it over the index and middle fingers of the left hand, under the ring finger and over the little finger.

Use the hook to catch the yarn held in the left hand and to pull it through the loop on the needle, then tighten the yarn by pulling the loose end downwards. Repeat until you have a chain of stitches.

finishing off

To finish your work, cut the yarn leaving a tail, then use the hook to draw the stitch through the final loop. Finally, use a darning needle to weave the tail into the work. If you are crocheting a large item or one with sections worked in different colors, you need to join the sections when they are finished. To do this, use the same type of yarn as you have been crocheting with. Use a slipstitch and don't pull on the yarn or you will bunch up your crochet.

This may sound gobbledegook as you read it, but all will become clear as you follow it through your promised ten rows! When you look at the beautiful, gossamer-fine, state-of-the art crocheted shawls that are made in places like the Shetland Islands you may think they are impossible to make but the old adage "practice makes perfect" was never truer than in crocheting.

incorporating new yarn

When you need more yarn, either to start a new ball or to add a different color, wait until you are at the beginning of a row then work a stitch with the old yarn and complete the same stitch with the new yarn, laying a longish length of the new yarn along the top of the row and working over it.

quilting

I have always maintained that if the world were peopled solely by women, apart from the obvious problem of reproduction, we would still live in caves, but what comfortable, decorative caves they would be. Nothing, I feel, illustrates women's natural instinct for creating comfort than the art of quilting.

the layers of a quilt

Quilts were originally made for use and warmth as well as for their decorative qualities. They can be as simple or as complicated as you want but basically they are made up of three layers: the top layer which is the decorative layer, the middle layer, which is usually a worn blanket or large piece of felt, and a backing layer of some neutral or toning color, often sheeting. If the quilt is mainly or purely for decoration then the middle layer should be of thin cloth.

It is the top layer that all the fuss is about. This is made up of different shaped pieces of cloth—squares, octagons, diamonds, indeed any shape you wish provided they are capable of having edges that align. Every household has a store of worn-out clothes, unused or stained table linen, or old curtains or sheets and any of these can supply the fabric you need to make your top layer. The trick when deciding which to use is to work out colors and patterns that go well together. Old jeans, for example, are good for providing neutral blocks of color to break up areas of patterned fabric.

making the shapes

When you have decided on the shape of the individual pieces of quilt, you must cut out templates of stiffish card stock in that shape. This is where you involve children, elderly relatives, harmless drunks, indeed everyone you know. Once you have your templates, you cut up your material, lay a piece over each template, turn the edges over the edges of the template, tack lightly to the template, and trim the edges. When you have assembled your fabric-covered templates, you then lay them out on a work surface or even on a bed and arrange them to your satisfaction. Once you are content with the layout, tack the fabric-covered templates together at the edges to make manageable groups. Then sew each tacked group to its neighboring group, according to your planned arrangement until you have completed your whole top layer. Turn this over, cut the tacking threads holding the fabric to each template, and remove the templates.

Lay the backing layer flat on your work surface or bed, place the middle layer on top and, finally, the decorative layer, then tack around the edges to hold the three layers together. Then sew through all three layers along the edges of the fabric shapes. This can be done by hand and reinforced by machine stitching unless the quilt is for display only, in which case it should be solely hand-stitched.

Have ready some plain binding in a color that will enhance your pattern and sew this carefully all around the edge of your quilt. If the quilt is to be used you can tack this and then oversew on a machine.

In America, quilts are often made on quilting frames and if you really take to quilting you may think of making one, but all my quilting experience has been with work laid on a flat surface.

quilt aftercare

When you store your quilt, don't put it in a plastic bag but instead use a large pillowcase or a bag made from sheeting, depending upon the size of your quilt. Fold the quilt with tissue paper to prevent permanent creases which will rub and cause damage, and re-fold them along different folds every three months.

If the weather is damp or humid, hang your quilt out to air from time to time, avoiding bright sunlight which will fade it. Don't store it where it may attract rodents or moths. When washing, don't put it in the machine but wash by hand, unless you are sure none of the materials will shrink or run. Lay it flat on the ground to dry.

quilting in America

In America there are museums full of quilts that pioneer women made in the little spare time they had to brighten and decorate their sparse cabins. Quilting in America is now a folk art and memorial quilts are very popular there. I remember, when AIDS first hit America badly, seeing photographs of wonderful huge memorial quilts being made for the victims. Curiously, quilting is much bigger in America than in England, although the finest English examples are to be found in Lincolnshire and East Anglia, the parts of the country that provided so many of the original settler families.

mending

"Make do and mend," read the wartime posters. "A stitch in time saves nine," my mother used to tell me. "We will mend it, stick it with glue," sang the Clangers, the small, pink mouselike creatures of the 1970s BBC television series. Today in the United Kingdom, no child learns to mend in school unless they go to a Rudolf Steiner school. In our throwaway society we don't mend. Instead we are clothed by the sweatshops of the Far East in cheap synthetic clothing that has no real life span and when it tears or wears out, we go out and buy something else.

Mending is to my mind the practice for sewing without wasting expensive cloth. Once you have perfected the techniques of mending, sewing is a cinch. My eldest sister and, indeed, my sister-in law both earn good money with their curtain-making businesses and my sister-in law hand-covers lampshades, too—a good home industry and one in much demand.

sewing on a button

Let's consider the different types of mending. First there's sewing on buttons. Buttons on manufactured garments are usually poorly sewn so they come off easily. "Easy peasy!" you cry, "What does one need to learn about sewing on a button?" Well, remember the thread. Don't sew back your button with white thread if all the others are sewn on with blue, green, or black. It will stand out like a neon light. Button thread is a special tough thread designed for sewing buttons on thick cloth, men's jackets, and ladies' coats. When sewing buttons on this type of garment you must remember to leave

higgledly piggledy buttons

Johnny and I were both given buttons by the Saltersgate Hunt at their Hunt Dinner after we filmed with them during the second series of *Clarissa and the Countryman*. Johnny was hunting the next day and was eager to have the buttons on his hunt coat for the occasion, so I got up early and painstakingly sewed them on. The Melton cloth of these hunt coats is very thick indeed and I had to use a glass for a palm—a block of wood set into a leather strap that's held in the palm—to push the needle through as I had no thimble. Looking at his coat six months down the line, I was horrified to discover the buttons were all higgledly piggledy, with the embossed crests on them at a variety of angles. It isn't enough to sew buttons on strongly; they must also all be facing the same way.

a long stem, or shank, of thread which you wind around with more thread to strengthen it. If you don't do this, the wearer will not be able to do up their buttons. You will also need a thimble or you will puncture yourself.

Thread your needle, make a small knot in the long end of the thread, push the needle through from the reverse side of the garment, and pull the thread through. Don't ever have your thread too long or it will tangle and knot. Put the needle through one eye of the button, back through another eye and through the material, leaving the thread slightly loose. Continue this process several times. When the button is secure, wind the thread around the shank several times and finish off securely.

mending a ripped hem

Where the material is actually ripped, open up the hem, insert a new strip of material under the rip, re-fold the hem, and sew the two sides together.

No-sew method
You can buy iron-on adhesive tape to take for hemming but frankly I find it more trouble than it's worth.

patching

When a piece of cloth is very badly ripped or a hole has formed and the edges of the tear can't be joined together, you may need to insert a patch. If you have a matching piece of cloth you can use that or you can chose a contrasting color and make a feature of it. If the hole is in an appropriate place, you could cover it with a pocket. I remember a young man in my youth who had ripped his good new jeans on the inside of the upper thigh. He had sewn a patch over it on which was embroidered with the words "Custer had it coming." I found it very distracting.

Cut out your patch so that it is slightly larger than the tear in the garment, then trim the edges of the tear carefully. Lay the patch on the reverse side of the cloth with the right side facing through the tear and tack carefully around it and the edge of the tear. Then hemstitch around it with small stitches. If you are making a feature of your patch, choose a vivid, contrasting thread and make your stitches larger.

Trim the edges of the patch on the inside. Sew a second line of stitches to strengthen.

sewing a hem

If a shirt or dress is too long or if fashions change, you will need to take up the hem. You could, of course, like one very grand and stylish lady of my acquaintance, simply cut off the excess with pinking shears but you need a lot of style to carry that off without looking a slut—and what if hemlines drop again?

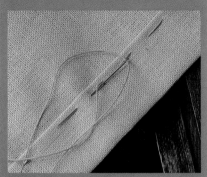

Using a tape measure, pin up the hem to the length you want, fold a narrow edge over, pin it, then tack it with long running stitches – – – – thus, which will be easy to pull out. You can now try the garment on and ensure it is even all around, either by asking someone to help you or by looking in a mirror. Once you are sure it is even, you will be able to hemstitch it. Yes, you can do this on a machine but hand-sewn stitches are stronger and neater—though not when I do them!

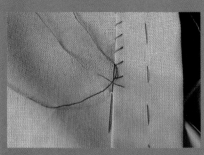

Hemstitch is a small, even, diagonal stitch / / / / thus, which joins the edge of the hem to the material of the garment. If the material is thick enough, you can hemstitch without going right through the cloth. Otherwise, make sure your stitches are small so that they don't show on the right side and don't pull them too tight or they will pucker the cloth. If you are right-handed, sew from left to right. Make sure the thread matches the cloth. When all is done, pull out the tacking thread.

Fallen hems need to be sewn up by the same method. Doing this is a good example of a stitch in time saving nine. Once a hem starts to unravel, pinning it up won't hold it long.

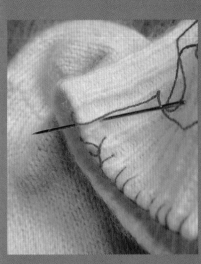

Blanket stitch is a strong stitch designed for hems that are under pressure, such as side seams which have undone. The technique is to make one stitch then loop the thread through itself before making the next stitch. Visually, blanket stitch looks like a line of capital T's all joined together TTTTTT thus. It is stronger than hemstitch.

Contrast patching

Contrast patching can be made from leather. Leather patches are placed over the hole on the right side of the garment and are then carefully sewn around the edge through the leather and the cloth.

You can also edge the frayed edges on cuffs and lapels in leather or cloth which can look very smart.

The practice of sewing leather or suede patches over the holes in the elbows of men's tweed jackets has become so fashionable in country clothes that tailors are now asked to sew them on new jackets, which I think looks quite ridiculous. Johnny has a favorite tweed jacket that is so beautifully patched, edged, and mended that it is an artwork in its own right.

> "The practice of sewing leather or suede patches over the holes in the elbows of men's tweed jackets has become so fashionable in country clothes that tailors are now asked to sew them on new jackets..."

Embroidery cover-up

An alternative to a patch if the mend is going to show is to embroider a motif over the top of it. I have an old and much-loved olive-colored vest with many pockets. It is of an irreplaceable type. I wear it every day at home instead of carrying a handbag around with me. I once caught the back of the vest on a nail, which left a jagged tear. The edges of the tear weren't going to meet, so I embroidered the word's "NO BAN" on the L-shaped tear. It makes me a lot of new friends. The enemies Ive made already! It's the same principle as those embroidered T-shirts that people pay a lot of money for.

If you are embroidering any motif, it is advisable to trace it on in pencil or ballpoint first and then sew, following the line. Use silk or cotton embroidery thread. Either use satin stitch, a simple embroidery stitch where the stitches are placed so close to each other that they appear to be joined together, or cross-stitch.

invisible mending

This is really darning (see below) but done with such care as to replicate the angle of the grain of the cloth and its texture so that you cannot see the finished result. It is best left to a professional.

where to learn to sew

I learned sewing in school, taught by a gentle aging Belgian nun called Mother Receiver. She must have bypassed any time in Purgatory that might have been pending for the pain she suffered watching our clumsy stitches. I was a poor, little rich girl. I didn't mend things as we had servants to do that and they, being Spanish, sewed beautifully. I embroidered and I did tapestry, but that was it.

The Women's Institutes in Britain and the Junior Leagues in America will teach you how to sew and mend and I bet there are women mending all over Iraq and Afghanistan. War and poverty teach you to make do and mend, though I'm not suggesting you move to a war zone to learn the skill.

"I was a poor, little rich girl. I didn't mend things as we had servants to do that..."

darning

Now that you are buying or making woolen cloth instead of the synthetic stuff, you will need to rediscover the art of darning. I love darning and even won prizes for it. When I was small I would make holes in my father's shooting stockings especially so I could darn them.

You will need a large-eyed darning needle and matching thread. If you haven't any, go mad and darn using some totally flamboyant color and flaunt the finished darn. Then you need a darning mushroom. If you don't have one, use a small saucer or anything you can stretch the hole and its surrounding edges tightly over. Thread your needle and start by running a line of stitches around the hole to stabilize the edges of the hole. Then, following the grain of the material as best you can, take the needle across the hole and through the material on the other side.

Reverse direction and repeat, working your way up the hole until all of it is filled with thread drawn across. Sever the thread then, starting at the top of the darn, repeat, working at 90 degrees to the first lot of stitching and weaving over and under the first threads. Continue until the hole is filled. It may then be necessary to weave in a few more stitches if there are any gaps. Remove the darning mushroom and, voilà! a perfect darn.

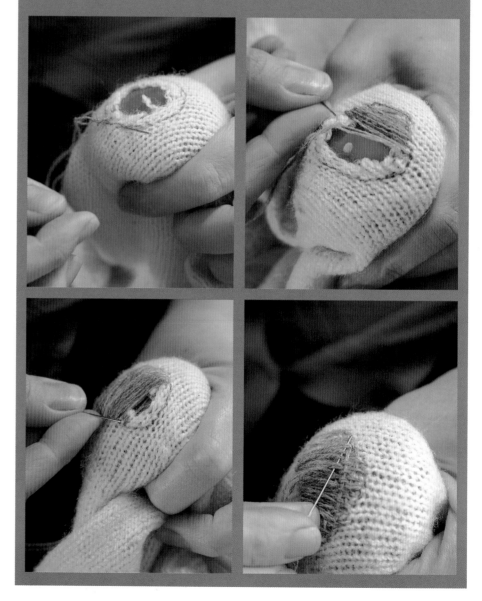

sewing in history

Saint Madeleine Sophie Barrat, founder of the Sisters of the Sacred Heart, wrote a short book of advice, some of which was read out to us at the start of the school year. She was writing before the French Revolution for the children of the well-to-do and was an advanced educator who wanted women to be taught the sciences. She also wrote of the importance of sewing and—one point I remember—of the dangers of carrying open scissors in your pocket.

There are displays of mending in local museums—children's work with exquisite tiny stitches practicing hem and buttonhole stitch, invisible mending, and darning.

At the turn of the 20th century, young ladies were sent to Holland and Belgium to learn the sewing techniques they would need in their married lives, but nothing like this happens any more.

My friend Arianne, President of the Scottish Embroiderers' Guild, tells me that during the Second World War, when things were in short supply, she used to wear the legs of her mother's old stockings—the feet had worn out—sewn onto the feet of her father's woolen shooting stockings that had shrunk in the wash.

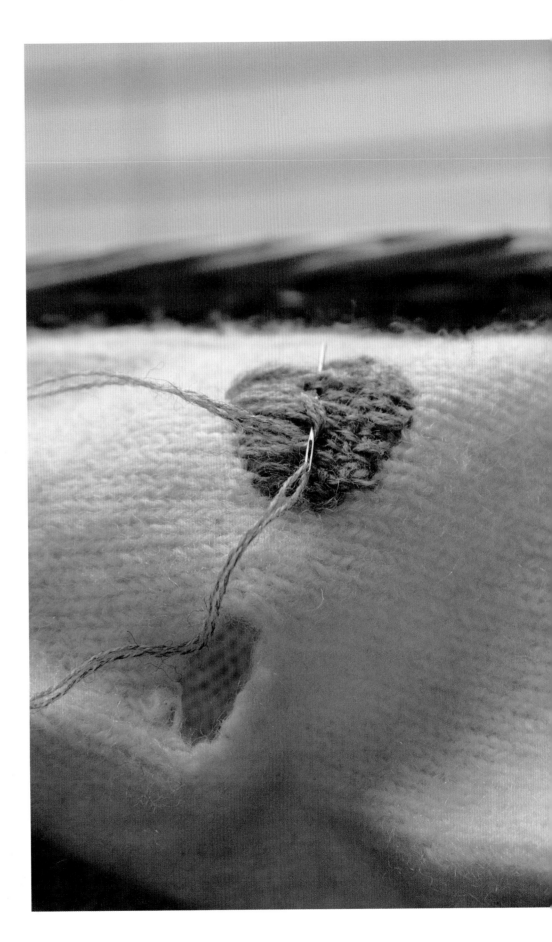

herbal remedies

There are literally thousands of different flowers and herbs. A hundred years ago, the countryside was a riot of wild plants, most of which were used either because they were edible (see page 78) or for their medicinal properties. The need for agricultural expansion, particularly after the Second World War, destroyed huge areas of rough pasture where these plants had previously thrived. Now that it is cheaper for the British government to feed the nation on imported food, and farming subsidies are directed towards landscape enhancement instead of farming, the countryside has once more become a herbalist's paradise.

the early history of herbalism

The first documentation in the Western world concerning the medicinal properties of certain plants were the writings of the Greek physician, Hippocrates, in 400 B.C. The next notable work, *Materia Medica*, was by his fellow-countryman, Dioscrides, in 100 A.D. The Roman, Galen, followed with a series of books on herbal cures written in the second century A.D. and these remained in use for the next fifteen hundred years. The Romans brought their extensive knowledge of herbs and their cures to Britain and we have them to thank for the introduction of many of the herbs that grow wild in this country today, thyme, rosemary, parsley, fennel, sage, and borage, to name only a few.

The great Norman religious houses brought an immensely sophisticated standard of herbal healing with them to England and every monastery had an

infusions from country lore

- For a head cold—leaves of agrimony, fennel, and sage, and the flowers of chamomile, linden (basswood), and verbascum.

- For a feverish chill or a cough—elderflower, peppermint, and yarrow.

- For catarrh—borage, hyssop, coltsfoot, and comfrey leaves.

- For flu and rheumatism—elderflowers mixed with honey.

- For constipation—dandelion and basil.

- For varicose veins—daisies.

- For colds and flu – eucalyptus leaves.

other country remedies

● For teenage pimples and acne—the sulphurous properties of gorse and broom flowers were capitalized on by being beaten into a paste with goose fat.

● For headaches and sleeplessness—a handful of lavender leaves, crushed and rubbed into the temples or sprinkled over hot water and inhaled under a towel.

● For insect bites and stings—fresh dock leaves and parsley juice.

● For a tick bite—bracken juice, once you had gotten the wretched creature off.

● To repel mosquitos—eucalyptus leaves and sweetgale.

● For pulled or stiff muscles—horseradish in a poultice.

● For chilblains—horseradish mixed with lard.

extensive herb garth or garden. The Augustinian monks at the 12th-century Hospice of Soutra in southern Scotland developed a form of anesthetic for amputations from black henbane, opium, and hemlock. Juniper berries and the fungus, ergot, were used to induce childbirth. St. John's Wort, nature's answer to valium, was used to treat melancholy. The little yellow-flowered tormentil was used to remove internal parasites and a diffusion of bracken fern cured bronchitis. Nineteenth-century colonists in America, Australia, and New Zealand were slightly nonplussed to find the aborigines there using it for the same purpose.

Over the last hundred years, modern medicine has suppressed much of the knowledge of natural cures that was detailed in the 16th-century works of Turner and Gerard and in Culpeper's more famous herbal of a hundred years later. The recent interest in holistic medicine is to be applauded.

the power of nettles

Old Joe, our gardener was a great believer in nettles, rubbing his hands with the leaves to ease rheumatism. He also used nettle leaves as a dressing for septic cuts, for the nettle beer he made in the spring as a post-winter tonic, and for the gray-green lotion he made from the boiled leaves, which he rubbed into his thinning hair, convinced that the astringent properties would activate the hair follicles and promote growth.

joe's sleeplessness

Like so many country people, Joe was a martyr to rheumatism—the "screws"—and on the nights he was unable to sleep, he would drink an infusion of valerian leaves and would lie on a pillow filled with hop flowers. In the morning he would be heavy-eyed and bad-tempered until the effects wore off.

using your produce

Apart from the real feeling of achievement a well-stocked
pantry and cupboard bring to the gatherer, there is the added
joy of exquisite tastes not often found in this modern world
of nasty supermarket foods. Refrigerators and freezers may
have brought new economies to distant lands but their
downside is obscene wastage of food and starving nations.
Do you really believe buying third-world vegetables feeds
those nations? Surely the money that is earned goes to
provide cars and palaces for the politicians whereas the
general populace would have prospered better eating the
food they grow themselves rather than exporting it to us.
Preserving your own produce not only makes you self-
sufficient but adds a whole range of different flavors to
your diet, whatever that diet may be. I have recently been
doing some vegan cooking for a friend (don't faint, dear
reader) and it is amazing what a spoonful of pickled cabbage
or a slice of preserved lemon will do to enliven that dullest
of diets. When food is preserved by one of the means
suggested here, it ripens and develops wonderful flavors that
our increasingly bland world has forgotten. And just think
how much electricity you save if you don't throw everything
in the freezer.

milk

In this sanitized, pasteurized, sickly age we have forgotten the joy of whole milk straight from the cow. Cooking with this wonderful milk, especially if it comes from Guernsey or Jersey cows, is like hearing the heavenly choirs singing the Alleluliah Chorus! Your sauces don't curdle and your rice puddings are a feast for the gods.

I have never believed the argument for skim milk. In my view, the increase in osteoporosis and depression that we see today is directly linked to the rise in the consumption of skim and low-fat milk and now, after all these years, the pundits are beginning to agree with me. According to the Royal Society of Chemistry and Dr. Harold McGee, the body needs the fat in the milk to absorb the calcium, hence the increase in osteoporosis in these days of low-fat milk. And the rise in depression is because the only substance that naturally stimulates the body's serotonin levels is animal fat. That's why you reach for ice cream when you're feeling low.

"In my view, the increase in osteoporosis and depression is directly linked to the rise in the consumption of skim and low-fat milk..."

selling your excess

You may want to sell your excess milk and if you pasteurize it, it is quite legal to do so. In Britain unpasteurized milk can be sold under license, the milking parlor must be checked by the Dairy Hygiene people and obviously your cow's inoculations must be in order. After that you can obtain a licence to sell milk at your farm gate but only to the end-consumer, not into restaurants or cafés. This is to ensure traceability in the event of any brucellosis outbreak. Unless you are truly dedicated to selling unpasturized milk it will cause you many headaches but those who prevail truly bring joy to mankind and cooks alike.

milk from other animals

Of course, milk from cows is not the only milk. My mother was so allergic as a child that she was fed on mare's milk, which she always reckoned accounted for her great love for horses. Then there is camel's milk, which is very rich in fat and makes great butter. Goat's milk and ewe's milk are more used in cheese production, the milk being less strong and less sweet than cow's milk. Sheep and goats will only milk for nine months in the year, unlike a cow who, once she has had her first calf, will continue to produce milk all year round. In recent years there has been a growth in the making of artisan cheeses from the milk of these beasts. I know of a goat farmer who makes over 200 blocks of goat cheese a day from his flock of 200 goats, each of which gives about three and a half quarts a day. He sells all he produces to a specialty cheese shop and delicatessen market, feeling, as I do, that supermarkets are the road to ruin for an artisan producer.

Vegans scream that drinking milk and eating butter and cheese is wrong as it deprives the calf of sustenance. As usual with such bigots, ignorance prevails. A dairy cow produces so much milk that the calf could not possibly consume it all so it is taken off its mother and fed separately. If it were not, the cow would not let down its milk to the machine and would suffer and even die.

cream

In the summer, when the cows are at pasture, you get a lot more cream than during winter feeding when they are on

hay and sugar beet. Fred, an 84 year-old farmer with six Guernsey cows that he now just keeps for pleasure, has a wonderful cream separator made by Alpha Laval about 120 years ago. It has 22 blades and at the turn of a handle can separate just over a quart of milk in five minutes. If you do not have such a machine, you must separate the cream by pouring the milk into a large shallow glazed earthenware dish and let it stand in a cool pantry. The cream will then rise to the surface. It takes 12 hours for light cream and 24 for heavy. Then you must scoop the cream off with a specially designed flat ladle with holes. Cream separates naturally from unpasteurized milk as the fat globules are too large to remain suspended in the emulsion. Industrially produced cream is separated by centrifugal force. This pasteurizes it instantly and so the cream does not have time to ripen and the taste is quite inferior. You will know once you have tried the real thing.

Some historians allege that clotted cream came to the West Country of England via Phoenician tin traders. They would have been used to the Middle Eastern kaymac, a very similar cream made with water-buffalo milk. It is nice to think of Joseph of Arimathea and Jesus sitting down to a Cornish cream tea!

To make clotted cream you put the whole milk in shallow pans to allow the cream to rise. It takes 12 hours in summer and 24 in winter. You then heat the whole to 180°F and keep it at that temperature for half an hour. Let the cream cool overnight, then skim it off in layers and cut it with a knife.

cream in different countries

In Britain, single cream is about 20 percent fat, double is 48 percent fat, and clotted cream is about 55–60 percent fat. In the US, light cream is between 18 and 30 percent fat while heavy cream is between 36–40 percent fat.

butter

Butter is a universal of any dairy culture. I remember at school being quite turned against the ancient Greeks when I discovered that they ate olive oil and kept the butter as an ointment. In the West Country of England they used to make a very rich butter with clotted cream. Thomas Hardy describes the dairymaids plunging their linked hands and forearms into the cream until the butter was formed. No wonder dairymaids were so sought after; they had lovely soft skin and great upper-body development!

Fred and I used to make butter together in a wonderful old butter churn, the likes of which I have never seen since. It was a chest about two foot square, made of thick elm planks and inside, turned by a handle, were four latticed paddles, side by side and two by two. Butter is made from ripened cream so Fred and I kept the cream in an earthenware crock standing in a cool place for three days before we used it.

It is the lactic-acid bacteria present in milk that cause the fat globules to cohere and make butter. Commercial butter made from pasteurized milk needs the addition of milk acids for the process to occur. Butter made from fresh cream is sweeter and keeps for less time.

yogurt

In this day and age we have gotten used to yogurt but when I was young it was a rarity that was only eaten by eccentric ladies wearing sandals and floral wrap dresses, and smelling vilely of stale lentils. In the 1960s I was introduced to commercially produced yogurt for the first time. With its chemical flavoring and strangely vivid coloring, it put me off yogurt for years. Then, like so many other people, I went to Greece on vacation and discovered what yogurt really should taste like.

making butter

You can churn butter in a jam jar, shaking it to and fro until the butter sets, or you can use a glass jar with paddles on the top turned by hand. When the butter sets, drain off the buttermilk. This contains the lactic acid and can give a sour taste to unsalted butter. Then you need to squeeze the excess buttermilk from the butter. I am the proud possessor of an antique butter table with hand-turned rollers, designed for squeezing butter, but more usually the squeezing is done with wooden butter pats. Divide the butter into half-pound lumps. Put a lump between the pats and keep patting it into a block, pressing as you go to extrude the excess liquid. It is quite a knack. The French wash their butter to remove any remaining buttermilk.

At this stage you can add salt to help preserve the butter longer. This is purely a matter of taste; the Welsh, for instance, like their butter quite salty but I, being a hedonist, like almost none. You can then wrap your butter in waxed paper, or put it in a crock, or even stamp it with a pretty pattern.

The buttermilk that remains is great for baking and is very healthy to drink.

Real yogurt is wonderful—a marvellous gift from Asia Minor to the world. It is great for cooking and is the alleged reason for so many centenarians fathering children in Bulgaria. Yogurt is digestible by people with lacto intolerance as the heating and fermentation involved in its preparation cause the bacteria in the milk to convert most of the lactose to lactic acid.

To make the yogurt you will need to keep back a little live yogurt from your last batch as a starter. Heat your milk to 180°F. You must use a thermometer as overheating will kill the bacteria and underheating will not start the process. Middle-Eastern nomads put the milk out in the sun. Pour the heated milk into clean containers and let the milk cool to between 106°F–109°F. Take some of the cooled milk and stir in half a teaspoon of starter for each pint of prepared milk. Distribute this evenly between the containers and stir well.

Place all the containers in a pan or baking tray to hold them steady, cover with a linen cloth and wrap in a blanket. The temperature must not drop below 60°F so you may need to stand the containers on top of the kitchen stove. The yogurt will set in eight hours. Be careful not to jolt it during this time or the yogurt-making enzymes will stop working. Store in a covered container once it is set.

which milk to use for yogurt?

All milk can become yogurt but if you are using cow's milk, it is better to use low-fat as it will keep better. Goat and sheep's milk give a more stable product, especially for cooking, and just in case you need to know, yak and camel milk are so rich in fat that it is better to use them skim for making yogurt.

buttermilk scones

(MAKES APPROXIMATELY 10)

These little griddle scones are found all over Ireland and are very good. You can also substitute buttermilk with milk when making any conventional sweet or savoury scones.

3½ cups all-purpose flour
1 tsp baking of soda
1 tsp cream of tartar
1 tsp salt
⅓ cup (¾ stick) butter
1¼ cups buttermilk

Sift together the flour, baking soda, cream of tartar, and salt. Rub in the butter and mix to a soft dough with the buttermilk. Roll out to ⅝ inch thick and cut into small flat circles using a biscuit cutter. Cook on a hot griddle for about 2 minutes until golden brown or bake at 425°F for 10 minutes. Eat when they are cool.

cheese

In your new greener life you can make cheese from any of your ruminants, though probably not from the yaks or camels. Cheesemaking is as varied as there are countries with ruminants to supply milk and manuals (mostly unhelpful) for the aspirant cheesemaker.

Making cheese
The first stage of cheesemaking is to let your milk ripen, allowing the lactic-acid-producing bacteria to sour it. Keep the milk fairly warm during this time, then raise the temperature to lukewarm. Now you must set the curd with the help of rennet. This process involves the casein fraction of the protein in the milk coagulating and shrinking, forcing out the whey and trapping the fat globules.

With the milk lukewarm, add the rennet and the curd will separate from the whey fairly speedily. You must then cut the curd with wire harps into smaller flakes or grains which you then lift from the whey. One exception is curd cheese or the very soft French-type cheeses in which the curd is simply lifted from the whey with a perforated ladle and hung in a cloth or other perforated mold to drain.
Once the curds are removed, they are salted and, in the case of hard cheeses, the salted curds are added to the cheese. Hard cheeses such as cheddar are then piled into molds and a weight applied to drive out still more whey. You can still find hand cheese presses for sale. The pressure applied to a full-sized cheddar may be as

great as a ton and a half. The pressed cheese is then wrapped in a bandage and heat applied with an iron to seal the cheese and stop mold getting in.

For semi-soft cheese, the salt is rubbed on the outside, while for soft cheese, the cheese may be immersed in brine for hours or even days.

Once the cheese is formed and removed from its mold, it must be matured. Hard cheeses are kept in cool, dry conditions but for soft cheeses a moist environment helps ripening and aids the growth of surface organisms.

rennet

Rennet is usually obtained from the lining of the fourth stomach of a ruminant calf. It can be dried and reused many times. Nowadays one buys it commercially in liquid or powder form. There is also vegetarian rennet, obtained from the infloresence of various plants. The most successful vegetarian rennet comes from my old friend the cardoon, although in Britain, yellow spring bedstraw (*Galium verum*) was most commonly used. Vegetarian rennet is harder to use and is more commonly confined to the making of goat's and ewe's milk cheeses.

whey

This is what is left after the curds have been removed. It is also what Cleopatra and Mary Queen of Scots are said to have bathed in as it is supposed to give wonderful skin tones. Italian ricotta is a whey cheese—the name simply means re-cooked. To make whey cheese the whey is heated to a high temperature then allowed to cool slightly and some sour whey or other coagulant is added. The resulting curds are then lightly pressed and eaten "fresh," in other words, unsalted, or they can be more heavily pressed and salted, and used in cooking. In Italy fresh ricotta is eaten as a dessert with sugar or honey.

eggs

Primitive people have always regarded eggs as a symbol of fertility and magic. The Romans, for example, kept sacred chickens for divination purposes and the egg crop was the preserve of the priest in charge! Christians are supposed to abstain from eating eggs during Lent. This has religious significance but more probably it was to allow the first eggs of the spring to hatch. Yeastre, goddess of fertility, had as her symbols the hare and the egg; these were speedily adopted by the early Christian church as the Easter egg and the Easter bunny. The taint of the old religion accounts for a number of superstitious links between eggs and witchcraft—for instance children are sometimes told to bash the bottom of their empty eggshell to stop witches using them as boats or, the white of an egg dropped into water on New Year's Eve by a young virgin is supposed to show, in the patterns formed, her marriage prospects. In Brazil young children are given dew collected during a full moon in an eggshell to help their speech development.

Your worry as a new henwife however is what to do with your egg glut while the hens are laying. First you need to test your eggs for freshness. The simplest way to do this is to put the egg into a deep bowl of water; a really fresh egg will sink virtually flat but as it ages the pointed end will sink and the egg eventually will stand upright. If an egg floats on the top then save if for throwing at a politician.

We are told that eggs keep fresh at room temperature for about 12 days, and three weeks in a refrigerator or at 45–46°F. However the reality is that kept in a cool, slightly damp cellar or garage, they will keep for up to three months and I have incubated pheasant eggs kept in such conditions after four weeks.

cooking with your egg glut

Homemade pasta is a great way of using up eggs and freezes well, either cut into strips or as sheets for dishes such as lasagne. Eggs cooked into prepared dishes will also freeze but do check that the recipe is suitable for freezing. Other ways of storing eggs are to make mayonnaise or curd with the yolks, and meringues, which keep well in airtight containers, with the whites.

Another good use for whole eggs is to convert them into crêpes, which freeze perfectly, or will keep in an airtight container for about two weeks. Not all methods are advisable—the islanders of northern Scotland and Ireland stored their eggs, probably seabirds' eggs, between layers of peat ash in underground chambers known as souterraines. Sir Lindsay Scott, who I am convinced must be related to Johnny, visited the islands in the 1690s and reported that the eggs were kept for six to eight months, after which they became very appetizing and satisfactorily loosening, especially those that were on the turn! I must remember to get some in for Johnny's next visit.

Top center: Burford brown chicken egg;
Top right: Old Cotswold legbar chicken egg;
Bottom right: duck egg; **Bottom left:** quail's eggs; **Top left:** goose egg

pancakes

MAKES 8–12

Crêpes are hypnotically pleasant to make, but always remember the first one is for the dog as it never seems to work! Crêpes are not fried in fat; the pan is rubbed with fat merely to stop them sticking. Use a 6-inch cast iron pan or a special omelet pan. Some people prefer to use half milk and half water for a lighter batter, extra butter or oil for a richer crêpe, and cream for some recipes. This is, however, the best batter for freezing. Instead of stacking the crêpes between paper before freezing, you can freeze them individually and then stack them afterwards.

A rather charming recipe I came across from the days of harder winters suggests briskly beating 3 tablespoons of snow into the batter just before cooking. As I found this recipe after I stopped skiing, I haven't tried it yet.

3/4 cup all-purpose flour
salt, a pinch
1 medium egg
1¹/4 cups milk
1 tbsp oil or melted unsalted butter, for frying

Sift the flour and salt into a bowl, make a well in the center and drop in the egg. Add a little milk and stir gradually, drawing the mixture in from the sides. When it has become a thick cream, stir in the oil or butter and beat well, then stir in the rest of the milk. Strain the mixture into a pitcher for easier pouring and to ensure there are no lumps. Heat your pan and grease it with a smidgen of butter or oil. I use two pans the same size and turn the crêpe from one to the other as tossing wastes a lot of time and crêpes unless you are incredibly adept. Grease your pan between each crêpe and if you aren't using two pans, use a spatula to turn them.

an excess of eggs?

Apart from cooking delicious dishes using your eggs, there are several ways of keeping your glut.

● Preserving—Eggs to be preserved whole in the shell should be clean and dry, but do not wash them as the shell is porous and this practice can cause disease. Instead, wipe them with a damp cloth and then a dry one. You can then rub them with buttered paper or kerosene so that all air is excluded and they will keep for six months or longer.

● Storing in isinglass—When I was a child we used to store eggs in isinglass (see page 119), which can be bought from a good pharmacist. The eggs are layered, point downwards, in an earthenware crock or glass jar. You pour in the cool liquid, ensuring the top layer of eggs is completely submerged, and then cover to keep out bugs and dirt and prevent evaporation. Eggs stored like this will keep from six months to a year, but they should be used for baking or prepared dishes as they have a slight taste if boiled or poached and the shells will crack if boiled. After six months the whites go a little thin so they are not really suitable for whipping.

● Freezing eggs is another successful way of preserving your glut. Remove them from the shell and freeze them individually or, if you are freezing larger numbers, beat them together, adding a teaspoon of salt or sugar per 5 eggs. Make sure you label them carefully as to whether sweet or salty and how many eggs are in each package. Eggs treated in this way are good for scrambling or baking and you can even fry or poach them straight from the freezer.

Yolks and whites can be frozen separately, too—add sugar or salt to yolks and, as usual, don't forget to label them.

bread

In these days of Chorley Method baking when dough is steamed and glutens are stretched, it is difficult to remember how delicious properly baked bread is. I can remember driving down from London with a school friend and stopping in Uckfield to buy a loaf of white bread from the baker for her mother. The smell of the warm bread was so wonderful that we stopped in a lay-by six miles further on and ate it all just as it was, and then had to go back for more.

The great thing about breadmaking is that it gets rid of anger and lowers your stress levels. This is thanks to the kneading, which distributes the yeast evenly through the flour and helps to develop the gluten. Kneading is an almost hypnotic practice that requires intense energy. I once shared a house with a woman who would get up at three in the morning when she couldn't sleep and make bread to relieve the tension caused by her nasty divorce.

bread in history

Historically, bread was, quite literally, the staff of life. Shortage of flour for its making invariably led to rioting in the streets. The Romans conquered North Africa and Egypt because the area was the bread basket of Italy, providing huge amounts of grain. "Bread and circuses" was the motto for government and they used both as a way of subduing the mob just as social services today ensure the poor have a television. In the Middle Ages your wages from the great household you worked for were partly paid in loaves of bread. I never cease to be amazed at how much of it people ate then.

what flour can I use?

Bread can be made from all sorts of flour, some of which you may be growing yourself.

First and foremost, wheat has been a staple provider of flour for centuries. It is a good source of fiber, protein, and vitamins B and E.

Barley flour (known as bere in Scotland) gives a dense, heavy loaf and has a mealy flavor. It is good when mixed with other flours. Barley is low in gluten which means that it may be tolerated by celiacs. Bere cornmeal or maize flour are not to be confused with the thickening agent cornstarch.

Cornmeal must be mixed with wheat flour for making leavened bread but is used for flat breads and tortillas, mostly in the southern states of America, and in Mexico, Italy, and Africa.

Oatflour is most easily obtained by grinding rolled oats. It is used to make oatcakes. An enzyme in oats is good for lowering cholesterol and healing wounds and adhesions. Oatflour can be added to wheat flour for flavor and nutrition.

Rye flour is the staple of much of Eastern Europe. It gives a dense, chewy dark loaf that can be eaten by celiacs. It is often mixed with sourdough for flavor.

Buckwheat is obtained from a plant of the rhubarb family and is native to Asiatic Russia. It is generally used to make blinis and crêpes and has a distinctive flavor.

Millet flour, or spelt, is the earliest known grain, high in protein, vitamins and minerals, but so low in gluten it is almost invariably mixed with wheat or rye so that it makes a risen loaf. In its natural state, it is very suitable for celiacs.

white versus brown

White flour has a lot less fiber—only about 75 percent—and most of the bran and wheat germ have been removed. If you buy stone-ground white flour—much more of the kernel is left. This type of flour is usually from stone-grinding mills.

Brown flour retains about 85 percent of its kernel but some of the bran has been removed, hence the theory that brown bread is better for you. Sadly, that is only true of properly made bread. I won't tell you what they do to the commercial stuff.

Wholemeal or whole wheat flour contains 100 percent of the kernel, and is sold in either coarser or finer varieties. The bran will hinder the development of the gluten and hence the rising of the bread, which is why a wholemeal loaf tends to be heavy. Hard, or bread, flours will rise better as they are made from hard wheats which have a higher proportion of protein to starch.

getting the bread to rise

To make leavened bread, you need to add yeast. It was the Egyptians who first made yeasted bread and it is generally believed to have happened by accident when some yeast spores floated across from a brewing plant. Beer is really bread without flour, or so a lot of my drinking friends try to tell me.

Yeast is a living organism and needs gentle warmth, sugar, or flour to stimulate its growth. It is the carbon dioxide it produces while growing that causes the dough to rise. It is most important to get the temperature right: too cold and it inhibits the yeast's growth and too hot and it dies. The ideal temperature is 98.6°F or, as it is usually referred to, blood heat.

Bread rises in the warmth but some advocate a slower, cooler rise for a better-tasting loaf. I don't know if my nerves could take it! Cover your dough while it is rising or you will get an impenetrable crust. If dough rises too long it will collapse in on itself while cooking.

You have a choice of fresh or dried yeast. Fresh is better but is not always available. Using too much yeast causes the bread to become stale more quickly.

greasing the pans

When greasing my loaf pans, I use unsalted butter as I find there is less sticking, but vegetable oil or lard will do.

be consistent

Once you have made dough successfully, remember its consistency. That is the consistency you should always aim for and you may find that you need to add more or less liquid than a recipe dictates to achieve it.

basic white loaf

MAKES A 2-POUND LOAF

1 (0.6-ounce) fresh yeast cake
5¼ cups unbleached white flour
1 tablespoon salt
1¾ cups water
unsalted butter for greasing
flour for dusting

Crumble the fresh yeast into a bowl and add 4 tablespoons lukewarm water. Cream it to a smooth liquid. Sift the flour into a larger bowl, add the salt, make a well in the center and pour in the yeast, then pour in the remaining lukewarm water. With your hands, draw the flour into the liquid and mix thoroughly to form a smooth, thick batter in the well, with flour still unmixed around the outside. Sprinkle the wet center with a little flour to prevent a skin forming. Let the mixture stand, covered, for half an hour during which time it will become frothy and aerated.

Now mix the remaining flour into the batter. Form the dough into a ball, adding a little more water if it is too dry or a little more flour if it is too sticky. Knead the dough on a lightly floured surface. Stretch it away from you, form it back into a ball then give it a turn and continue for about 10 minutes. Fascinatingly, the dough will change texture, becoming elastic and glossy.

When you have finished kneading, form the dough into a smooth ball. Put it into a lightly greased bowl to prevent sticking and cover with a clean lintfree towel. Let it stand for anything up to two hours, depending how warm the place is where you have left it. It will double in size. Place on a lightly floured surface. If properly risen the dough will not spring back when you stick a finger in it.

Punch the dough with your knuckles to flatten it. This is known as punching down in the US, and knocking back in

England. Gently knead the dough to shape it into an oval. As if practicing a karate chop, make a good crease lengthwise along the dough with the edge of your hand, then fold over and roll into an oval ballotine. Slash the top of the dough diagonally two or three times, cover with a damp lint-free towel and let it rise again to double its size. Meanwhile, lightly grease a baking sheet, transfer the risen dough to the sheet, and bake in a preheated oven at 425°F for about 15 minutes. Reduce the heat to 375°F for another 20-25 minutes.

If you are using a loaf pan, lightly grease a 9 x 5 x 3-inch loaf pan, put the risen dough in the pan, and bake in the same way.

Remove the loaf from the oven and from the pan, if used. Tap the underneath of the loaf and if it doesn't sound hollow, return it to the oven for another 5 minutes. Cool on a wire rack.

granary loaf

This is a good nutty brown loaf that isn't too heavy.

MAKES A 2-POUND LOAF

1 (0.6-ounce) fresh yeast cake
5¼ cups granary flour
½ tsp salt
1¾ cups water
1 tbsp vegetable oil
unsalted butter for greasing

Make as for the basic white loaf. When you add the last of the water, also add the oil. Let the dough rise until it has doubled in size. Meanwhile, lightly grease a 9 x 5 x 3-inch loaf pan. Knock the dough back and gently shape it to fit the tin. Place the dough in the pan, seam side down, and let stand for about 1 hour, until it has doubled. Bake in a preheated 450°F oven for 15 minutes. Lower the heat to 400°F and bake for another 25–30 minutes until the loaf sounds hollow when tapped underneath. Cool on a wire rack.

cottage loaf

There is something very cosy about a cottage loaf, especially eaten by a winter's fire with lashings of butter and jam. I suppose it is the shape that makes it so cosy. The Germans would call it gemütlich.

MAKES A 2-POUND LOAF

1 (0.6-ounce) fresh yeast cake
5¼ cups unbleached white flour
1 tablespoon salt
1¾ cups water
unsalted butter for greasing
flour for dusting
1 egg, beaten

Lightly grease a baking sheet. Proceed as for the basic white loaf. When you reach the punching-down stage, punch down the dough and pull off one-third. Form both pieces of dough into balls. Set them on the baking sheet, leaving plenty of room in between, and cover with a lint-free towel. Let it rise for about 40 minutes; they will not quite have doubled. Gently flatten each ball and put the smaller one on top. Push your thumb and first two fingers into the middle of the loaf and let it rest for another 10 minutes, no longer. Glaze with the beaten egg.

Slash around the edges of both layers with a very sharp knife. Bake for 15 minutes at 450°F then reduce the heat to 400°F and bake for 25–30 minutes until the loaf sounds hollow when tapped underneath. Cool on a wire rack.

baps (bread rolls)

In Scotland we eat baps at breakfast. When I was in charge of the catering at the Museum of Flight in East Lothian, we were voted as having the best bacon butties, but actually they were baps.

MAKES 12

1 (0.6-ounce) fresh yeast cake
1¾ cups lukewarm milk and water mixed
3½ tablespoons cut-up lard
680g unbleached white flour
½ tsp salt
1 tsp sugar
milk for glazing
flour for dusting
unsalted butter for greasing

Crumble up the yeast and mix it to a paste with 2 tbsp of the milk and water mixture. Rub the lard into the flour until it forms a fine crumb. Make a well in the center, add the salt and sugar, and pour in all the liquids. Mix to a soft dough. It should not stick to you or to the bowl. Knead for 10 minutes on a floured surface until silky, put into a lightly greased bowl, and cover

with a damp towel. Let it rise until about double the size. Meanwhile, lightly grease 2 baking sheets. Punch down the dough and knead briefly, then divide into 12 portions.

Pat each into an oval about ½ inch thick. Place on the baking sheets, glaze with milk, and sift a fine dusting of flour over them. Let stand for 30 minutes until doubled in size. Flour them again and press your thumb into the middle of each bap so that it stays flat. Bake in a preheated 425°F oven for 15 minutes. Transfer to a wire rack and eat when they can be handled.

swedish rye bread

My dear friend the Swedish food photographer Carin Simon introduced me to the joy of this delicious bread.

MAKES A 1-POUND LOAF

1¼ cups white flour
2¾ cups stoneground rye flour
1½ tsp salt
2 tbsp unsalted butter
1 (0.6-ounce) fresh yeast cake
⅔ cup lukewarm milk
⅔ cup buttermilk
1 tbsp treacle or molasses;

Put the flours and salt in a large bowl and mix in the butter with your fingers to make a fine crumb. Cream the yeast with the milk and pour it into the flour. Add the buttermilk and treacle and mix together. Work the mixture until you have a soft, sticky dough. Turn onto a floured board and knead for 10 minutes. Return to the bowl, cover with a damp lint-free towel and let rise for 2 hours or until the dough has doubled. Meanwhile, lightly grease a baking sheet. Punch the dough down, turn it onto a board, and shape into a loaf. Place on the baking sheet and slash the dough straight down the middle lengthwise with a knife. Cover and let rise until it has doubled again. Bake in a 400°F preheated oven for 40–45 minutes until it sounds hollow when tapped underneath. Cool on a wire rack. Do not cut this bread warm.

spelt bread

You will either love it or hate it, but if you're a celiac it's safe.

MAKES A 2-POUND LOAF

1 (0.6-ounce) fresh yeast cake
2½ cups water
½ tsp salt
1 tbsp vegetable oil
5¼ cups spelt flour
unsalted butter for greasing

Lightly grease a 9 x 5 x 3-inch loaf pan. Mix the yeast with half the water. Mix together the remaining water, the salt, and the oil. Pour the yeast liquid into the flour and mix roughly. Add the remaining liquid and mix thoroughly by hand for 5 minutes. The dough will cease being sticky as you work it. Pour the mixture into the pan and smooth the top with a damp pastry brush. Cover with a lint-free towel and let rise for 35–40 minutes, or until the dough reaches almost to the top of the pan. Bake for 45–50 minutes in a 400°F preheated oven until the loaf sounds hollow when tapped underneath. Cool on a wire rack.

corn dabs

Flour was scarce in the early American Colonies. The main crop was maize or Indian Corn as it was known, but if a woman had followed her man halfway around the world in appalling conditions, she wasn't going to let a little thing like the lack of flour deter her. I love corn bread. It's a thing you scarcely ever find in Britain unless you make it yourself and it's delicious with fat pork and collard greens or clam chowder.

This recipe has no leavening agent and should be made in muffin pans or the sort of shallow loaf pan you use for tea breads. Muffin tins will do. If you are visiting a historic house in America, you can buy corn stick pans. If you aren't

grinding your own maize yet, you can buy your cornmeal instead.

I copied this recipe into my own book from an American Heritage book but cannot this far on remember which historic house it came from. It works very well but you must guard against scorching.

MAKES ABOUT 6

1 cup yellow cornmeal
pinch of salt
¾ cup boiling water
¼ cup sour cream
1 tbsp bacon fat, plus extra for greasing
1 medium egg, beaten

Add the salt to the cornmeal, then pour the boiling water over it and let it stand for a few minutes. Stir in the cream. Mix well and leave it for another 10 minutes. Meanwhile, brush your pans with melted bacon fat and put them into a 425°F preheated oven to heat up. Stir the bacon fat and the egg into the corn mixture. Spoon the mixture into the pans and bake for about 15 minutes or until an inserted knife comes out clean. The pans should be very hot when you put the mixture in. The recipe works on the same principle as Yorkshire pudding. Serve warm.

sourdough bread

This is the most ancient way of making leavened bread and is probably the same as the method used by the ancient Egyptians. It involves using a "starter" made of unbleached all-purpose flour and water, which you can then use with any other flour—though wholewheat or rye flour are more commonly used—to make your sourdough bread. To make a starter takes three days but with any luck you will only make it once and you can then keep it going and leave it to your grandchildren. It is also used for making friendship cakes—so called because you

give a piece of the starter to a couple of friends before adding all the fruit and other goodies that make the cake.

When you make your starter, remember that it picks up fresh yeast from the air, so when you leave it to stand, cover it with a damp cloth and re-dampen it daily—no nonsense with plastic wrap or foil. The famous Poulin bakers of Paris, who only make sourdough bread, bake their bread in a cloth-lined basket.

Sourdough bread has amazing keeping qualities. In that lovely book, *A Wild Nettle Soup*, the family who live in the French mountains were snowed in all winter and baked their sourdough bread in October to last them until the snows melted. They stored it in a wooden chest where it went hard, not bad. You know when it tells you in soup recipes to place some bread in the bottom of the soup bowl and pour in the soup, and you wonder why it doesn't work with modern bread. Well, those recipes really call for hard sourdough bread which people sometimes had to chip with an axe.

Yukon miners used to carry a piece of sourdough starter under their shirts to prevent it being stolen and to stop it from freezing. Now there's a gourmet flavor for you.

To make the starter
Take 1¾ cups unbleached all-purpose flour and 1 cup lukewarm water. Mix these together into a thick batter, cover with a damp lint-free towel, and leave at room temperature in your kitchen for three days, re-dampening the towel each day. After this, the batter should smell sour but not bad and should be slightly gray and bubbly. If it smells bad it has failed, in which case throw it out and start again.

On the fourth day, pour the starter into a larger non-metal bowl and add ⅔ cup lukewarm water and 1⅔ cups of the same flour. Mix thoroughly with your hand, cover with a damp lint-free towel, and leave it for 24–36 hours, depending upon how strong you like your bread. The starter is now ready to use and will be spongy and slightly bubbly.

To make the sourdough bread
Stir the starter well and add 1/4 cup lukewarm water and up to 1²/3 cups flour to make a soft but not sticky dough. Knead for 10 minutes and return to the bowl. Cover with a damp lint-free towel and let it stand for 8–12 hours until it has doubled in size. Meanwhile, lightly grease a baking sheet. Punch down the dough and cut off an 8-ounce piece to keep as your future starter. Form the rest into a ball and stand it on the baking sheet. Cover with a damp lint-free towel and let it stand for another 8 hours or until it has doubled in size. Slash the top 4 times with a very sharp knife; the loaf may collapse if the dough is dragged. Bake for 20 minutes in a 425°F preheated oven. Reduce the heat to 375°F for another 40–55 minutes, until the loaf sounds hollow when tapped underneath. Turn onto a wire rack and do not eat until completely cool.

Your saved starter will keep for 3 days in a plastic bag in the fridge or 2 days at room temperature under a damp cloth. To re-use, start the process as at the fourth day above.

soda bread

This is probably the easiest bread to make. The recipe was given to me by my friend Marianne whose mother's family came from Drina in Northern Ireland. Isabel of the weeds (see page 24) tells me that she used to make her soda bread in an old terracotta flowerpot, but you had to put a tin lid in the bottom to stop the dough coming through the hole.

Fried soda bread cooked in hot bacon fat is the best. My maternal grandmother came from Gory in County Wexford, Ireland and there they make soda bread farls (triangles) on top of the stove in a frying pan with a metal lid. To make them, form your dough

---

upsizing a cake recipe

Mary Berry once gave me a great tip for working out how to upsize a cake recipe. Fill the tin you usually bake the cake in with water up to the level that the cake mixture usually occupies. Pour the water into the bigger tin and repeat until the bigger tin is filled to the same level. The number of times you have to do this gives you the multiplier for the larger cake recipe.

---

into a 1-inch-thick disk and cut it into 4 triangles. Cook in a frying pan in hot bacon fat over a medium heat, turning every 5 minutes.

MAKES A 12-OUNCE LOAF

1²/3 cups stoneground white or wholemeal flour
3/4 cup self-rising flour
1 tsp salt
1 tsp baking soda
2 tbsp unsalted butter, chopped up small
sour milk or buttermilk, as required
flour for dusting

Put the flours, salt, and the baking of soda into a mixing bowl, rub in the butter, and add enough sour milk or buttermilk to make a stiff dough. Knead until the dough is smooth, shape into a flat loaf, and put on a baking sheet. Sprinkle with flour and cut a deep cross into the loaf. Bake in a preheated 400°F oven, with a large cake pan over the top for 20–25 minutes until the loaf sounds hollow when tapped underneath. Wrap it in a lint-free towel to cool or the crust will be very thick.

home baking

Well, you now have a good cross-section of breads to try your skills on so let us move on to home baking. I learned to make cakes one frenetic weekend when I was in my thirties and about to start my first domestic job. My new boss said, "We always like to have a cake knocking about the place." I froze. Though I had made

---

bread and puddings, I had never baked a cake. I fled to my friend, the author and poet Christine Coleman, and we spent an intense weekend baking, since when I have never looked back.

One thing you need to remember about cakes is that you can make them in any old container but for an easy life, buy springform pans. These have springs on the side and detachable bottoms. Remember, take care to line and grease your cake pans before use. Otherwise, the pain of breaking a cake when you take it out of the pan is indescribable.

singing hinnies

I love the name of these little Northumbrian teacakes. When they are cooked you cut them into wedges, butter them, stick them back together again, and eat them warm by a roaring fire after a day's hunting—or should I now say hound exercising—on the cold Northumbrian hills.

MAKES 6–8

3¹/3 cups self-raising flour
1 tsp salt
1/2 cup lard
1/2 cup caster sugar
1¹/4 cups currants
2 medium eggs, beaten
2/3 cup milk
unsalted butter for greasing

Grease and preheat a griddle. Sift the flour and salt together, then rub in the lard. Mix in the sugar and currants. Make a well in the flour and add the eggs and the milk. Mix thoroughly into a soft, elastic dough. Roll out to ³/4-inch-thick and cut into 2 circles. Cook on the griddle for about 10 minutes until golden brown, turning them over halfway through.

boiled fruit cake

This is a very easy cake believed to hail from Gloucestershire, England.

MAKES A 6-INCH CAKE

1/2 cup sugar
3 1/2 tbsp unsalted butter
2 1/2 tbsp golden syrup
3 medium eggs
75g dried fruit
50g plain flour
1/4 tsp bicarbonate of soda
1 tsp mixed spice
unsalted butter for greasing

Grease a 150mm cake tin. Boil the sugar, butter and syrup in a pan and set aside to cool. Beat in the eggs and add all the other ingredients. Spoon into the cake tin and bake at Gas Mark 4/180°C/350°F for 1 1/2–2 hours. Turn out and cool on a wire rack.

devon black cake

This is a wonderful cake that should be stored for a year, then covered in marzipan and royal icing. The Cornish version has no black treacle. Black Cakes, like Scottish Black Buns, are made to be eaten at New Year rather than Christmas. This very rich cake is great to wrap and take in your pocket when you are out shooting or walking.

The idea of beating the eggs over hot water is not to cook them but to warm them through slightly and stop them curdling when they are added to the butter and sugar. If you are nervous about this, beat them into the mixture instead, adding a little flour before each egg.

MAKES A 230mm CAKE

350g unsalted butter
350g caster sugar
12 medium eggs
225g plain flour, sieved
3/4 tsp baking powder
1/2 tsp baking soda
1 tsp apple pie spice
1 tsp grated nutmeg
2 tsp ground cinnamon
1 2/3 cups rice flour
6 1/2 cups currants
3/4 cup chopped raisins
2 1/2 cups chopped golden raisins
1 1/2 cups chopped candied orange peel
1 1/2 cups chopped candied lemon peel
1 1/2 cups blanched, chopped almonds
2 tbsp brandy
1/2 cup black treacle (or molasses)
unsalted butter for greasing

Double line with parchment paper and grease a 9-inch round cake pan. Cream the butter and sugar well together. Beat the eggs into a large bowl over hot water until they are creamy, then whisk into the butter and sugar mixture. Fold in the sifted flour, baking powder, baking soda, the spices, and the rice flour. Finally add the fruit, the brandy, and the black treacle

Pour the mixture into the pan. Bake in a 350°F oven for 3 hours. Let cool slightly in the pan for 30 minutes, then turn out and cool completely on a wire rack.

marlborough cake

Marlborough in Wiltshire, England was once a great coaching stop. This Georgian cake was offered to stagecoach passengers with a mug of beer while their horses were being changed. The caraway seeds would have provided a good palliative against the nausea caused by traveling.

MAKES A 9-INCH CAKE

4 medium eggs
1 1/4 cups plain flour
1 cup sugar
1/4 cup caraway seeds
confectioners' sugar for dusting
unsalted butter for greasing

Grease and flour a 9-inch cake pan. Beat your eggs over a pan of warm water until creamy and thick enough for the beaters to leave a trail. Remove from the heat and sift in half the flour and all of the sugar. Add the caraway seeds with a metal spoon, then fold in the remaining flour. Bake in a preheated 425°F oven for 10 minutes. Turn out and cool on a wire rack. Sift confectioners' sugar over the top when cool.

crumpets

It always seems to amaze people if you make your own crumpets, but it isn't hard and they are much nicer than the storebought ones.

MAKES 18–20

1 (0.6-ounce) fresh yeast cake
2 1/4 cups warm water
4 cups all-purpose flour
1 tsp salt
unsalted butter for greasing

Preheat a griddle or large frying pan. Grease and preheat the crumpet rings. Dissolve the yeast in a little of the warm water. Sift the flour and salt together, then stir in the remaining water. Add the yeast liquid, cover with a cloth, and keep in a warm place until the dough is well risen. Thin the mixture to a batter consistency with a little warm water and leave for 5 minutes. It is a good idea to try cooking one crumpet first; if the batter is too thick the holes will not form, in which case add a little more water and console yourself by eating the imperfect one with butter.

Place the crumpet rings on the hot plate and fill them half-full with batter. When the mixture is dry on top and slightly browned on the underside, turn the rings over to cook the other side. Remove the crumpets from the rings and serve with butter.

preserving in salt

Quite when salt was first used to preserve food has been lost in the mists of time. What is certain however, is that for thousands of years, until the invention of refrigeration in the late 19th century, salt was essential to the winter survival of people living in temperate latitudes. Salting and pickling of meat and fish was still commonplace in rural areas well into the 1980s in Britain and still is across large parts of Europe and rural North America, with many farm workers making their own bacon and hams and pickling mutton and beef.

salting

Salt works as a preservative by draining moisture from fresh meat or fish through osmosis. Without water, access is denied to bacterium and so decay is prevented. The removal of superfluous water also means that the flavor is better as it is more concentrated.

Traditionally, cattle and beef were slaughtered in October, when they were fat from summer grazing and before the grass ran out, with pigs slaughtered a month later. This is the best time to salt: the cooler the weather, the less bacteria and the lower the risk of contamination from flies.

dry-salting

This method involves rubbing a cut of meat with a mixture of salt and sugar over a period of several weeks. The juices are drawn out of the meat and allowed to drain away. At home, I have an old stone larder next to the cellars, with deep, slate curing shelves. These have channels that direct fluids to holes above a drain. A simple alternative is a grid made of several wooden rods, sterilized by boiling, and placed across an old earthenware sink or shallow wooden box.

bacon flitch (belly pork)

I am lucky to have eaten bacon like this for much of my farming life. It is delicious and bears no resemblance to that insipid muck they sell in the supermarket. A ham can be cured in the same way, although it must be pressed with heavy weights balanced on a board to hasten the de-moisturizing process. A leg of mutton or venison may also be cured this way to make mutton and venison hams. Simply add dried juniper berries to the mixture. Many hill shepherds, who could not keep a pig, made mutton ham and ate it fried it for breakfast like bacon.

FOR AN 11-POUND BACON FLITCH

2¼ pounds sea salt (or kosher salt)
1 cup Barbados sugar (or dark brown sugar)
1 bay leaf

Mix all the ingredients together. Take half the mixture and divide it into 3 batches. Rub one batch well into every crevice of the flitch. Layer the second batch across the bottom of the sink or box. Lay the flitch on top, cover it with the third batch of mixture and cover with a cheesecloth.

After 3 days, repeat using half the remaining mixture. Leave it for a week and repeat. If you find that you have run short of the salting mixture, simply make up some more.

Leave the flitch, well covered in the mixture, for 3 weeks. If your flitch happens to be smaller than this, leave it for 2 days per pound.

After 3 weeks, wipe off with a dry cloth, then put it in a muslin bag and hang it in a dry place. It will last like this for ages, getting harder as time goes on. If it becomes too hard, you may have to soak it overnight before frying it.

pickled meat

This is a recipe I have adapted from Jane Grigson, which we often make for Christmas. It is absolutely delicious and, if kept in cool place, will easily last through Christmas and into the New Year.

FOR A 6½-POUND TOP ROUND CUT

½ cup Barbados sugar (or dark brown sugar)
½ cup sea salt (or kosher salt)
¼ cup freshly ground black pepper
⅓ cup juniper berries, crushed
3 tbsp crushed allspice
chopped suet, for covering

Rub the meat all over with the sugar and leave it in a deep pot for 2 days. Mix together all the other ingredients except the suet and rub well into the joint every day for the next 10 days. Keep the pot covered. The mixture will soon turn to liquid. Do not discard but continue to rub it into the meat.

Preheat the oven to 275°F. Remove the meat from the pickling mixture and wipe clean. Stand it in a deep pot with 1–1½ cups water. Cover the top of the meat with suet. Fix the lid of the pot on with foil so that it is tightly sealed and no moisture can escape. Bake in the preheated oven for 45 minutes per pound. Let it cool in the liquid. Drain, place on a dish, and cover with a wooden board with a weight on top. Leave it for 24 hours after which it is ready to eat.

fish fillets

Fillets of salmon, bass, or sea trout are very good cured using a similar method to the pickled meat. They will keep for about 5 days.

FOR A 2¼-POUND FILLET OF FISH

2¼ cups sea salt (or kosher salt)
2½ cups raw sugar
1 tsp ground black pepper
zest of a lemon
1½ oz. chopped dill

Mix all the ingredients together. Divide the mixture into 2 batches. Lay half of the first batch in the bottom of a glass or porcelain dish and put the fillet on top. Smother with the remainder of the first batch. Put a weighted board on top. Leave for 36 hours then drain off the liquid and remove the fillet. Put half the remaining batch of mixture in the dish, replace the fillet in the dish, turning it over, and cover with the rest of the mixture. Leave for another 36 hours.

salted cod

Smother cod fillets in salt in a wooden box or similar receptacle that will allow the fluid to drain away. Leave it for two weeks, then hang up somewhere cool and dry, shaking off any excess salt. When you want some cod to eat, hack off a piece and soak in water for 48 hours, changing the water at least twice.

meat in brine

Some of the great recipes of English cuisine, which you rarely see nowadays, involve boiled salt meats, for example boiled salt beef and carrots or boiled salt mutton and caper sauce. A properly made and well looked-after brine tub is a wonderful way of preserving a variety of meats through the winter.

FOR A 9-POUND CUT SUCH AS BRISKET OF BEEF, HAM, OR A LEG OF MUTTON

5 cups sea salt (or kosher salt)
1 cup Barbados sugar (or dark brown sugar)
2 tsp black pepper
2 tsp juniper berries
2 tsp mustard seeds
2 tsp coriander seeds
2 tsp cloves
2 large bay leaves, crumbled

Mix together all the ingredients. Rub a handful of the mixture into your meat and let it drain for 24 hours to draw out the moisture.

The following day, bring the rest of the mixture to a boil in 4¾ quarts water. Simmer for 30 minutes. Pour into a glazed crock or other non-metallic container—your brine tub—large enough to submerge the meat. When the mixture is cool but not cold, put the meat in. Keep the meat below the surface of the brine with a board weighted down with a stone. Cover to exclude the light.

As a rule of thumb, small cuts of meat should be kept in the brine for 2 days per pound, larger cuts for 3 days. The longer the better. Turn the meat every 4 or 5 days.

Remove the meat from the brine and hang it up somewhere cool and dark in a muslin bag. It will keep for a long time in a cool, dry place but is best eaten within 6 months. Generally, brisket of beef and leg of mutton are eaten fairly soon or are smoked (see page 196). York hams were traditionally buried in oak sawdust after they had been brined.

The brine will stay good for several months and can be used over and over again. If it happens to turn viscous, boil it up again, this time using half the recipe quantity. Sterilize the crock and return the brine to it.

using a drying box

Dried meat delicacies are the specialty of countries with arid climates. They are produced by air curing, where moisture is drawn out by the sun. This process is simple to replicate—and well worth the time and expense—if you build or buy a drying box or dehydrator. Virtually any meat or fish can be dried in this way as long as it is taken off the bone and salted for a couple of hours first. The options for the marinades are endless.

biltong

A delicious type of biltong or "jerky" can easily be made in a drying box. Use any lean red meat—venison is delicious, while the best South African biltong is made from antelope. Cut the meat along the grain into 1/2-inch-thick strips 8 inches long. Smother in sea salt and leave for 2 hours. Brush off the salt and lay in a marinade of your choice for 24 hours. Hang up to drain and when dry, roll in bruised peppercorns. Transfer to a drying box for 4 days.

sausages

One of life's never-ending adventures is making sausages. There is an enormous range of cured salamis— saucissons de montagne, morcillas, chorizos, to name but a few. They are preserved by a combination of a fermenting agent, drying, smoking, and storing. The permutations for experimenting are endless.

The acidophilus guarantees the necessary fermentation and I recommend its use if you live in a temperate climate. In the arid country areas of places such as France, Spain, and Italy, they can rely on the bacteria forming naturally.

MAKES A 3 1/2-POUND SAUCISSON DE MONTAGNE TYPE

3 pounds fatty boneless pork
9 ounces pork fat back
6 cloves garlic
1/2 cup red wine
1/3 cup bruised peppercorns
3 tbsp sea salt (or kosher salt)
6 1/2 tbsp cayenne pepper
6 1/2 tbsp caraway seeds
sausage casing
1/2 tsp acidophilus (optional)

Coarsely grind the pork. Cut the fat back into 1/4-inch chunks and mix with the pork. Add all the remaining ingredients. Stuff the casings with the mixture and hang it in the drying box for 2 days. If you live in a dry, arid environment, hang outside for 2 days. Then smoke (see page 196) using beechwood sawdust for another 3 days. Tie with string and hang somewhere dry, airy, and with a constant cool temperature for 6 weeks. The sausages will now be ready to eat, but will continue to mature the longer that you leave them.

making a drying box

Make or buy a tightly sealed wooden cupboard, with a hinged door. The cupboard should be 32 inches high by 2 feet wide and 2 1/2 feet deep. Drill holes at 2-inch intervals along the bottom and at the top of the sides of the cupboard.

Fix two hanging rails 6 inches apart near the roof, and a removable 2-foot by 2 1/2-foot perforated board 1 1/2 feet from the bottom. Rest the board on battens fixed to the walls. Connect a light fixture to the middle of the bottom with an 80-watt bulb pointing upwards. Keep the box in a dry dark place. When the light is switched on, warm dry air rising from the bulb circulates around the box, drying whatever is hanging up inside.

fish

You can cure any easily skinned fish such as salmon, pike, perch, or cod.

FOR 3 1/2-POUND FISH

2 quarts water
1 1/2 cups sea salt (or kosher salt)
juice and zest of 1 lemon
handful chopped fresh dill
lemon juice for seasoning
ground black pepper or chili powder for seasoning

Skin the fish and fillet it. Mix together all the ingredients except the seasoning. Soak the fillets in this brine for 8 hours. Remove from the brine and drain for 12 hours. Season with the lemon juice and pepper or with chili powder if you prefer. Cut into 1-inch strips, then hang in the drying box for 3 days.

smoking

Smoking as a form of preserving became popular where there was not enough salt for either a prolonged dry-salt or to make a large quantity of brine. The anti-oxidants in the smoke preserve the flesh and the fact that they add a delicious flavor to fish and meat is an unintentional bonus.

Chimneys in many old houses had a recess in which hams were hung for smoking, which people have often mistaken for priest holes. The two crucial factors for smoking are the sawdust—beech and oak are best but any will do as long as it is hardwood—and that the temperature does not rise above 77°F.

A smoker does not need to be elaborate or complicated to do the job. All that is required is an enclosed chamber, in which a small sawdust fire can be lit, and an outlet for the smoke. At one time I used to use an old 24-gallon beer barrel.

kippers

Can you imagine anything nicer than a home-smoked kipper? Buy really fresh herrings. Gut them, cutting right up through the ribcage so they can be flattened out. Wipe clean and place in a brine solution made by mixing 1 1/3 cups sea salt (or kosher salt) per litre of water. The quantity required will depend on the number of fish you are preparing. Weigh the fish down with a board and a stone on top, to stop them floating to the surface. Leave them for 30 minutes, or longer if you like them salty. Hang them up to drain. Then suspend them in the smoker by their mouths and smoke for 12–16 hours.

salmon

For a bigger fish, like a salmon—the ultimate one-upmanship is to smoke your own catch. Follow the instructions for smoking kippers but immerse in the brine for 3 hours, or longer if you like your fish salty. Hang the fish up to drain, then smoke it for 3 days. If you want, you can make the following, more adventurous brine. It only suits salmon though.

1 quart strong beer
1/3 cup crushed juniper berries
1/4 cup black pepper
1 cup sea salt (or kosher salt)
1 cup Barbados sugar (or dark brown sugar)

Mix all the ingredients together, bring to a boil, and simmer for 10 minutes. When cool, use it to cover the salmon fillets for 12 hours, then smoke them for 3 days. A rule of thumb for judging when the fish are ready is to weigh them just before they go into the smoker, then weigh them at 12 hour intervals. When they weigh just less than 75 percent of their original weight, they are done.

beef

You need a well-aged, fat-free fillet of beef for this. Prick the beef all over with a thin needle to facilitate the penetration of the brine. Place in a brine solution made by mixing 1 1/3 cups sea salt (or kosher salt) per quart of water for 3 hours. Drain for 12 hours, then smoke it for 5 days.

chicken

Prick the chicken with a thin needle down either side of the breast bone. Soak in a brine solution made by mixing 1 1/3 cups sea salt per litre of water for 3 hours. Hang to drain in a cool, dry place for 12 hours, then smoke for 24 hours.

You can use the same instructions to smoke pheasants, but soak for 2 hours and smoke for 18 hours.

goose and duck

You should only smoke the breasts. Cut the breasts from the carcass by slicing lengthwise down either side of the breast bone and around the wish bone. Soak the breasts in a brine solution made by mixing 1 1/3 cups sea salt (or kosher salt) per quart of water for 3 hours, then smoke for 36 hours.

to make a smoker

Build or buy a hut, 6 1/2 feet high and with an area of 5 square feet, made of untreated wood and with a hinged door. Drill a couple of smoke holes on the three plain sides just below the roof. Place two cinder blocks end to end on either side and put a 3-foot-square perforated metal plate on top. Three feet above this, hang a rack with hooks to hold the food to be smoked.

Place a gas burner under the metal plate and a bucketful of sawdust on top. Light the gas burner and let the sawdust smoulder away with the door of the smoker closed.

potting

Today we think of potted meat or potted shrimps as a delicacy but originally potting was developed as a means of preserving fish or meat. It is first recorded as a means of taking food to sea for long sea voyages. The food to be preserved was immersed under a layer of oil, clarified butter, or lard in an earthenware pot (i.e., jar) whose top was sealed with a parchment cover tied tight with tarred twine. This excluded the bacteria, rather as canning or vacuum packing does today. Salmon was even exported "potted" in red wine. Writing in 1609, Sir Hugh Platt, the Naval Secretary, recommends parboiling chickens, coating them in lard or clarified butter, and laying them in stone pots filled to the brim with the same fat flavored with some cloves and salt. These, he says, will keep for a good month.

The trick with potting is to cook your food with butter or lard, then mash it up and put more of the same fat as a seal on top. It is particularly pertinent if you keep ducks and geese, both of which exude large quantities of fat when cooked. The resulting confit is a great delicacy, as are rillettes, potted meat, still sold universally in Scotland, and of course potted shrimp.

glass or china?

So great was the clamor for potted goods that by the late 18th century the demand transformed the output of the pottery towns of Stoke-on-Trent and Coalbrookdale. When cheaper glass jars became available, the demand for the china pots declined.

confit of goose

Confit is the most useful commodity to have on hand. It is an essential ingredient for mutton stews, cassoulets, and so on, but also makes a delicious quick meal. Simply dig out the number of pieces required and warm in the oven. Use some of the fat to reseal the jar and the rest to sauté some potatoes. Confit will last for several months.

The same recipe may be used for duck by cutting the ingredients and the cooking time in half. The legs, wings, and thighs of a roast duck or goose—pieces that are so often left—also make excellent confit material.

FOR A 10-POUND GOOSE

½ cup sea salt (or kosher salt)
¼ cup freshly ground black pepper
1 tsp grated nutmeg
2 bay leaves, crumbled
2 sprigs thyme, leaves removed

Preheat the oven to 325°F. Mix together all the ingredients. Cut the goose into 8 pieces—thighs, drumsticks, wings, and breasts cut in half. Place on a baking sheet and cook in the preheated oven until the fat runs freely and the pieces are browning. Lower the heat to 250°F. Add more goose fat, if you have some, or lard, until the pieces are completely covered. Cook for 5½ hours.

Remove the duck pieces and pour some of the fat into the bottom of a sterile terrine or large canning jar. Add the pieces of goose in layers, ensuring that they do not touch the sides of the container. Cover each layer with fat. Seal and store in a cool dark place.

rillettes

Basically, this is a coarse meat paste preserved in fat in a sterile container. Cook pieces of rabbit, pork, duck, and goose in the same way as you would for the duck confit (see above), adjusting the cooking time according to the weight of meat. When the meat is browned and running with fat, remove the meat from the baking sheet. Break it up with a fork and pot it and cover with fat as above. Rillettes will last for a couple of months in a cold dark place but must be eaten quickly once the seal has been broken.

potted shrimp

This recipe may be adapted to virtually any fish. It will keep for two weeks or so in cool, dark place.

MAKES ABOUT 2¹/4 POUNDS

1¹/2 cups (3 sticks) unsalted butter
2 tbsp ground allspice
2 tbsp freshly ground black pepper
2¹/4 tbsp sea salt (or kosher salt)
2 tbsp freshly ground nutmeg
cayenne pepper, a good pinch
2¹/4 pounds cooked miniature shrimp

Preheat the oven to 425°F and sterilize jars of a convenient size. Melt the butter in a saucepan and mix with all the remaining ingredients except the shrimp. Place the shrimp in an ovenproof dish. Pour three quarters of the melted butter over the shrimp and bake for 1 hour. Tip into sterilized jars and use the remaining butter to seal.

pickling, fermenting, and ketchups

pickling

Pickling became popular in England in the 16th century when it largely replaced the salting of vegetables among the better-off. As pickling had been practiced in China and Japan for centuries before, I like to think that, given the century and its improving trade routes with the Far East, someone may have brought back the idea but I'm afraid I have no proof.

Capers—the unopened flower buds of the Mediterranean shrub *Caperis spinosa*—became hugely popular in the 18th century but people who couldn't afford them made substitutes with pickled nasturtium and gorse buds, and very good they can be. Elder and hop shoots are also good pickled as are the unopened crosiers of ferns, picked before any green appears. If you have a walnut tree, pick the fruits in their casings while they are still green and soft. They seldom ripen in Britain anyway. Prick them all over with a needle and leave in a brine solution (1 pound salt to 4³/₄ quarts of water) for 3–4 days, then rinse them off and let them dry on trays for a few days. When they turn black, pickle them in malt vinegar or wine vinegar.

Shallots are best for pickled onions and the Elizabethan society hostess Dame Eleanor Fettiplace pickled crab apples. Johnny made me some and they were very good but took a long time to mature. I suppose the most famous pickles are cucumbers or gherkins. Cleopatra apparently regarded them as a great beauty aid, which just shows how fashions change. History doesn't relate whether she ate them or added them to her ass's-milk baths. As W.C. Fields once said, "Remember girls, you are born beautiful and if you ain't too bad but a good pickle cellar will still entice a man!"

Jars for pickling must be glass or stoneware as the vinegar reacts negatively with metal and the pickle will spoil. You can use any old jars really, as long as they don't leak. The trick lies in keeping the pickled object below the level of the vinegar so that the air can't get at it.

To sterilize your jars and seals, wash and rinse them in hot water, then fill with boiling water and let stand for 10 minutes. Then empty them and dry them in a cool oven.

sweetish pickle

If you are using this recipe to pickle fruit, add more sugar and use cinnamon, fresh ginger, and allspice instead of the bay leaf, peppercorns, and cloves.

MAKES 1¹/₂ QUARTS

1 bay leaf
10 black peppercorns
6 allspice
6 cloves
7 cups vinegar
1³/₄ cups brown sugar
1¹/₂ tsp salt
3 pounds prepared vegetables

Crush the spices slightly. Put them, along with the vinegar, sugar, and salt into a pickling pan and bring to a boil. Add your vegetables and simmer for 5–10 minutes uncovered. Transfer to the pickling jars and pour in the hot vinegar to cover. Leave for 6 months before eating. The longer you leave them, the better they will be. They keep for several years if you let them.

sour pickle

Make as for sweetish pickle but omit the sugar and add 7 small fresh or 10 small dried chiles instead. You can also add blades of mace, coriander seeds, and fresh ginger, according to taste.

ketchups

The name of these vinegar-based sauces may have originated in the Far East but, like kedgeree, they owe little else to the original. The Eastern "ketsiap" is a type of fish sauce.

In the 19th century, Britain became a haven of different sauces for the growing luxury food trade. The most favored of these was perhaps mushroom ketchup.

Because the tomato is a relation of the deadly nightshade, the American settlers believed that it was only safe if cooked for several hours—hence the development of tomato ketchup. The original tomato ketchup was sharp but an American businessman called Davidson, recognizing his nation's passion for sugar, added lots. Now you wouldn't eat a hamburger without tomato ketchup. Curiously, British food snobs hate it while top French chefs adore it. Reading an English translation of an early Joel Reblochon book I was amused to find the translator writing, "the chef only ever uses fresh tomato concasse." The French original clearly had the chef using ketchup!

mushroom ketchup

You can use any mushrooms you like but the original mushroom ketchup called for horse mushrooms (*Agaricus arvensis*), the large, flat, black-gilled wild mushrooms that can grow to the size of a dinner plate. The mushrooms are called by that name as it was believed the spores had to pass through the digestive system of the horse.

3 pounds horse mushrooms, sliced
2 tbsp salt
2 shallots, peeled and chopped
1 garlic bulb, cloves separated and crushed
3¹/₂ cups white wine vinegar
¹/₄ cup port
3 anchovy fillets, preserved in oil
2 bay leaves, lightly crushed
6 cloves
10 white peppercorns
10 allspice
¹/₂ tsp freshly grated horseradish

Sterilize glass bottles or jars without metal lids. Cover the mushrooms with salt and leave in a cool place overnight. Remove from the bowl then throw everything into a pan, bring to a boil and simmer for 30 minutes. Let cool, then return to a boil and cook for another 30 minutes. Mix well in a blender, return to a clean pan, and boil to reduce by one third. Strain into the bottles or jars and seal. Keep for 1 month before using.

tomato ketchup

You will need really ripe tomatoes for this so let them go soft on the vine.

10 pounds tomatoes
1 tsp white pepper
1 tsp ground nutmeg
1 tsp ground cinnamon
1 tsp allspice
2 tsp paprika
2 tsp salt
6 cloves garlic, chopped
1 cup sugar, or according to taste
³/₄ cup white wine vinegar or cider vinegar

Sterilize glass jars without metal lids. Put all the above ingredients into a pot, bring to a boil, and simmer gently to reduce by one third, uncovered, for 2–4 hours. The slower you reduce it the better. Put everything through a strainer or food mill and if it is too thin, simmer strongly to reduce it further. Bottle in jars, seal, and store for 10–12 months without opening, but shake the jars every 3 months.

walnut ketchup

MAKES ABOUT 1½ QUARTS

5½ pounds green outer shells of walnuts
1½ pounds salt
2 ounces bruised ginger root
2 ounces whole allspice, lightly crushed
¼ cup freshly ground black pepper
⅓ cup cloves

Sterilize glass bottles without metal lids (see page 201). Layer the walnuts in a tub with salt sprinkled between each layer. Let it stand uncovered or covered with a cloth for 6 days, stirring and mashing occasionally until all the shells are soft and pulpy. As liquid appears, drain it away but reserve it. The mixture should produce several quarts of liquid, with the amount varying from year to year. (You can put the rest of the walnuts on the compost heap.) Simmer the liquid in a cast iron pan until the scum ceases to rise, then add the ginger, allspice, pepper, and cloves. Bring to a boil and simmer for 30 minutes. Strain and bottle, sealing with a cork and wax. Leave for 6 months.

pickled lemons

My favorite thing to pickle is lemons. The best and easiest recipe comes from my great heroine Claudia Roden. Hopefully some of you reading this have a lemon tree in your garden or even your conservatory.

6 thick-skinned lemons
6 tbsp sea salt (or kosher salt)
fresh lemon juice, to cover
4 tbsp olive oil (optional)

Wash the lemons if waxed, otherwise leave unwashed. Cut the lemons into quarters, but not right through so that the pieces are still attached at the stem end. Stuff each lemon with plenty of salt. Put them in a sterilized glass jar, pressing them down so that they are squashed together. Seal the jar. Leave for 3–4 days. The skins will soften and the juice will be drawn out of the fruit. Press the lemons down as far as they will go in the jar, placing a stone inside to hold them down. Add fresh lemon juice to cover them entirely, close the jar, and keep in a cool pantry or garage for at least 2 months, the longer the better. Wash well to remove the salt before using. You can also add olive oil at the end to keep the air out if you like.

myths and cabbages

The cabbage is a curious plant. We all love to hate it but it has survived since early Egyptian times. The ancient Greeks believed it sprang from the sweat of Zeus's armpit. One can see why. The smell of the Inner London Sessions when I was a barrister was actually like boiled cabbage but was indistinguishable from the sweat of the prisoners in the cells below! I am not sure whether cabbage has survived because it is an excellent anti-scorbutic or because of the myth that it diminishes the after-effects of alcohol.

fermenting

Fermentation uses micro-organisms to ferment food rather than turn it into poisonous substances. It is a means of processing that is well suited to cold, damp climates with long unproductive winters. It is still used in Scandinavia where the surströmming, or sour herring, of the Swedes and the rotted shark of the Icelanders are still national delicacies. The Finns, too, have a type of fermented small fish which I actually quite enjoyed but I desperately needed to call for the Epsom salts the next day.

Russian borscht is another example of fermentation. The reason it tastes different and better than ordinary beet soup is that the beets are packed in barrels and left on the roof of a shed to freeze. This causes fermentation without the tedium of distilling, rather like making applejack—a brandy very like Calvados—where the apples receive the same treatment.

Two staple foods are fine examples of the fermentation process. The first is kimchi, the Korean pickled cabbage which is placed in pots and buried in the ground to ferment. Koreans are still given time off work at the appropriate time of year to make their kimchi and would not eat a meal without it.

tofu

I know you can buy tofu in all its guises in Chinese supermarkets but you have just harvested a crop of soybeans, so why not make your own? The development of tofu, according to my late friend Yan Kit So, parallels the spread of Bhuddism in China and Japan with its vegetarian precepts. The similarity between cheese-making and tofu is quite noticeable. Once the curds are made they can be eaten soft, pressed, smoked, flavored, and fermented, just like cheese.

Take your dried beans and grind them quite finely. Add water to cover and bring them to a boil, stirring well so that they form a milk. This is of course soymilk, much used for dairy-allergic people and added to the tea and coffee of vegans.

You must now set the curds in the same way as cheese, but using either calcium sulphate or a substance called nagari, obtainable from Chinese and Japanese grocery stores, in place of rennet. Nagari is, as far as I can tell, sea salt with some added dry seaweed and I have no doubt that you could use sea salt just as efficaciously.

Once the curds are set you can eat them soft as a sort of pudding with honey or as a savory dish with a little chili and soy sauce. Or you can lightly salt them, wrap them in cheesecloth, and press them. Before pressing you can add flavorings according to taste.

The other, and much more familiar example, is sauerkraut. For centuries, this has been the staple peasant food of central Europe, Germany, and Russia, and the making of sauerkraut is a serious matter. Once the potato harvest was over, the peasant communities pulled together to make their stores of it. Originally sauerkraut was made in large pits in the ground lined with boards, but as barrels became more available, these were used instead. The cabbage was chopped and packed in layers in the pits or barrels with salt, then it was kept warm for a few days either in the kitchen or in some cases in the living room where a fire was lit specially. It was then transferred to a cool cellar for a month or two before broaching. Caraway or dill seeds were added and sometimes gherkins. The liquid remaining in the barrels when the sauerkraut was taken out was used as a flavoring. The smell must have been awesome. Maybe it is my Danish great-grandmother's genes, but I do love sauerkraut and in the dark days following Christmas I sometimes have an overwhelming compulsion to eat it.

sauerkraut

2 heads of cabbage
salt, 1 tbsp per pound cabbage
2 tbsp caraway or dill seeds

Core and finely shred the cabbage. Sprinkle a layer of salt on the bottom of a large non-metallic container. Layer the cabbage with more salt and the caraway or dill seeds. Place a plate or board over the top and weigh it down with a non-metallic object. Cover and leave in a warm, dark place for 2 weeks, to ferment. Then either move the container to a cellar or repack in sterilized jars and store it. Don't eat it for several months. It will keep at least a year.

drying fruit and vegetables

drying fruit

As a child I was fascinated by the differences between golden raisins made from the white grapes of Smyrna in Turkey, Malaga raisins made from Muscat grapes, and currants, which are also actually dried grapes and have nothing to do with red, white, and black currants. The smell of dried apricots takes me to warm sunny days with the fresh fruit ripening against a south-facing wall and dried prunes remind me not of the sanatorium but of boxes of sugar plums at Christmas. Also reminiscent of Christmas are dried dates in long sticky boxes.

If you live in a sun-drenched climate anywhere in the world, in most years you will have the advantage of being able to dry fruits in the sun. You can dry any fruits in this way. Lay them out flat on wooden wattles and leave them in the sun, turning them once or twice. You will, of course, have to fight off wasps, bees, birds, and other predators. In North Africa they wash their figs in seawater before drying them, which seems to help.

If you don't live somewhere with enough sun, then you can always dry your fruit in an oven or kitchen range. For a four-door range, 15 hours on a rack in the bottom oven or in a cooling bread oven will do the trick. If you only have a two-oven range, close the oven lids and lay the fruit on racks on top.

If you have an old-fashioned oven, you can try drying your fruit in it at 250°F. If you have a modern one and make meringues in it, dry your fruit at the same setting, but do experiment first with a small quantity. I am lucky to live in a stone-built 17th-century cottage and I find that things just dry naturally hanging about the kitchen.

climate change?

I imagine the British habit of turning their fruits and vegetables into jams, chutneys, and fruit leathers is dictated by the climate, though the ever-optimistic Scots surprised me by producing a 600-year-old recipe for drying haddock on the rocks in the sun. Can't you see it now? "Willy haste and bring in the fush? It's raining again!"

dried fruit tricks and tips

● Cut the peel of oranges and grapefruits into strips with the pith removed and dry them for adding to desserts and stews. Lemons will dry whole and can be added to stews or stick one in the cavity of a stewing chicken before poaching.

● If you live where your figs ripen, dry them, flatten them, then mix them with toasted sesame, anise, fennel, and cumin seeds. Form them into balls, wrap them in fig leaves, then store them in stone jars. The Romans were very fond of eating figs this way. They go brilliantly with ham.

● Apples can also be peeled and cored and threaded on strings to hang by an open fire, as can mushrooms. The smells will permeate the house all winter and make it wonderfully cosy. In England, there is a particular type of apple called the Norfolk Biffin which was traditionally grown for drying.

● If you have a plum tree and want to dry your plums, let the fruit fall from the tree rather than pick it so that they are completely ripe for drying.

drying vegetables

Drying vegetables is much the same as drying fruit. I know the Poles dry green beans in the pod, but don't rush for them. Tomatoes should be dried in the oven, as can bell peppers or chiles. The latter two can also be dried on their own on a rack or hung in a bunch to dry.

Sun-dried tomatoes for soups and stews take about 15 hours. Sun-blushed or semi-dried tomatoes, which are good for salads and risottos, take less time and should be

making fruit "leather"

Another good way of drying fruit is as fruit leather—you may know this as "fruit roll-ups." I love the name of the South African *plat perskie*, or flat peach, which is really just a fruit leather.

Any fruit can be made into a leather. Cut the fruit into pieces, put in a saucepan with a little honey or sugar, and simmer gently for 5 minutes to make a puree. Put a silicon mat or sheet of parchment paper on a baking sheet and pour on your purée. Cook at 250°F for about 6–8 hours. The leather should be tacky but not sticky. Remove from the paper, roll the leather up, and store in a cool place.

watched to make sure they don't get over-dry. Once dried, sun-blushed tomatoes should be stored in jars of oil. When the tomatoes are eaten, the oil, gently infused with the tomato flavor, is a great addition to dressings.

Dried strips of parsnip, carrot, or beets make good suckies for children as they are full of sugar. A Swedish friend of mine remembers them as substitutes for candies during the war. Sweet potatoes cooked as a fruit leather also keep well and can be reconstituted or added to soups and stews.

Legumes and pulses should be dried carefully, either in the sun or the oven. If they are not properly dried they will start to sprout.

a long tradition

The staple diet during the Middle Ages, in the days before potatoes, was pease pudding, and your mess of pottage is found in the Bible as the price of an inheritance. Before you turn up your nose and say how old-fashioned, just ask yourself how often you feed your children baked beans! Nice to think you are joining a 4,000-year-old tradition. Incidentally, legumes were sacred to Apollo and a "bean feast" was one where you drank pea soup together with your hallucinogenic mushrooms!

mincemeat

So called because the original contained minced beef, mincemeat nowadays is a mixture of spices, dried fruits, and suet, all chopped together. The basic recipe is as follows, but I have seen raspberries, prunes, dried apricots, and russet apples added.

MAKES 1³/₄ POUNDS

3/4 cup currants, finely chopped
3/4 cup golden raisins, finely chopped
3/4 cup raisins, finely chopped
1/2 cup chopped suet
3/4 cup candied peel, finely chopped
3/4 cup finely chopped tart apples
1/2 cup raw sugar
1/2 tsp apple pie spice
grated rind and juice of 1 orange
grated rind and juice of 1 lemon
4¹/₂ tbsp rum
4¹/₂ tbsp brandy

Mix together all the ingredients except the liquids. Add the rum and and juices and mix well. Leave 2–3 days before potting in sterilized jars.

canning

When I was a child, my mother's family farmed in the Hunter Valley in New South Wales. Back then, it was a long way from anywhere with bull dust roads. My aunt spent a lot of time canning the produce of her vegetable garden. The sun is both friend and enemy out there and growing any food meant fighting the elements as well as the bugs and other predators, so she was particularly proud when admiring the canned fruits of her labors.

canning in brine or syrup

Use perfect, unbruised specimens. Wash vegetables in a solution of permanganate of potash (follow the instructions on the bottle) to kill any organisms, rinse in cold water, then dry. Wash and dry fruit and if you are using stone fruit, cut in half and remove the pit. In the case of fruit, make up a syrup of 2 cups sugar to 4 cups water. (Some fruits of very high acidity can be canned with no sugar at all.) For vegetables, make a brine of 3 tablespoons salt to 4 cups water. Put the fruit or vegetables in the jar, then pour in enough salted water or syrup to cover.

Cover the jars loosely. In other words, don't screw the lids down, just place them on top. Put some wooden slats or a thick layer of paper or cloth in a large fish poacher or a canner to stop the jars cracking. Stand the jars on top and add cold water up to the necks of the jars.

Bring the water gently to a boil and simmer until the fruit or vegetables are cooked—between 10 and 30 minutes for fruit, an hour for vegetables.

If you are canning ready-cooked food, put it into the jars hot and proceed in the same way.

Screw the lids down as soon as they are cool enough to handle. They will take up to 24 hours to cool completely and can then be stored indefinitely. In the case of vegetables it is recommended that you bring them back to a boil for a few minutes before finally sealing and storing but I don't really find it necessary.

canning in oil, honey, or alcohol

Fruit and vegetables can also be stored by immersing them in oil or honey. These practices were beloved by the ancient Egyptians and Romans. There are two methods for immersing in oil, the first of which is suitable for mushrooms, artichoke hearts, and so on, in other words, for harder vegetables. First simmer the vegetables in brine for about 10 minutes, then put them into sterilized jars (don't touch them with your hands at this stage). Pour in good virgin olive oil and let cool before sealing.

The other method for vegetables such as red peppers, eggplants, zucchini, and so forth is to charbroil them a little first, and in the case of red peppers, peel them after charbroiling. I'm sure you know the method where you keep turning your pepper under the broiler until it is black all over, then put it straight into a plastic bag, after which the skin simply washes off. They can then be put in a sterilized jar with the oil.

Sun-dried vegetables are, of course, partly cooked already, so they can go straight into the oil. In the case of completely dry vegetables, it is a good idea to steam them a little to rehydrate them before putting them in the oil.

If you wish to can in honey, choose perfect specimens of fruit—nectarines, apricots, peaches, and dates are all delicious. Wash and dry them, then put them in sterilized jars and cover with honey.

learning from the past

The first known recipe for canning gooseberries, from 1680, suggests putting the bottle in cold water which is then brought to a boil. The gooseberries are simmered until they turn white and then stored. The same recipe was still being published, unchanged, 200 years later.

hermetic jars

The best bottles to use are hermetic jars, that is canning jars with wire bail. They have screw lids, metal clips and rubber washers, all of which need to be carefully sterilized with boiling water before use. To do this, fill the jars to the brim with boiling water and leave for 10 minutes. Let dry in a warm place or a cooling oven. Then you are ready to fill the jars with the fruit or vegetables of your choice.

high altitude tip

Remember if you live at a high altitude that you need to adjust the timings as water takes longer to boil. Allow an extra five minutes per 1,000 feet for any altitude over 1,000 feet.

an unusual reason to freeze meat

Freezing is also, in hot climates, a good way of tenderizing beef and lamb. There, butchers cannot hang meat unless they have a cold store, so in more primitive countries the meat is cut up and sold almost at once, consequently it can be very tough. If you freeze it, defrost it, and repeat the process two or three times, the meat becomes quite tender. Before the health police yell at me, I learned this trick in the West Indies in the mid-1970s and it has never hurt me yet.

canning in alcohol

Alcohol is another great preserver and is good for storing soft fruit. Cherries or peaches are particularly good stored in brandy and pears in eau de vie. I am always fascinated as to who came up with the idea of a rumtopf, in which fruits are layered in alcohol and sugar as they come into season. The whole is broached in an alcoholic daze by Yuletide. I have also eaten, in Lebanon, lemons bottled in brandy and sugar, and quite delicious they were, too. You can drink the liqueur afterwards or use it for flavoring desserts.

freezing

This is not really the book for writing about freezing. The practice does, after all, increase food miles, prevent local sourcing, use extra electricity and enable huge food mountains to be preserved almost indefinitely. It also encourages intensive farming and negates seasonality *and* does nothing to enhance the taste of food—in other words, it is definitely not very green. However, home freezing has the advantages of being an easy way to store your gluts, which will encourage home production, and it is also very labor-saving.

To freeze your vegetables, you must first blanch them. Take the largest pot you have and fill it with water. Bring to a boil. Meanwhile, fill your sink with very cold water. Fling a batch of vegetables into the boiling water and leave for 1 minute. Using a slotted spoon, scoop the vegetables out and throw them into the cold water. Let the water come back to a boil before blanching the next batch. Remove the vegetables from the cold water, drain, and pat dry before freezing. Let the water cool and pour it on your compost heap.

● Always divide the vegetables into batches for blanching. If you blanch too many at once, you will lower the water temperature and they will go soggy.

● Break cauliflower or broccoli into florets and top and tail your beans.

● It is a good idea to "open-freeze" vegetables and herbs on baking sheets before transferring them to freezer bags.

● You can freeze fruit to turn into jams later or for cooking, but they don't eat successfully once they have been frozen. "Open-freeze" soft fruits (see above) before bagging them.

● If you are freezing meat, it must be well wrapped to prevent ice burn. Fish can be frozen in the same way as meat. It freezes very well.

● Don't forget to label and date everything clearly or you may have some interesting surprises.

jams, marmalades, and chutneys

jams

Jam making is a great way of storing your excess fruit. I once owned a rather pompous 1930s book which stated that, "If sound fruit and pure granulated or preserving sugar are used, jam making will always be a success." Through years of unset and burnt jams I have hated the author of that book, then I hit my alcoholic rock bottom over a pan of burnt jam and realized the problem was me. The author had forgotten to add that what you also need are patience and concentration.

Fruit for jam making should always be picked on a dry day and should be unbruised. If the fruit lacks acid, lemon juice or some fruit concentrate should be added. Our cook, Louise, didn't skim her jams while they were cooking as she said it caused waste; she just stirred the jam a lot while it was coming to a boil and the scum disappeared. I should add that she won prizes for her jams.

apple jam

This is an unusual way to use up apples but I grew up with it and rather like it.

Take good cooking apples, peel, core, and thinly slice them, then weigh. Stew until tender in a double boiler. Do not overcook. Transfer to a large heavy pot and add 2 cups granulated or preserving sugar and the juice of half a lemon for each pound of fruit. Add the zest from half a lemon, a 1¹/₂-inch piece of peeled ginger root and three or four cloves. Bring to a boil and simmer for half an hour, then apply the cold plate test (see opposite) and can it.

currant and raspberry jam

In a world where there are always too many currants and never really enough raspberries, you will welcome this very delicious recipe! It is important to gather the fruit on a dry day, especially the raspberries.

Use 1 pound currants—red, white or black—to every ¹/₄-pound raspberries, and 2 cups granulated or preserving sugar to this amount of fruit. De-stalk the fruit. Bring to a boil in a large heavy pot with the sugar and simmer gently for 40 minutes. Apply the cold plate test (see opposite) and can it.

mulberry jam

In my childhood garden we had a 400-year old mulberry tree which would have seen the capture of Babbington in the reign of Elizabeth I on that self same spot. To commemorate the coronation of another queen Elizabeth in 1953, I, with a little help from the gardener, planted another mulberry tree, so I have always been very attached to mulberries.

This jam is made partly with fruit juice and partly with fruit. Use 2 cups granulated or preserving sugar and 2¹/₂ cups juice from crushed mulberries to every pound of whole fruit. Put the juice and sugar in a large heavy pot and simmer to dissolve the sugar. In this case, do skim off the scum. Add the whole fruit and simmer rather fiercely for 30 minutes stirring well. Apply the cold plate test (see right) and can it.

plum jam

All jams of fruit of the plum family—plums, greengages, myrtles, damsons, and so on—benefit from the addition of the kernels. However, the EU in its wisdom, frightened by the minuscule amount of cyanide in plum pits, will not allow you to sell jam made like this, so if you are making jam to sell, leave out the kernels. It is alright to include them for your own use.

Weigh the plums, cut them open, and remove the stones. Keep about half the pits. Allow 2 cups granulated or preserving sugar to each pound of fruit—less if the fruit is very sweet. Put a layer of plums in a dish and sprinkle with sugar. Continue until both are used up. Leave it until the next day. Place the fruit and sugar in a large heavy pot and simmer gently for about 15 minutes. Meanwhile crack the reserved pits and blanch the kernels in boiling water. Add the kernels to the jam and cook quickly for another 15–20

when is it ready?

No precise time can be given as to when a jam sets; there are so many different variants of fruit type and weather conditions during the growing season that the plate test is the only safe method. Put a little jam onto a cold plate and if it sets as a jelly, it is done. If not, keep cooking.

minutes, stirring repeatedly as this jam tends to burn. Apply the cold plate test (see above) and can it.

raspberry jam

Pick the fruit on a dry day, ensure it is ripe, and use at once. Remove the stalks, add a scant 2 cups sugar to each pound of fruit plus 1 cup of raspberry or red currant juice for each pound of fruit. Bring to a boil and simmer for 35–40 minutes. Apply the cold plate test (see above) and can it.

decanting and storing your jam

When the jam is done, remove from the heat and let it stand for a few minutes before decanting it. The jars you use for storing your jam should be clean and perfectly dry as the slightest moisture will cause the jam to turn moldy. Our cook, Louise, always made a great ritual of washing them the day before, setting them to dry and covering them with a cloth to keep out bugs and impurities.

Use screw-top jars where possible, pour the jam in but don't fill the jars too full. Once the jam has cooled, lay a circle of waxed paper over the top, then close the jars. If you don't have screw-top jars, tie the waxed paper covering down securely. Label the jam with the date and type before storing in a dry, airy place.

marmalade

Marmalade can be made with all citrus fruits, but their skin is tougher than other fruits and has to be softened. Apart from the marmalades below and marmalade made from quinces, all fruit marmalades are technically jams, although I have seen them referred to as marmalades as early as 1710 in a Scots household book.

orange marmalade

Weigh 12 Seville oranges, cut them up small and thin, removing but reserving the seeds. Put the oranges in a non-metallic crock and add 4³/4 quarts cold water for each pound of fruit. Let to stand for 24 hours.

Transfer to a large heavy pot and boil until the fruit is tender. Wrap the seeds in cheesecloth and boil them with the fruit for added pectin. Remove from the heat and let stand for a least 12 hours and no more than 24.

Remove the seeds. Add 2 cups sugar—I use half white and half muscovado (dark brown) to every pound of fruit. Boil, stirring constantly, until the fruit is clear, the liquid has reduced by half, and the syrup gels, about 1 hour. Apply the cold plate test (see page 209) and can it. You can add the juice and grated rind of 2 lemons if you want a sharper marmalade.

oxford marmalade

2 pounds Seville oranges
juice and grated rind of 1 small lemon
1½ tbsp black treacle
6 pounds preserving sugar
3½ quarts water
7 ounces candied ginger

Proceed as for orange marmalade, but add the ginger just before canning it.

three-fruit marmalade

2 grapefruits
juice and grated rind of 4 lemons
2 sweet oranges
6½ pounds granulated or preserving sugar
3½ quarts water

The total amount of fruit should weigh 3 pounds. Proceed as for orange marmalade.

chutneys

You either love chutneys or you hate them. Personally I am not a great fan but they are a splendid way of using up fruit and vegetables that are a bit battered and you can always give your chutneys away.

You can make chutneys with any fruits and vegetables—beans, beets and apples, blackberries, cranberries, gooseberries, pears, plums, rhubarb, and of course, tomatoes, both red and green. I particularly like quince and lemon with garlic, coriander seeds, and cloves. Whatever you make, the principle is always the same.

apple and marrow chutney

1½ pounds marrow, peeled, sliced, and cubed
1½ pounds peeled, cored and chopped
3 tbsp salt
2 medium onions, peeled and chopped
1¾ cups vinegar (any will do)
½ tsp salt
1 tsp mustard seed
1¾ cups brown sugar
1 tsp black peppercorns
ginger root, small piece

Put the marrow in a bowl, sprinkle with salt, and leave for 12 hours. Strain. Put all the ingredients in a large heavy pot, bring to a boil, and cook until tender and reduced to a thick consistency. Pour into sterilized containers.

jellies, curds, and cheeses

jellies

Making fruit jellies is another good way of keeping fruit. The jellies are delicious with hot or cold meat or can be eaten with bread and butter. The fruit must be skimmed while it is cooking to give a fine clear product.

crab apple jelly

Cut the apples in half, put them in a large heavy pot, and add 7 cups cold water to every pound of fruit. Boil rapidly for 30 minutes and strain through your jelly bag into a bowl. Measure the amount of juice you collect and boil it up with 2 cups sugar to every 2 cups strained juice. Bring to a boil and cook for 30 minutes, stirring well. At this stage you can add a teaspoon of lemon juice if desired. Apply the cold plate test (see page 209) and pour into sterilized jars.

You can use this method for all currant jellies, too, but reduce the sugar by 1/2 cup.

red currant jelly

You can either cook as for blackberry jelly (see opposite) or put your fruit in a large heavy pot with 1/2 cup water to every 2 cups of fruit. Cook until the juice runs freely and strain through your jelly bag. Measure the strained juice and add 1 1/2 cups sugar to every 2 cups juice. Cook gently until the sugar melts, then bring to a boil. Simmer for 30 minutes. Apply the cold plate test (see page 209) and pour into sterilized jars.

This method can also be used for black and white currants.

using a jelly bag

You will need a jelly bag, preferably on a stand, though you can hang it from a pole secured between two chairs or from a hook over the bowl in which it will drip. The fruit must be dry but I don't bother to remove any but the largest stalks. Having once had to deal with 78 pounds of currants in one session, I've learned to be quick. Don't squeeze your jelly bag or your end result will be cloudy. Just walk away and let it drip, giving it a stir with a wooden spoon occasionally.

blackberry jelly

Put the fruit in a double boiler or in a jar in a pan of boiling water and simmer for 30 minutes, until the juice flows freely. Strain though a jelly bag. Transfer the juice to a large heavy pot and boil up with 1½ cups sugar to every 2 cups juice. Stir well. Apply the cold plate test (see page 209) and pour into sterilized jars. This jelly is improved if you add equal quantities of bullace (wild plums).

Use this method for raspberries, strawberries, mulberries, etc.

quince jelly

Take ripe sound fruit, slice them, and put in a large heavy pot with just enough water to float them. Simmer for 2 hours until the fruit is a pulp. Strain twice through a jelly bag, rinsing the bag out between strainings. Boil the strained juice with 2 cups of sugar per every 2 cups juice for 45 minutes. Apply the cold plate test (see page 209) and pour into sterilized jars.

curds

This is a way of preserving food short-term when you have an egg glut. Curds do not have long eating qualities but they will add a few months to your eggs.

lemon curd

4 lemons
1¾ cups sugar
½ cup (1 stick) unsalted butter
8 egg yolks or 4 whole eggs, beaten

If the lemons are waxed, wash them, if unwaxed there is no need. Grate or finely peel the lemon rind. Squeeze the lemons. Mix the lemon peel with the sugar and place in a double boiler with the butter, lemon juice, and eggs. Place over a low heat and stir until the sugar is dissolved. Continue cooking over a low heat, stirring until the curd thickens. Pot as for jam (see page 209).

apple curd

2¼ pounds apples, any variety, pureed and strained
1 cup (2 sticks) unsalted butter
1 cup sugar
2 medium eggs, beaten
juice and rind of 1 lemon

Make as for lemon curd. You can also make apricot curd in the same way.

blackberry curd

1 pound blackberries
4 ounces green apples, pureed and strained
2 medium eggs, beaten
1 cup sugar
juice and rind of 1 lemon
½ cup (1 stick) unsalted butter

Cook the blackberries separately, then strain them. Mix with the apple pulp then continue as for lemon curd.

fruit cheeses

A fruit cheese is a thickly set fruit jelly that is made to be sliced.

basic fruit cheese

3 pounds fruit
2 cups sugar to each pound of fruit
olive oil for brushing

Brush sterilized containers with olive oil to enable the cheese to be turned out. Put the fruit in a pot with just enough water to cover. Simmer until soft. Strain through a nylon mesh strainer, measure, and add the sugar accordingly. Put the strained fruit and sugar in a large heavy pot and stir until the sugar has dissolved. Simmer until it reaches the required consistency. Put in the sterilized containers, cover, and store for at least 3–4 months to allow the flavor to develop.

damson plum cheese

3 pounds damson plums
2 cups sugar to each pound of pulp

Bake the whole fruit at 300°F until soft. Remove the pits and crack several for the kernels. Add these kernels to the pulp, then continue as for fruit cheese. Store for at least 6 months. It will continue to improve for up to 2 years.

farmers' markets

Eighteen years ago, as I came out of my alcoholic haze, the world and I became re-acquainted. I was appalled at the state of the food industry. Supermarkets stalked the land like great dinosaurs, keeping farmers and food producers in thrall. To all intents and purposes, farmers' markets had died out both in Britain and in the USA, whereas in mainland Europe, people had the good sense to hang onto and treasure them.

the start of the farmers' market movement

The Farmers' Markets idea started in America, and one name really stands out, that of Alice Waters, creator of the restaurant Chez Panisse in California. Alice was unable to find the vegetables she wanted. In the 1970s, what we now call New Wave American Cuisine started in California. It was the most important food revolution since the 19th century. New Wave took all the centuries' old national formulas and busted them, creating dishes that broke all the rules.

We forget how exciting it was. Alice, Deborah Maddison at Greens, Wolfgang Puck, Jeremiah Tower, and Mark Miller collectively took the ball and ran with it straight past the fullback. New wave led to the growth of fusion food, the pan-Asian movement, slow food, and, above all, of farmers' markets. The local farmers who grew for Alice and her friends found they had more food than they could use, so, in the 1980s, Alice encouraged them to set up local markets.

In the past two decades farmers' markets in America have rapidly regained popularity and have become an integral part of the rural/urban food chain once more.

Farmers find a number of advantages in selling at farmers' markets. By selling directly to their customers without going through middlemen, farmers can get a better price for their produce. A farmers' market is a good place for new growers who are perfecting their skills and growing crops on a small scale and learning which products customers want most.

For customers, too, the farmers' market is not just a place to buy food, but a social affair. A festive atmosphere helps to bring people to markets, where they can talk with farmers about how the produce was grown and how it can be prepared.

the introduction of certification in Britain

Certification was introduced in the UK in 2003 because the success of the farmers' markets had led to a proliferation of markets that weren't following our rigorous practices. An umbrella organization FARMA, the National Farmers Retail and Markets Association, maintains a code of conduct for farmers' markets, and acts as a certification body.

When visiting a market in Britain, look for the FARMA green-and-white logo. If it is not there, it doesn't necessarily mean the market is bad but just be more careful and question the producers before buying. After all, if you want to buy eggs brought from several hundred miles away, you can go to a supermarket.

In the United States, however, it is not so regulated and while some markets are carefully managed, with strict rules for pricing, quality, and vendor selection, others are much more relaxed. There is almost always an emphasis on locally-grown/produced organic food and many operate by important standard criteria that state that goods be locally produced and that vendors sell their own products. However, the specifics of these criteria do differ from place to place as the definition "locally produced" can sometimes allow a great deal of leeway. For example, in major urban areas, farms are of necessity some distance away, so the radius may be larger than that for smaller communities. As with the non-credited UK markets, it is probably a good idea to be a vigilant consumer and assess the quality of the product you are buying yourself.

"Eighteen years ago, as I came out of my alcoholic haze, the world and I became re-acquainted. I was appalled at the state of the food industry."

the farmers' market coalition

In the United States, The North American Farmers' Direct Marketing Association (NAFDMA) was established in 1986 as a non-profit association geared towards delivering farmer's produce direct to the consumer. Farmers' market enthusiasts have been part of NAFDMA's leadership and membership base since the beginning and now in six short years they have nurtured the creation of the Farmers' Market Coalition (FMC) that is now dedicated to strengthening Farmers' Markets for the benefit of farmers, consumers and communities.

beating the supermarkets

I know that we are winning because supermarkets try to woo us to hold markets in their forecourts, and also because of the lip service paid to local produce in supermarkets. Don't shop for food in supermarkets. They have an arrogant disregard for food miles, and I'm not talking just about their imported fruit and vegetables. One major British chain of supermarkets slaughters all its beasts at an abattoir in Cornwall, driving the cattle and sheep in trucks hundreds of miles, then driving the carcasses back all over the country.

Nor do supermarkets sell American organic food much because of appearance and price. Instead they import from suspect countries where you can use sprays that are banned in the US and then register as organic 3 days before harvesting. I could go on forever. Trust me. Don't shop there.

my favorite markets

When I was a child, my father would often take me to Petticoat Lane on a Sunday, a colorful place in London where Orthodox Jews with ringlets in their hair and curious clothes sold delicious pickled

cucumbers, gefilte fishballs, and tasty cold fried fish in matzo meal.

When I was young and wild, I would go off to Covent Garden, not then stuck out on the South Bank, and eat bacon butties (sandwiches) and drink at the late-opening pubs and talk to producers around the braziers.

Which brings me to that other great London food market, Borough Market, situated by London Bridge. There has been a wholesale fruit and vegetable market at Borough for centuries but in 1998, again under the auspices of Henrietta Green, Jennifer Paterson and I opened the Gourmet Food Market. The Council was unfriendly, the railway arches leaked, and we thought we'd last two years if we were lucky. I remember milking a goat to celebrate the opening. It wouldn't let down its milk, due to all the excitement, no doubt.

Today Borough boasts 70 stalls, and growing. It has 55,000 people a month visiting it outside the Christmas period, when there are more. Borough is a true London market. Here a man in a dish dash will sell lemons next to a stallholder from Devon selling fallow deer. Peter

Gott, in his moleskin britches, red socks and brown Derby, discusses his bacon with an apple brandy seller from Hampshire or with Alastair from Brindisia, who is arguing about Cumbrian ham versus Pata Negra. I go whenever I'm in London and feel very proud to have been involved.

selling your own

You may wish, when your self-sufficiency is producing more than you need, to sell at a farmers' market in your area. You can contact local organizations for advice.

christmas markets

Another place you might think of trying to sell your produce are Christmas markets. These are much more successful in mainland Europe, especially in Germany and Eastern Europe. Prague has a famous Christmas market but they are growing in the US. They are a good outlet for specialty goods and can bring in much-needed cash in the period before Christmas for the dark unproductive days of January and February. Whether you go as a supporter or a stallholder, if you want a greener life, markets are where you must do your food shopping.

home brewing

One of the many wonders of nature is the existence of sugar in plants and fruit and the presence of the yeast fungus in the atmosphere. Quite when it was discovered that yeast ferments sugars to create alcohol has been lost in the mists of time, but that discovery has been a most powerful influence on civilization. As well as giving us "the cup that cheers," it is a valuable source of vitamin B and provides the wherewithal to preserve food. When the fermenting action is negated by exposure to air and vinegar is created, it also provided the earliest form of antiseptic and household cleaning fluid. The art of making wine, beer, cider, mead, vinegar, and verjuice was once a common household skill. The old recipes were faithfully recorded and I offer a few here to tempt the home producer into an immensely rewarding, if bibulous, new hobby. Though I have not drunk alcohol for over 20 years, I was once a dedicated home brewer.

beer

The difference between ale and beer is that beer uses hops as a flavoring. Hops came into Britain from the Low Countries during the reign of Henry VIII. Before then, ale was flavored with a variety of different plants, depending on where you lived and what grew locally. Germander, a small, yellow-flowered woodland plant, was once popular, giving ale a dark color and a bitter taste. Germander would probably be used in commercial brewing today, if hops had not been introduced. Heather and bracken (ferns) were used to

flavor ale in the north of England and Scotland. Bracken is still used in Norway and Russia. It might help to get rid of the pernicious stuff if someone starting manufacturing bracken beer here. Monks were great brewers and made particularly potent ales flavored with cinnamon and other spices. For centuries, the county of Kent was famous for its cherry ale.

In my grandparents' day, there was a brew house at the Home Farm. Here beer was made for the hundred or so farm men, gardeners, and household staff. They made a light, thirst-quenching beer for harvest time, a stronger beer for the autumn, and a type of stout called October Ale for Christmas and the winter months. As machinery replaced manpower, the estate brew houses became redundant, but the old recipes survive.

Home brewing is easy, enormous fun, and the results of one's labors are infinitely better than anything mass-produced.

beer (pale ale)

The following is the simplest, most traditional recipe for making beer. There are many permutations to achieve a different texture, taste, or strength by increasing the quantity of hops and sugar. You can also add black malt granules to make stout.

MAKES 4 QUARTS

2¹/₂ cups Barbados sugar (or dark brown sugar)
1¹/₄ cups malt extract (malt syrup)
1 ounce hops, plus an extra handful
4 quarts water
1³/₄ tsp granulated yeast
8 scant tsp unrefined sugar

Dissolve the brown sugar and malt in 4 cups of warm water and pour into a sterile gallon container. Boil the hops in 4 cups of water for 10 minutes. Strain through a fine mesh strainer into a sterile pitcher and then into the gallon container. Re-boil the hops twice more, adding 4 more cups of water each time. Add all the hop liquid to the "wort" in the container. Seal the container with a bung and airlock to which you have added a little water mixed with a drop of bleach. Let cool overnight. Next morning, add the yeast to the wort with a handful of hops, and replace the bung. Fermentation will start in a few hours. Leave until fermentation ceases.

Rack, or bottle, the beer using a syphon tube, into sterile pint bottles to within ⁵/₈ inch of the top. Make sure to keep the tube clear of the sediment in the bottom of the container. Add a level teaspoon of sugar to each bottle and seal. The sugar creates a secondary fermentation in the bottles without which the beer would be flat and lifeless. Stand the bottles somewhere cool.

The beer will quickly clear to a healthy brilliance as the yeast deposit settles to the bottom of the bottles. It will be drinkable in two weeks, but infinitely better the longer you leave it. It is advisable to refrigerate the beer for a day before you drink it. This stops the yeast sediment from rising and makes the beer easier to pour.

"Home brewing is easy, enormous fun, and the results of one's labors are infinitely better than anything mass-produced."

wine

Virtually all the country people who worked on the land when I was a child made wine from a wide range of plants and flowers, to recipes that were centuries old. The different varieties—flower wines, like cowslip and dandelion, or berry wines such as elderberry and blackberry—brought the scent and taste of spring, summer, or autumn, to bleak mid-winter evenings. Other wines—such as parsnip, potato, birch, and rhubarb—were more full-bodied.

Country wines are delicious, easy to make, and considerably better for you than anything bought from a liquor store. And they are a fraction of the price. The main considerations in wine-making are sterility—boil everything well—and avoiding contaminants like fruit flies.

elderflower champagne

Elderberry trees grow wherever the nitrogen content of the soil is high. Typically, this might be where there once was an old household midden (refuse heap) and the soil has been enriched by the breakdown of organic matter. They also often grow beside churchyards, deserted gardens, rabbit warrens, and badger setts. In early summer, the trees are covered in heavily scented white flowers that are rich in vitamin C. These can be used in an infusion, to treat coughs (see page 172). The flowers also make a delicious, slightly effervescent, refreshing wine, not unlike a Frontingac. No yeast is required as the flowers provide enough.

MAKES 4 QUARTS

15 elderflower heads
3¹/₂ cups unrefined sugar or honey
2 lemons, juice and zest
4 quarts water, boiling

Pick the elderflower heads when they are in full bloom, on a warm day when the scent is at its best. Remove any leaves and twigs and shake out any insects that may be feeding on the nectar. Place in a gallon crock and scatter the sugar or honey over the flowers. Add the lemon juice and zest to the crock. Pour in the boiling water and stir well. Let cool for at least 24 hours, stirring occasionally. Strain through cheesecloth and decant into sterile screw-top bottles. Leave it for 2 weeks and drink it over the following 3–4 weeks.

elderberry wine

This is a beautiful, rich, port-like drink and well worth the effort. It can be made using any berries—raspberries and blackberries for example.

MAKES 4 QUARTS

6³/₄ pounds elderberries
4 quarts water, boiling
3 pounds unrefined sugar or honey
2 lemons, juice and zest
piece of toast
2 tbsp wine yeast

Pick the elderberries—about two bucketfuls. Remove any leaves and twigs, and cut the stems holding each little cluster. Spread the clusters on a baking sheet and warm in a 350°F oven until they start to split. Mash with a heavy wooden spoon, scrape into a gallon crock, and cover with boiling water. While they are still warm, scatter in the sugar or add honey. If using honey, warm it slightly so that it is runny. Add the lemon juice and zest. Stir well and leave it for 24 hours. Add a piece of toast spread with the wine yeast, cover with a cheesecloth and leave in a warm place at 70°F until fermentation ceases (2–3 weeks).

Once all signs of fermentation have ceased, rack the wine into sterile bottles, making sure to leave the lees (sediment) behind. Leave the wine at least 12 months—the longer you leave it the better it will taste.

dandelion wine

Dandelions were traditionally picked and the wine made on St. George's Day, April 23rd, to be drunk at Christmas. When you pick the dandelion heads, take the opportunity to gather some dandelion leaves for a salad, too. This recipe can be used to make wine from any flowers—elderflower, cowslip, broom, gorse, rose petals—whatever catches your fancy.

MAKES 4 QUARTS

4¹/₂ pounds dandelion heads
4 quarts water, boiling
3 pounds unrefined sugar or honey
2 lemons, juice and zest
piece of toast
2 tbsp wine yeast

Fill two buckets with dandelion heads in full blossom, picked on a warm day in the early afternoon. Remove as much greenery as possible and shake out any insects. Put the flowers into a gallon crock and pour in the boiling water. Cover and leave for 2 days, stirring occasionally. Transfer to a large pot, add sugar or honey, and the lemon zest. Bring to a boil and simmer for 1 hour. Return to the crock and let it cool. Add the lemon juice and wine yeast on toast. Cover with cheesecloth and let it ferment out in a warm place at 70°F.

Once all signs of fermentation have ceased, rack into sterile bottles, and store in a cool place. It is ready to drink at 6 months but, like most wine, it improves with maturity.

parsnip wine

This was a great favorite with Joe the gardener but his version was dangerously potent. Traditionally, it was made in winter after the first hard frost. Any vegetable wine can be made the same way. Try celeriac, turnip, rhubarb, potato, or beets. Beets make a lovely heavy port-type wine. The beets need to be boiled and mashed before straining.

MAKES 4 QUARTS

4¹/₂ pounds parsnips
4 quarts water
4 pounds unrefined sugar or honey
2 lemons, juice and zest
3³/₄ cups wheat
3²/₃ cups best raisins
piece of toast
2 tbsp wine yeast

Chop the unpeeled parsnips, add the water, and boil until al dente. Strain the liquor into a gallon crock. The parsnips can now be eaten if you wish. Add the sugar or honey and stir until dissolved. Add the lemon juice and zest, together with the wheat, raisins, and yeast on toast. Cover with a cheesecloth and let it ferment out in a warm place at 70°F.

Once all signs of fermentation have ceased, rack into sterile bottles and store for 12 months.

mead

This is the oldest known fermented drink. It was certainly being drunk in vast quantities in the heyday of Babylon. There it was sometimes mixed with borage to give it an extra kick and to enable the revelers to keep going, when they might otherwise have rolled under the table. Newlyweds were recommended to drink mead every night for a month after the nuptials to ensure a fruitful union, hence "honeymoon."

If you want to make sack, a very sweet, almost liqueur wine that was popular among medieval clergy and nobility, simply double the quantity of honey. Metheglin, a type of invalid's tonic, was made by adding nutmeg, coriander, cinnamon, and cloves.

MAKES 4 QUARTS

3 pounds heather honey
4 quarts water
18 ounces crab apples, mashed
3 lemons, juice and zest
2 big pieces ginger root, bruised
pieces of comb honey (optional)
piece of toast
2 tbsp wine yeast

Bring the honey, water, crab apples, lemon zest, ginger, and any pieces of comb honey you may have to a boil. Simmer for 30 minutes. Pour into a gallon crock and when cool, add the lemon juice and yeast spread on toast. Cover and let it ferment out in a warm place at 70°F. It can ferment for a long time and often a double or triple fermentation takes place. Once fermentation appears to have stopped, syphon the mead through cheesecloth into a demijohn with a fermentation lock. Nothing is more alarming or messy than bottles of mead exploding all over the place. Leave them for a few weeks.

Once fermentation has ceased, rack into sterile bottles and store for 12 months.

vinegars and ciders

verjuice

Verjuice is the naturally fermented, acidic juice of crab apples, cider apples, or sour grapes. It had hundreds of culinary and household uses until well into the last century, when lemons became a readily available alternative. The best verjuice is made from crab apples. The word "crab" means sour and in Scotland, a "crabbit woman" is to be avoided. Pick ripe crab apples in October and pile them in a heap, somewhere dry and under cover, to sweat. After a few days, discard any that are rotten, remove the stalks and stems, mash them, and put through a cider or fruit press if you have one. If not, mash until very fine and squeeze through sacking. Strain through fine cheesecloth into sterile bottles, seal, and store. Verjuice may be used to substitute vinegar or lemon juice in any recipe.

vinegar

Any bottle of red or white wine, rice wine, cider, mead, or beer will turn to vinegar if it is left for 24 hours with the top off. Exposure to air negates the fermenting action and allows the bacteria, acetobacter, to turn the alcohol to the acid we call vinegar. You can let your wine, beer, or cider do this naturally, but it is much easier and more effective to create your own acetobacter.

Sterilize a one-gallon glass, porcelain, or plastic container. Pour in 2 cups of the alcohol you wish to turn to vinegar. Add 2^1/$_2$ cups pasteurized vinegar and ^{2}/$_3$ cup water. Stir vigorously. If you are using some cheap, store-bought wine, this will help remove any gas that may have been added as part of the manufacturing process to protect it against the very bacteria you want to form.

Cover with cheesecloth to allow air in and keep vinegar flies out. Place in a dark place where the temperature is a consistent 80°F. Leave it for a month, checking regularly. During this period, a whitish gelatinous scum will appear. This living bacterium is known as "the mother." You may now add 2^1/$_2$ cups of the same alcohol you started with together with 4 cups water.

Cover with clean cheesecloth and return to a dry dark place for 1–3 months. During that time, the mother will thicken and eventually sink to the bottom. Another will form in her place. Take this off to start the next batch of vinegar. When the mixture tastes strong enough, pour it through several layers of cheesecloth and bottle it.

To stop a mother forming in your bottled vinegar, store it in a cold place or pasteurize it by bringing it to a boil. Let it cool, then bottle and store it.

For much of history, the antiseptic properties of vinegar have been highly valued and it was frequently used as the mixing agent with medicinal herbs. Vinegar can also be sweetened with honey or spices, or heated with chiles. If you want to flavor your vinegar, simply add any seasonal herb or fruit to the vinegar and leave it for a month.

flavored vinegars

Nothing is more delicious than the flavor of herbs infused in white wine vinegar.

Herb vinegars are so simple to make and a bottle makes a wonderful Christmas present. The variety and permutations for different flavors from herb garden or hedgerow are endless.

elderflower vinegar

This is delicious with salads and, curiously enough, a small amount adds a certain nimbus to strawberries. You can use this recipe for any flower-petal vinegar.

Fill a sterile 1-quart canning jar with elderflowers. Cover with 2^1/$_2$ cups good white-wine vinegar. Seal and store in a cool dark place for 3–4 weeks, the longer, the better. Decant through cheesecloth into a sterile bottle.

tarragon vinegar

This is probably the most traditional herb vinegar. It is ideal for making salsa verde to go with head cheese and cold meats.

Pound a double handful of chopped tarragon leaves, stripped off the stalks, in a big stone mortar. Bring 2/3 cup white wine vinegar to a boil and pour into the mortar. This has the effect of utilizing all the herb oils that have accumulated on the sides of the mortar. Continue crushing the tarragon in the vinegar for a few moments and let it cool. Pour into a wide-necked sterile container and add another 2 cups wine vinegar. Seal and store in a cool dark place for 3 weeks, giving the container a shake every day or two. Decant through cheesecloth into a sterile bottle and cork.

garlic vinegar

Garlic vinegar is always useful for salad dressing on its own and is one that lends itself to additions of pretty well anything—basil, burnet, dill, chiles, and so on.

Peel and chop 5 large cloves of garlic. Pound and crush in a mortar. Bring 2/3 cup white wine vinegar to a boil and pour it over the garlic. Let it cool. This is when the garlic flavor is absorbed. Pour into a sterile wide-necked container. Store and seal for 3 weeks, giving a shake every so often. Decant through cheesecloth into a sterile bottle and cork.

fruit vinegars

Raspberry, blueberry, black currant, and strawberry are among the fruit vinegars that are delicious with duck and roe deer.

Wash 2 cups of the fruit of your choice and place in a large ceramic or glass bowl. Pour in 2 3/4 cups white wine vinegar, cover with a cloth, and leave for 10 days, stirring periodically as the fruit breaks down. Strain into a heavy pot and add 2 1/3 cups

unrefined sugar or, better still, honey. Bring to a boil and simmer for 10 minutes, stirring to dissolve. Let it cool and decant into sterile bottles, and cork. Store in a cool, dark place for 3 weeks.

hard cider

Cider is autumn's golden liquid. Historically, the French have always produced wonderful, high-quality ciders, particularly in Normandy and Brittany. Up until about 50 years ago, before farming in Britain became so mechanized, every farm had its apple orchard and the centuries-old culture of cider making remained still very much intact, with each region growing its own variety of apples—Foxwhelps, Woodcocks, Rusticoats, White Swans, Kendrik Wildings, Jews' Ears, and dozens of others. Many of the old orchards fell out of use, were grubbed out, and the land used for other purposes, but a surprising number have survived and there is now a renaissance in cider making, particularly in North America.

A small orchard always had a mix of cooking and eating apples and homemade cider was made from a mix of the windfalls of both, to get the right combination of sweetness and acidity, with some crab apples thrown in, to provide extra tannin and tartness.

MAKES 4 3/4 QUARTS

Pick 13–14 pounds assorted ripe apples. Pile them in a heap for 3 days so that they "sweat," or soften a little. Roughly chop the apples. Putting enough as will fill a shallow box on the ground and chopping them with a clean spade is the most popular method. Shovel the apples into a fruit press and squeeze the juice into a 4 3/4 quart fermentation container. The apple pulp can be fed to the pigs if you have any, or added to the compost heap.

Put the fermentation container into a sink as there will be rapid natural fermentation

which will froth over the sides of the container. Once this ceases—in roughly 48 hours—decant the apple juice through cheesecloth into another bin, to start the real fermentation.

Add 1 tbsp dried yeast and 5 1/4 cups raw sugar mixed in 2 1/2 cups boiling water. Put a tight-fitting lid on the container and store it somewhere warm for 3 weeks or however long it takes the sugars to convert to alcohol and the bubbling to stop.

When the bubbling has completely ceased, move the container to a cool place and syphon the cider into sterile bottles. To ensure a nice fizz, add 1 level tsp unrefined sugar to each bottle. Seal and store in a cool place for 12 months.

perry

This is a wine made from pears and was another very popular drink. The Roman historian, Palladius, refers to a beverage called castomoniale, which was made from fermented pears. In a burst of spirited creativity during the early Middle Ages, the monks at the monastery of Grand Saint Michel in Normandy were responsible for developing pear orchards specifically for perry making. The Cistercian monks brought many varieties with them when they established their abbeys in Britain and more were introduced during successive reigns—particularly Henry VIII's. However, pears for perry making are tart and they were gradually replaced by the sweeter eating varieties. There are, though, enough of the old varieties to be found, particularly in Gloucestershire. They have splendidly evocative names—Mumblehead, Merrylegs, and Devil Drink, for instance. The art of perry making was taken to America by early colonists and is now enjoying a revival in popularity.

Perry is made in the same way as cider but replacing the apples with pears.

the green house

alternative energy

With a world energy crisis and ever-escalating fuel bills, it seems crazy not to utilize nature's resources—the sun, wind, water, or biomes, in the form of waste woods or bracken—to generate our own power. Even here in the north there is enough daylight through the winter to warm solar-heating panels and there is no shortage of wind, water, or bracken (ferns).

water power

Water power depends on a constant flow of water and if you are lucky enough to have a stream through your property, however small, it is well worth making use of it. To calculate the strength of water flow, start by measuring the depth of the stream from bank to bank along a given length. Area equals depth multiplied by width. A corked bottle is then timed as it floats along the measured length of stream and the flow is calculated by multiplying 75 percent of the time the bottle takes to cover the distance, by the area.

Harnessing your water power will almost certainly involve building a simple dam to provide increased velocity and, possibly, a trench or leat to carry water from the dam to the turbine, but the initial outlay is more than compensated for by a continuous supply of free electricity. A further requirement will be a shelter to protect the generator from the elements. Such a shelter can range from a tin shack to the sort of brick, stone, or wooden building that develops into a summer house and becomes something of a feature of your property.

Renewable energy, and mini-hydro electric generators in particular, have become such a science in the last 20 years, that there is no shortage of specialist surveyors to accurately assess the electricity-generating potential of your water supply and to give advice on the most suitable turbine.

wind power

The power of wind has been harnessed since the dawn of time and windmills were a common sight everywhere until electricity became the universal source of energy. Now, of course, clusters of huge wind turbines are sprouting across the countryside, destroying some of the most beautiful landscapes in the world. Although I abhor industrial wind turbines, there is a place for small domestic ones and these are becoming increasingly sophisticated and affordable. A turbine with a 5-foot, three-bladed propeller mounted on the roof of a house or on an exposed area of wind-catching high

some historical notes

Having always lived beside running water, I am fascinated by the historical uses of water as a source of energy as well as water's potential today. For centuries, any farm that grew grain had its mill pond—a lagoon of water that could be used to drive a water wheel for grinding corn. Incredible feats of engineering went into harnessing water in the early days of the Industrial Revolution during the 19th century—the nearby town of Hawick is built on a complex labyrinth of tunnels that used to carry water from the River Teviot to drive the machinery in dozens of tweed mills.

ground, and connected to the conversion box by cables will supply about 1kw of electricity, supplementing the property's supply from their commercial power supplier and reducing bills by a third. Rough electricity generated by the turbine is converted directly to household current via the conversion control box. The average householder in the UK can expect to recoup the cost within about five years.

solar power

Sunlight—the solar power that is the basis of all life on earth, even in Scotland, where there is not much of it—can now be utilized to generate electricity and heat water via solar panels. The technology is improving all the time and solar panels are commonly used in the UK to generate heat for water in high-usage situations like apartment buildings and hospitals.

For domestic use, solar panels represent an enormous eco-friendly saving in electricity. The beauty of them is that they sit outside, sucking up sunshine. They are sufficiently recognized as simple energy-saving devices for grants to now be available in parts of Europe for their installation. Solar panels have really come into their own in America, Australia, and New Zealand where many new lifestyle homes are not connected to outside power supplies.

Another method of utilizing the sun's power is through a Trombe wall—a south-facing wall of the house built with a double skin. The inner skin is traditional masonry fitted with ventilators and painted black, to act as a thermal mass to absorb heat. The outer skin is sheet glass that increases the heat in the cavity between the two skins. Warmth is released into the house through the ventilators. A strategically placed conservatory can be a marvellous heat trap for even thin winter sunlight.

fossil fuel alternatives

Alternatives to fossil fuels are being sought all the time and biomasses as fuel for heating are easily accessible to the home producer. Those that were commonly utilized in the past are now being looked to again to generate energy. In the days when hazel, poplar, willow, and chestnut were all cut for wattle fencing, baskets, paling, and charcoal, any waste was scrupulously saved, taken home, and burnt. A hedger carrying a bundle of trimmings home on his back was once a familiar sight in the winter. Dried ferns, which gave a fierce heat, was burnt in brick kilns and the ash was used in soap making. Gorse, another fierce burner, was cut and used in bread-baking ovens. Grown timber was rarely used as fuel. It was far too precious and was saved for ship and house building.

Poplar and willow are now being grown again as short rotational crops to be harvested for fuel use, as is miscanthus, a woody perennial grass which can be baled and harvested. Aberdeen University has carried out research on using ferns, dried and compressed into cubes, as an alternative to coal. Gorse could also easily be used in the same way. Both these plants have become damaging, invasive pest species on a global scale so this would be an excellent use for them.

So what should you, the home producer, burn your biomass fuel in? I have several friends who have installed Scanfield boilers imported from Denmark, of which there are now any number of different makes and sizes designed for the domestic market, which will burn virtually anything—bales of straw and ferns, timber offcuts which are of no commercial value, even dried chicken dung and leaves.

a variety of turbines

There are a number of different turbines available to suit different water-flow strengths.

● The Pelton wheel turbine is driven by water forced through a nozzle at high speed into spoon-shaped deflector buckets set around the periphery of the turbine wheel. The revolving wheel turns a generator which converts mechanical energy into electrical energy, either via a shaft or through a system of pulleys, depending on where the generator is sited. The Pelton is designed for fast-flowing water and is 80 percent efficient, producing 1.8 horse power which equates to 805 watts.

● A propeller turbine is the next best converter. Water passes down an outlet pipe set below the water level at the bottom of your dam and rotates a propeller positioned inside the pipe and connected to the generator. This suits slower-flowing water and is a correspondingly less effective generator, operating at about 75 percent efficiency.

● The Banki turbine looks like a miniature water wheel and works in much the same way. It is positioned beneath a sluice. Water channeled down a chute strikes curved fins set at angles around the periphery of a wheel. The weight of water revolves the wheel, which in turn charges a generator. This is the simplest form of hydroelectric turbine, operating on the least volume of water pressure, and is the easiest to

natural paints

If you use natural paints, you can experience much the same thrill of creativity, using almost identical materials, as the first caveman artist did 50,000 years ago. Natural paints are basically made from chalk, water, a binder of some sort, and a pigment, while mass-produced paints are based on derivatives of the petroleum industry—polyurethane, acrylic, synthetic latex, and vinyl. Natural paints have the advantage in that they are porous, allowing the surface underneath to breathe. This was an important consideration in old buildings that had no insulating layer. What is more, the chalky, matt finish of natural paints is infinitely more attractive than the modern equivalents.

Painting with natural materials is enormously rewarding but anyone embarking on it must appreciate that it is going to be an adventure that is full of experimentation and, unlike what most people have come to expect from modern barrier paints, the fruits of one's labors never last for long.

limewash

The most ancient form of weather-proofing is limewash, used by the ancient Greeks and Romans to protect statuary and commonly used on all buildings until well into the 19th century. It is made by crushing and burning limestone or chalk and slaking it with water to produce slaked lime, otherwise known as lime putty. The lime putty is then diluted with water to make a thin paint—basic limewash. Tallow or linseed oil were sometimes added to the water, to improve waterproofing, particularly for painting woodwork. In some areas, horse and cattle hair, gleaned from tanning-yard waste, were mixed in to strengthen the wash.

Color, in the most basic form, was provided by whatever soil was handy, washed several times and then added (see below). Different colors were obtained by burning earth containing different minerals—for example, soil from areas where iron oxide was present produced the different hues of ocher. Umber and sienna are derived from other different clays.

basic earth coloring

For coloring your limewash, use your own soil. It will be fun experimenting with the different color permutations.

Fill a half-gallon bucket with soil and sift it to remove the stones, etc. Boil the soil three times in 5 quarts water. Strain off the water and replace it after each boiling. After the third boiling, strain off the soil and mill it as finely as you can with a block of wood (correctly known as a maul) on a board. Either add the milled soil straight to the limewash or, put it in a cast iron pot over a fire and see what the heat does to the color.

soft distemper

Soft distemper is a lovely natural paint with a soft matt finish for interior walls. It is made with a fine powdered chalk, known as "whiting" and rabbit glue as the binder. All the ingredients can be obtained from specialty art stores. Several hours before you need it, mix the pigment with water to make a runny paste. This will allow the color to "breathe."

COVERS THE WALLS AND CEILINGS OF AN AVERAGE ROOM

3¹/₂ ounces pigment powder
12 pounds whiting
12 ounces rabbit-glue granules

Put the whiting in a bucket, covered with water, and let it soak for a couple of hours. Pour off the excess water. Using another bucket, mix the glue granules with just enough water to soak and, after a few minutes, add 3 quarts boiling water. Stir until completely dissolved. Let cool then add to the whiting paste. Mix thoroughly, then add the pigment paste. Continue to mix until thoroughly incorporated.

non-earth colors

The quality and range of pigments that have survived in murals from the Egyptian, Minoan, Phoenician, and Roman empires are extraordinary. Although the peoples of the East retained the knowledge of how to make vivid colors from the murex shellfish, and from cinnabar, lapis lazuli, lead, and malachite, this knowledge was lost to the West during the Dark Ages and had to be laboriously learned all over again. Many of the following pigments can still be obtained from specialty suppliers and may be used to color a variety of different washes and paint bases.

● Until the Industrial Revolution, when paint coloring became a by-product of the chemical industry, white was made from burning lead ore.

● Green came from the verdigris formed on copper by soaking it in verjuice (see page 151).

● Red, the color most sought after by artists, came from cinnabar, a soft red mineral that is the principal ore of mercury.

● Orange was achieved by heating white lead.

● Yellow came from gamboges, a resin from trees in Asia and later, in the 1700s, Indian Yellow was made from the urine of cows denied water and force-fed on mangoes .

● Blue, so precious to early manuscript illuminators that they only painted the hem of the Virgin's robes with it, was made by grinding up lapis lazuli, mixing it with beeswax, and repeatedly washing it.

● Charcoal, lampblack, and scraps of ivory, fired in a kiln, created the important base color, black.

Dyes made from plants, fruit, and flowers (see page 161) may also be used with some of the finer non-lime-based washes for beautiful soft interior coloring, although they are not lightfast and tend to fade. However, this is an effect that I find extremely attractive.

Grouse, 91
Growbags, 19
Guernsey sweaters, 162
Guinea fowl, 120
Guyanan beef stew, 100

Hanging baskets, growing fruit and vegetables in, 19
Hard flooring, 239
Hazelnuts, 80
Headaches, herbs for, 173
Heating, saving on, 237
Hemlock, poison, 81
Henbane, white, 81
Herb bag, 150
Herbalism
  country remedies, 173
  history of, 172, 173
  infusions, 172
Herbs
  angelica, 68
  anise, 68
  basil, 69, 240
  bath oil, scented, 151
  borage, 69
  caraway, 70
  coriander, 70
  drying, 68
  flower fennel, 69
  freezing, 68
  French tarragon, 69
  growing, 68
  hyssop, 69
  lavender 70
  lemon balm, 69
  lovage, 70
  melissa, 69
  mint, 70
  parsley, 70
  pennyroyal, 71
  pests, deterring, 46
  rosemary, 71
  rue, 71
  sage, 71
  summer and winter savory, 70
  sweet cicely, 71
  thyme, 71
  wild, growing, 68
  windowsills, growing on, 19
Highgrove Estate, 12
Hindle wakes, 121
Home baking, 190, 191
Honey
  canning in, 206
  extracting from hive, 129
Horseradish, 18, 173
Horses
  adult, for, 114
  breed, choosing, 116
  child, for, 114
  disabled, riding for, 117
  horsiculture, 114
  looking after, 117
  milk, 176
  uses of, 114
Horticultural fleece, 42
Hose, garden, 15
Hot beds, 43
Hot walls, 43
Houseplants, 240
Hydroponic cultivation, 12
Hyssop, 69

Insect bites and stings, herbs for, 173

Insect pests, 45
Insecticides, 46
Insulation, 238
Iron deficiency, 25

Jackdaws, 45
Jam
  apple jam, 208
  currant and raspberry jam, 208
  decanting, 209
  excess fruit, using, 208
  mulberry jam, 209
  plum jam, 209
  raspberry jam, 209
  setting, 209
  storing, 209
Josie's chicken, 122

Kale, 63
Kippers, 196
Knitting, 162, 163
Knotgrass, 25

Ladybugs, 45
Lamb
  Armenian lamb stew, 112
  deviled lamb cutlets, 113
  mutuk, 112
Lambsquarters, 82
Lavender 70
Leeks, 19, 58
Legumes
  beans. See Beans
  peas, 65
Lemon balm, 69
Lemons, 53
  duck with quinces and preserved lemons, 125
  lemon curd, 213
  pickled lemons, 201
Lighting, greener alternative, 237
Limewash, 233
Livestock. See also Horses, etc.
  animal health, 94
  autumn, 246
  chickens, 118-123
  cows, 96-101
  ducks, 124, 125
  geese, 128
  goats, 108, 109
  guinea fowl, 120
  horses, 114-117
  ill-health, signs of, 94
  pigeons, 128
  pigs, 102-107
  sheep, 110-113
  spring, 244
  summer, 245
  turkeys, 120
  winter, 247
Loam, 24
Locust wood, 35
London food markets, 216
Lovage, 70
Lunar planting, 13
Lye, 148

Magnesium deficiency, 25
Magpies, 45
Manganese deficiency, 25
Manure, 28
Marigolds, 46
Marmalade
  making, 210

orange marmalade, 210
Oxford marmalade, 211
Marrows, 66
  apple and marrow chutney, 211
Mayweed, 25
Mead, 223
Meadow saffron, 81
Meat
  freezing, 207
  in brine, 193
  pickled, 192, 193
Melissa, 69
Melons, 52
Mending
  button, sewing on, 168
  cover-up embroidery, 169
  darning, 170
  hem, sewing, 169
  invisible, 170
  learning to sew, 170
  patching, 168, 169
  ripped hem, 168
Mice, 140
Midges, herbs for repelling, 173
Milk
  butter from, 178
  camel's, 176
  cheese, making, 180
  cream, 176, 177
  ewe's, 176
  excess, selling, 176
  goat's, 176
  mare's, 176
  skimmed, 176
  whole, 176
  yogurt from, 178, 179
Mincemeat, 205
Mint, 70
Moles, 141
Mollison, Bill, 12, 13
Moss, dried, 25
Moths, 141
Mulberries, 52
  mulberry jam, 209
Mulching, 28
Muscles, pulled or stiff, 173
Mushroom compost, 28
Mushrooms
  edible, 85
  mushroom ketchup, 200
  mushroom pies, 87
  wild mushroom crêpes, 86
Mustard, 46
Mutuk, 112

Nasturtiums, 18, 46
Nettles, 25, 46, 82
  nettle beer, 82
  uses of, 173
Nitrogen deficiency, 25
Non-earth colors, 234
Nut trees, 35
Nuts, 80

Oak, 35
Oats, 74
Oil glaze, colored, 235
Onions
  companion planting, 57
  cultivation, 56
  pests, 57
  seed, growing from, 56, 57
  sets, growing from, 57